Hardcore Fanzine

Good and Plenty, 1989-1992

Christopher Sleboda
Kathleen Sleboda

With text by
Walter Schreifels

Hardcore Fanzine

Good and Plenty, 1989-1992

With contributors
Kristian Henson
Briar Levit
Ian Lynam
Gabriel Melcher
Anthony Pappalardo
Nate Pyper
Ali Qadeer
Gabe Rodriguez

Draw Down

It was thirty years ago today, or so the song goes. Looking back on the years when I was working daily, hustling *Good and Plenty Zine*, going to shows, writing reviews, thinking and living hardcore, I can recall the thoughts of that 18-year-old who didn't know what the hell he wanted to do with his life. I just knew I wanted to listen to some good music and hang with good friends at shows.

I wish I had a better memory so that I could relive those days. Going to shows in the Midwest, taking trips out east to see historical shows, then coming home and documenting everything with dummy mock-ups of my zine. The things you can do with a Sears typewriter and a blue pencil—tricks of the trades.

Regrets? Maybe the Chain Gang interview: a bunch of us got ripped off on some mail-order records or something, and like the young adults that we were, we embellished a little. I should reread it and see how harsh we were really; I think people understood what was going on there.

I'm proud of the fact that the first time I took a trip to experience some New York hardcore on the East Coast, I spent a week with friends who were vegetarian and vegan. On the eighth day, when I returned home, I said to myself, "I didn't eat any meat for a week—I think I really can live without it." Twenty-nine years later, I can say that I was right: the streak is alive.

I didn't know it was possible until I met people who showed me it was.

I met fine people doing *Good and Plenty Zine*, and I made some hefty record trades as well. Heck, I gave away a *New York City Hardcore: The Way It Is* 7" test pressing in a contest! What was I thinking? And I owned a test pressing of Judge's *Chung King Can Suck It*. The records came and went, but I wouldn't trade the experience I had running *G&P* for anything.

I was even able to travel the world, tour managing Local H, my friends' band, in the late 90s, all because I came out of my shell after doing *Good and Plenty Zine*. I was a shy kid from Zion, Illinois. But somehow, I grew the balls to approach Billy Joe Armstrong and ask for an interview. I may have lost the tape with that interview, but I kept the memory.

Those were the days: lots of friends, lots of shows. Still straight edge. Some have passed on now, and some have drifted out of the scene. Last night I watched an interview with Ritchie Birkenhead, Mike Judge, and Paul Bearer on YouTube. Paul Bearer said it pretty well, something like, "Hardcore will live on with me and without me." I couldn't agree more. I'm glad to have had a small slice of the pie. Sometimes I think—what if I had the technology that kids have today? What kind of zine could we do now?

GORILLA BISCUITS INST

BROTHERHOOD BOLD

JUDGE

The Perfect Hardcore Fanzine

Christopher Sleboda
Kathleen Sleboda

Opposite: Detail from paste-up for cover of *Good and Plenty*, issue 3, 1989.

As a piece of graphic design, it's a thing of beauty. Modest in size, straight-forward in execution, and reliably legible.

Released in September 1989—photocopied, folded and stapled in Zion, Illinois by Gabriel Rodriguez—*Good and Plenty Fanzine* issue 3 is the perfect hardcore fanzine. It is impressive as documentary evidence of a thriving music subculture in its prime. And it offered an incredibly useful design that wholly encapsulated the spirit and the style of a moment and a movement that was both simultaneously thriving and fleeting. In spread after spread, the margins overflow with an innocence and a sincerity that's difficult to duplicate.

Black and white drawings illustrate the issue: X'ed up fists (fig. 1); a hardcore kid in a hooded sweatshirt (the Champion logo's C modified to GP); and an angry mouse in a Bold band t-shirt (fig. 2) all appear. Each piece of art was a unique creation, keyed to appeal to a particular subculture: straight edge.[1] In a pre-internet/pre-digital world, there was far less content circulating about unsigned and underground bands. Access to the photographs, interviews, and reviews that did make their way into the world could be equally hard to come by. Determined teenagers—ambitious despite the barriers, and enthusiastic about anything related to their musical landscape—would mail well-concealed dollar bills to zinemakers around the world, then keep watch on their mailboxes for manila envelopes bursting with unfettered creativity in printed form.

G&P employed text produced on a typewriter, physically cut into a variety of column widths and pasted into each spread. Interview headlines were created by photocopying official band logos from album artwork. This sleight of hand lent the zine a professional feel as if it was produced in part by a computer, something out of reach of many at the time. Gabe Rodriguez published the third issue of *Good and Plenty* the same year that Apple released the Mac IIci, a personal computer that cost $6,269 in 1989 (equivalent to over $12,000 today). QuarkXPress 2 had just been released, and Photoshop was on version 0.87, an Alpha version that wasn't yet publicly available.

Fig. 1. GXP Straight Edge Fist, *Good and Plenty*, issue 3, p. 3, September 1989.

Fig. 2. Illustration for Show Reviews, *Good and Plenty*, issue 3, p. 36, September 1989.

1. Straight edge is a subculture of hardcore punk whose adherents refrain from using alcohol, tobacco, and other recreational drugs.

9

Despite the odds, *Good and Plenty* achieved a surprising sophistication within its limited means. Every spread was graphic and bold, well-balanced in variety and pacing. And issue 3 was affordable with a cover price of less than a dollar.

Hand-drawn titles were a regular feature, conjuring visual references familiar to readers. The masthead on the cover of the third *G&P* evoked the lettering of the Misfits logo (itself a reference, drawn from the masthead font of movie magazine *Famous Monsters of Filmland*), but without the jagged edges (fig. 3). Lettering throughout evokes graffiti and high school notebook doodling, like the letters filled with a city skyline that introduce *G&P*'s show reviews.

The original script for record reviews displays formal qualities that have more in common with the expressive forms of Art Nouveau (fig. 4), rather than the hard-angled typography of Slayer or Metallica.

Fig. 4. "GP Record Reviews" section heading, *Good and Plenty,* issue 3, September 1989. Théophile Alexandre Steinlen, *Motocycles Comiot* (detail) from *Les Maîtres de l'Affiche,* 1899.

Original and never-before-seen photos, including mailed-in submissions from around the world, filled *Good and Plenty*. While issue 3 lacked halftones and Xerox photocopying compromised overall image quality, the reproduced photos still offered readers a rare glimpse of what their favorite bands looked like. It was this kind of on-the-scene reportage that zines, made and distributed by fans, could provide.

Gabe's introduction to his interview with the Gorilla Biscuits (fig. 5) interview notes, "This was my first run in with da' Biscuits and I was surprised at what I saw. I expected them to be upbeat, hyper people, but they were the opposite. As a matter of fact, they were laid back and mild guys." The honest, in-the-moment approach continues with the Insted interview, when at the end, Gabe writes, "The interview was cut off there because Upfront started their set." The editorial objective appears to be complete authenticity.

The cut and paste layout was just as straight-forward and transparent; *G&P* did not subscribe to the chaos and anarchy of the punk rock ethos but instead embraced the earnest application of a grid. How could a straight edge zine not choose to utilize an organized and logical grid, rejecting the ransom note aesthetic of the dirty and delinquent? This underlying organizational approach arguably mirrored straight edge's reaction to the excess of punk. The grid, in this instance, became a tool of optimism and hope.

Good and Plenty (fig. 6) captured a quintessential moment of straight edge and youth crew,[2] when New York hardcore burned at its brightest, in a moment now etched into hardcore history. This single issue serves as a time capsule with interviews and original photographs of the scene's most iconic bands: Gorilla Biscuits, Judge, Bold, Insted, and Brotherhood. Three decades later, these bands continue to be influential.

Produced between 1989 and 1992, the seven issues of *Good and Plenty* grew more satisfying with each new edition. The trim size grew, and as Rodriguez's technical abilities and access to printing options also improved, the last four issues were offset printed instead of photocopied. Interviews increased in length and depth; photos multiplied like gremlins—and they were sharper, printed using halftones. Content and coverage expanded to include new styles of underground music, including Into Another, Iceburn, and Sacred Reich. *G&P* was a reflection of a living scene, one always in flux—as well as a reflection of one music fan's evolving personal taste.

The wonderful thing about a zine like *Good and Plenty*, produced quickly and modestly but with passion and heart, is that it functions as a time machine. The sequel to *Back to the Future* was released the same year as *Good and Plenty* issue 3. The movie follows characters as they travel into the future—first to 2015, and then to previous dates; they must repair the future while avoiding their past selves. Nostalgia is part of the time travel dilemma. But *Good and Plenty*, especially issue 3, is a DeLorean—and you're about to hit 88 mph.

Fig. 5. *Gorilla Biscuits* self-titled 7" EP, 1988, with artwork by Brian A. Clark (Billy Sidebyside).

Fig. 6. The cover of *Good and Plenty*, issue 3, released in September 1989, showed a clear reference to the *Gorilla Biscuits* self-titled 7" released by Revelation Records the previous year.

2. Youth crew is a music subculture of hardcore punk attributed to bands who were primarily active during the early to mid-1980s, particularly in the New York hardcore scene (NYHC). Youth crew is distinguished from other hardcore and punk scenes by its optimism and moral outlook. Many youth crew bands and fans were straight edge and advocates for vegetarianism/veganism.

A Paean to the Photocopier

Briar Levit

In the age of iPhones, Chromebooks, and Kindles, we take the humble photocopier for granted. But without this machine, the legendary output of punk zines like *Good and Plenty* may never have happened. Of course, punk fans weren't the first to publish their ideas independently of the mainstream press. Not by centuries. They weren't even the first to print fanzines—those began in the 1930s with sci-fi fanatics. But it is punk zines, no doubt, that most people associate with this particular corner of the independent publishing domain. Their influence on subsequent zines, but also on graphic design in general, has been immense, and *Good and Plenty* was printing at the height of the phenomenon in the late-1980s to early-1990s.

Punks emerged at a perfect storm of circumstances of Western culture and technology in the mid-1970s. They were tired of the state of the world around them—even their own subcultures—and were looking for creative ways to channel their ideas and energy. Meanwhile, "access to tools," as the *Whole Earth Catalog* put it, was easier than ever (fig. 1). A fan could conceive of, lay out, and reproduce a publication within hours (if they were particularly disciplined), without the services of a third party, save the use of a photocopy machine—accessible in copy shops around town, or even better, sitting idly at the day-job office after hours.

It's common knowledge now that only minimal tools are required to produce punk zines. All that's needed is a sharpie, perhaps a typewriter, some scissors and some glue to paste it all down. The more elaborately produced zines employ photos, magazine clippings, and sometimes clip art or dry transfer type, like Letraset. The one thing they all need, of course, is a photocopier.

The first photocopier—the Xerox 914—went on the market in 1959. But it would take some time for it to fully invade the existing suite of common office gadgets like typewriters and adding machines. They were, for a time, only able to make a limited number of copies,

Opposite: Detail from paste-up for *Good and Plenty*, issue 5, p. 47, 1990, featuring a collage of photographs from *G&P* issues 1-3.

Fig. 1. *Whole Earth Catalog: Access to Tools*, Fall 1970.

and at a higher price per sheet than existing options like spirit duplicators and mimeographs.

These precursors to the photocopier—duplicators—were democratizing forces. Librarian and archivist, Lincoln Cushing, notes in an essay about the use of duplicators by a print shop to serve the needs of the Bay Area "hip community," aka hippies—

> Every society has its pecking order, and printing is no exception. Equipment matters. At the top of the heap are the big presses—the giant Goss web machines that churn out daily newspapers...the elegant Heidelberg letterpresses for art prints. At the bottom are the lowly duplicators... But even below these machines, at the very dark recesses of the reproduction food chain, lie the spirit duplicators and mimeographs.

Depending on the model, they could be relied upon to reproduce tens to thousands of copies. Counter culture communities realized these duplicators were relatively affordable; paired with a typewriter, or better yet, an IBM Selectric Composer (which allowed for proportionally spaced type and justified alignment), they could create publications with reasonably "professional-looking" production quality.

But these presses still took some degree of experience, money, and space to run. The process could be messy and required supplies like ink, stencils, and carbon paper. Various levers and buttons to adjust the print quality and methods of masking to clean-up layouts took time to get accustomed to.

Meanwhile, the photocopier quickly caught up in affordability and accessibility. By the 1970s, they were ubiquitous in offices, not to mention, you could walk into a copy shop and run the machine yourself! The best part was that it took only minutes to learn to run a copier. Rest an original piece of art face down on the glass, close the lid, enter the quantity, and hit the "copy" button. As print historian, Frank Romano, wrote, "The critical innovation in xerography was eliminating the plate (and, of course, plate preparation) from the reproduction process." It is truly a democratic method of print reproduction. It was the photocopier that was used in 1976 to reproduce the first punk zine in England, *Sniffin' Glue* (fig. 2), and it was a photocopier that reproduced thousands of other zines after, including *Good and Plenty*, starting in 1989.

So, it's not surprising that punk zinesters are indelibly linked to this machine. But it's more than just the fact that they were democratizing printing presses. It's that they played a critical role in establishing the very visual language that defined zines. You can see it clearly in *Good and Plenty*, from blown-out images

Fig. 2. First issue of *Sniffin' Glue*, 1975 July 13.

14

to streaked and mottled black toner coverage. You can see it in the roughened line quality of the sharpie-scrawled headlines, and the fuzzy black edges delineating cut paper pasted on the layout. These so-called imperfections—overlooked in offices due to the ephemeral nature of the documents copied—were not only embraced, but were encouraged by zine makers. Photocopiers just naturally reproduced the angst, energy, and immediacy of the punk culture they helped cultivate.

Even when *Good and Plenty* moved to offset printing on issue 4, the designers maintained the visual language they had established with the help of the photocopier. The final issue almost feels more photocopied than the actual photocopied issues—perhaps, a result of using the photocopier to create original artwork that was then offset printed?

Now, that same visual language is imitated digitally to varying levels of success. Infinite sets of Photoshop brushes and stock images mimic the qualities the photocopier once created through trial and chance, allowing designers to carefully craft an 'analog' look for their website or Instagram post. And who can blame them? The sterility of the computer weighs on us.

But diehard zinesters are persevering at the beds of photocopiers around the world. Today, even though 77% of Americans have internet access in their homes—and all have access to it in their local library—zines and their associated communities continue to flourish. Why haven't blogs, Twitter, Tic Toc, and the rest, *totally* wiped out this slow, somewhat laborious physical method of communication? We must crave the process of making and watching our ideas and designs come together on the page. We must appreciate the intimacy of someone's handcrafted words and images on paper. It must be a relief to see a page exploding with texture and honesty on top of an obliterated grid.

We generally seek order in the things we look at, but ultimately, we also seek out the humanity. Zines are humanity in book form.

ALEX

LUK

Good and Plenty

Walter Schreifels

"But now I would like to talk about Chicago. A very prosperous scene with open minded people, full of different bands, and always fun shows. The only thing Chicago needs is for more bands to come through more often and play shows. So bands pleease [sic] come to Chicago! —Gabe Rodriguez, March 1989

Opposite: Detail from paste-up for *Good and Plenty*, issue 5, p. 18, 1990, featuring photographs of members of Gorilla Biscuits; bottom photograph of Gorilla Biscuits at The Safari Club in Washington, D.C.

Hardcore music developed as an offshoot of the North American punk scene in the early 1980s. The term "hardcore" originally caught on when D.O.A., a punk band from Vancouver, Canada went on a full U.S. tour in support of their *Hardcore '81* album (fig. 1). Along with a handful of other punk bands like Southern California's Black Flag and the Dead Kennedys from San Francisco, D.O.A. were the among the first to put out their own records and tour from coast to coast. While artists like Iggy Pop, The Ramones or The Damned still had the clout from their 1970s successes to tour nationally, there was zero support from the music establishment to help bring up the wave of new punk bands they had inspired. Refusing to die on the vine, the bravest of the bunch collected all the phone numbers they could find and built a network of highly motivated punk kids to secure venues and promote shows. The butterfly effect of this new punk rock silk road was truly revolutionary, giving rise to a thriving independent music scene that, for the most part, had never seen itself in the same room before. It was the advent of D.I.Y. culture, where the new ethos was you no longer had to ask permission—form a band, start a record label, book a show, and for those who wanted to write, this gave rise to the *fanzine*, like a website without the internet. And for a time it was glorious.

Fig. 1. Cover of D.O.A., *Hardcore '81*, Friends Records, FR 010, 1981.

    Now, fast forward eight years to March 1989. You're in Zion, Illinois, a town of roughly 20,000 about an hour's drive north of Chicago. Many if not most of the *Hardcore 81* generation kids are in their mid to late twenties by now, stooped over, losing their hair, over it. Sure the DKs, Black Flag and D.O.A. can still tour but years in the van have taken their toll, and there's not much left in the tank, the larger effect of which is that without a steady flow of nationally touring bands that can draw bigger crowds it's tougher for local scenes to spark up. By March 1989 the infrastructure for hardcore was still in place, but like Japan, it's population was in decline. It was in this bleak environment that Zion's own Mike "Good" Good and Gabe "Plenty" Rodriguez decided to step up and be part of the solution, and so began *Good and Plenty* zine.

Issue 1: Inspiration

First produced in Philadelphia in 1893, Good & Plenty, *the candy*, is believed to be the oldest branded candy (fig. 2) in the U.S. Until the company was sold in 1973 there used to be a cartoon character named "Choo Choo Charlie" who appeared in their T.V. commercials, Charlie was a train conductor if that tells you anything about the old-timeyness of G&P. I never saw Choo Choo Charlie growing up but was the prime age for the iconic 1970s redesign which remains indelibly imprinted in my mind in the very form it appears atop the masthead of *Good and Plenty* Issue 1, "NET. WT. 1.8 oz. (51g)." By 1989 repurposing the art of a very out of fashion black licorice-based candy from the 1970s, "soft and chewy" might appear a curious choice for a new zine. Though to anyone born in the late 1960s/early 1970s, which was pretty much the average age of everyone interested in hardcore at this time, it struck an immediate chord. In truth, I preferred Mike & Ike's (fig. 3) which was exactly the same shape and dimensions as G&P only with a variety of fruit flavors instead of the old Bob Dole, penny candy licorice taste of G&P (fig. 4). That said, there's something classic and cleverly understated about G&P, *a less is more* type of greatness, like *OK Computer* or Public Image Limited, that leaves room to the imagination only to blow your mind.

Fig. 2. Detail of typography on Good and Plenty candy packaging, 1969. Candy boxes during this period featured the G&P mascot Choo-Choo Charlie, a cartoon engineer.

Fig. 3. Detail of typography on Mike and Ike candy packaging, circa early 1980s.

Just below the masthead, the cover illustration shows a gang of faceless figures to outline a hardcore crew that does not yet exist. While the figures appear to be male, they might not be. There are no hairstyles or signs of ethnicity save for what looks like an Africa medallion on one figure in the front, a likely tip of the hat to the popular Native Tongues movement in hip hop who, along with Public Enemy's *It Takes A Nation Of Millions To Hold Us Back* and N.W.A.'s *Straight Outta Compton* (both released in 1988, had given suburban teenagers their first insider look at the black experience in the United States that both shocked and excited them in a way that hadn't occurred since the civil rights era. The X on the hand of the figure next to the Africa medallion guy could be a nod to Malcolm as much as to Ian MacKaye, the former being a 1960s leader of the Nation Of Islam, assassinated by one of his own flock; the latter being the originator of the "don't smoke, don't drink, don't fuck" straight edge movement within hardcore that he would just as soon disassociate himself from. Two powerful leaders with problematic relationships to the movements they had created.

Fig. 4. Collage from *Good and Plenty*, issue 1, p. 2, 1989.

In its early days hardcore was more Orwellian with it's "Fuck Reagan" socio-political paranoia and *Maximum RockNRoll* ink-stained fingers, it was dirty like *Oceania* was dirty, but as the cover for issue 1 signals, by the late 1980s this mood had cleaned itself up a bit. Both in an aesthetic and philosophical sense, *1984* had given way to *Brave New World*, *Two Minutes Hate* was out, *Soma* was in. Like candy cigarettes once taught kids to smoke real cigarettes, 1970s Good & Plenty candy looks like the Jr. version of Wellbutrin. Where Orwell feared the burning of books, Huxley suggested no one would want to read anyway, perhaps this is why *G&P* issue 1 of March 1989 was offered for FREE!

Perusing the playlists of issue 1, you wouldn't be crazy thinking the crew over at *G&P* came from a metal background. The playlists are split 60/40 hardcore to metal with a few rap mentions mixed in. Metal was a great feeder for hardcore at this time, before that it was hard rock like Ted Nugent, Alice Cooper, AC/DC. Hardcore scenes weren't exactly easy to find, most cities didn't have them, and there was no internet to search it for you. Metal records, on the other hand, were available everywhere with regular concerts in big venues. For those who dug deep into the genre, they were bound to bump into punk and the hardcore ghetto at some point. Suicidal Tendencies from Venice, California—who had an early MTV hit with "Institutionalized"—were a gateway band to hardcore for many; D.R.I. from Texas, whose albums *Four Of A Kind* and *Crossover* had a foot firmly in both genres, also introduced the hardcore scene to kids who might have only listened to metal. In the big cities, there were kids who came to hardcore through boarding school, broken homes, and runaways, but this was fading by 1989. The group that was making the shows bigger were coming from the metal scene in the suburbs and bands took note as witnessed in Gabe Rodriguez's review of Chicago's own Life Sentence who played Blue Oyster Cult's *Godzilla* as their encore or when Ludichrist from Long Island, New York, covered Cheech & Chong's *Earache In My Eye*. These comforting echoes of junior high gave everyone a chance to let their guard down, celebrate their former selves, and mix it up with their new tastes. Unlike punk, hardcore was bare-bones, void of pretense. To not shy away from one's pre-punk past was healthy and respectable, something *Good and Plenty* got right from the jump.

"Welcome to the 2nd issue of *Good And Plenty* magazine. If you have the first issue you can tell this issue is a lot bigger and we believe better."

May 1989, issue 2, still FREE, special and expanded and arriving just a few months on the heels of *Good and Plenty* 1, no small feat in the fast-paced world of hardcore. Gone were the handwritten, all caps of its predecessor, in its place a fully typeset and artfully pro new look for issue 2. I love the light tracing coming off of Chuck from Only The Strong's clothing on the cover photo. This effect is achieved by using a slower shutter speed, which acts as a visual reverb on the subject. This style of photography became popular following the Washington, D.C., band Dag Nasty (fig. 5) using it in the artwork for their game-changing debut album *Can I Say*. Like the music on *Can I Say* itself, the light traces added a bit of art and intelligence to an otherwise standard hardcore photo.

Fig. 5. Back cover of Dag Nasty, *Can I Say*, Dischord, 019, 1986. Photographs credited to John Reardon and Ilisa Katz. Graphic design by Jeff Nelson.

Another format change of note is the addition of a thanks list on page two. The hardcore thanks list is an art form in itself and can read like a map or tea leaves. As a staple feature of any hardcore record or zine, it's more than saying thanks, it's an endorsement, it's bread crumbs, it's a humblebrag, an inside joke, it shows who you respect, where you came from and where you aspire to be. *G&P* didn't have to thank all the members of Only The Strong individually, *but they did*. that's a strong endorsement, a classy gesture and I'm sure it was appreciated. Gabe also singled out Jimmy G from Murphy's Law with a "big yahoo" for diving on him from the P.A. speakers, showing that hardcore is the kind of scene where you thank someone for diving on you. I also like "thanks to Jen Bittner (we still need a ride to Metallica)"—it says so much in so few words. First, it tells me *G&P* have females in the crew, that Jen drives, is into Metallica and probably has a good sense of humor. She must have been cool to hang out with, I wonder where she is now?

"Welcome to the 3rd issue of *G&P*.
It has been a while since the last one..."
Not really, it's only that time seems to pass slower when you're young but as you age and become more experienced at living time begins to speed up like in the film *Groundhog Day* with Bill Murray. In the film Murray's character, T.V. weatherman Phil Conners, travels to Punxsutawney, PA to film a piece on that city's famous weather-predicting groundhog but ends up stuck in a loop, living the same day over and over again. While certain details change and underlying truths are revealed, the experience of living the same day speeds up the montage every time the alarm goes off at 5:59 A.M. *G&P* 1 came out just six months before, at three issues already they were pretty much churning them out.

Fun fact: issue 3 was the first to cost money. 75¢ a copy. If you don't value your work, how can you expect others to do so? It was the right time, a fair price and a healthy decision, they were going pro.

The summer of 1989 was the peak of the straight edge hardcore movement sparked by bands like Uniform Choice on the West Coast and Youth Of Today in New York. To get a sense of what was going on, Gabe's piece "Trend or Way of Life" is insightful: "It doesn't make me any better than anyone else, it's just what I chose, and it works for me. I have nothing against people who drink but if you think you need to drink to have a good time, I know a lot of people who can tell you different."

The straight edge scene appealed to many who felt out of step with typical high school peer pressure bullshit party culture. Less talked about were the kids who had suffered with addiction at home—alcoholic parents or drug-addicted siblings. For me, it was the back to the roots style of music that grabbed me. Straight edge bands were the ones that took the most influence from the original hardcore sound. I was too young to see Minor Threat in 1982, so Uniform Choice would do. While straight edge challenged the nihilism of punk and had the best mosh parts, many on the outside considered it a conformist, elitist, consumerist and even fascistic movement. By identifying as straight edge, Gabe took the risk of alienating some *G&P* readers, but he was willing to make that claim anyway. So is it a trend or a way of life? For me it was the best of both; I'm not straight edge now, but I was from age seventeen to twenty, when time moved very slow.

"I'd like this zine to be remembered for it's open views, cheap prices and quick mail responses"

Unbeknownst to *G&P* readers Gabe studied graphic communications in high school and was heavily into printing. What's more, his father was a pressman at a family-owned print shop and got him a part-time job there where he could use the machines at night. This arrangement came very much in handy as the runs for *G&P* steadily increased. Issue 4 was up to 1,500 copies. While Gabe's connects took some of the sting out of it, there were still many hard costs that could not be gotten around—like paper, increased postage, something called collating and others—so with a run that big *G&P* had to increase the price to $1.25 per copy. No one complained.

Of course good mail-order etiquette was a point of pride at *G&P*. Anyone into hardcore in the 1980s has a war story of being ripped off through the mail, a subject of issue 4's "Good and Plenty Brainstorm." Gabe writes, "I know this subject relates to more people than you think, because if you are a record collector like me than you probably have been ripped off through the mail. Is there really a legitimate reason to wait for things ordered via the mail for six months? For eight months?" To avoid shifty operators, Gabe advises you to send a letter first just to say hi and then see how long it takes for them to write you back as a gauge of trustworthiness. He also suggests sending a check or money order whenever possible, and so I ask myself—*what the hell is a money order?*

For me, issue 4 shines for its extensive photo section. My favorite series was taken at The Anthrax club in Norwalk, Connecticut. There's a great photo of Kevin Egan from Beyond, microphone in hand, set directly next to a Gorilla Biscuits crowd shot taken on the same night. In the first, lead singer Kevin is the center of attention with the crowd just out of frame; in the second, he's just another body on the pile singing his heart out. This illustrates a beautiful pillar of hardcore's ideology: the band is the crowd, and the crowd is the band in a functioning utopia. One minute you're the singer, the next you're the stage diver, the merch seller or the *zine writer*. Everyone has a job, it's kind of Marxist.

"First, you may notice there are no record
or zine reviews in this issue."
The decision to drop the reviews section likely stemmed from the battering *G&P* gave Positive Approach for their *Just Hang On* EP in issue 4. Ironically for Positive Approach it was *they* who would need to just hang on after Gabe got through with them. With a taste for blood he writes, "This is not the most original record out today *but it works*. Nothing really grabs me, *sorry*." Wait, what?? This is actually the worst review anyone received in *G&P*'s entire run. Gabe just didn't have the heart *or* had *too much* heart to disparage someone else's artistic efforts in print, and by issue 5 he could no longer keep up the ruse: "It is very hard to give someone a bad review if you got it for free from one of the band members or the editors." Meanwhile, Pitchfork gave The Pixies a one out of ten for their comeback EP.

The decision to quit reviews wasn't the only thing Gabe wanted off his chest in May 1990. While *G&P* always had female contributors, the regular reader might have noticed a lack of female faces in the show photographs. Some considered the hardcore scene to be sexist; maybe so, but not at *G&P*: "For those of you who still think there is no place for girls in the scene, screw you because there would be no zine without their help. This zine is 90% done by females." Gabe went on to explain that after issue 4 he had thoughts of quitting the zine but this "one person in particular, who he had met through the mail and got along with very easily" really helped him to keep on. "You're a true friend and those are hard to come by these days, thanks, you know who you are."

"I would be a fool not to voice my opinion, no matter how
you slice, dice or try to justify war, it just is not right."
I felt the same when the Gulf War started, and the U.S. bombed Iraq for the first time, you just knew it was wrong. We were post-Vietnam, Cold War kids and had no experience of war beyond what we were taught by *Platoon* and *Apocalypse Now*. Neither film

made war look any good at all, just cruel and misguided. With his anti-war statement and continued spotlight on sexism in the scene, Gabe found a new voice for *G&P*. By issue 6 there were apparently more pressing topics on his mind than straight edge and mail-order. He may admittedly have been too nice to give your record a bad review, but he was not about to keep quiet about the Gulf War.

The *G&P* playlist also got woke, shaking up the dominance of straight edge hardcore in favor of Belinda Carlisle ("notice, even top 40 made it in.") The straight edge wave of 1989 had peaked with issue 3; by 1990 the energy and creativity that had powered that movement had calcified into worn cliches. Case in point, Gabe had fun with a fake interview with a dishonest straight edge band from Southern California called Chain Of Strength. The Chain gang had apparently ripped off *G&P* by not paying for an ad they had placed. But in true Gabe fashion, the interview's not even mean. Besides a drawing of their lead singer strung up in a noose (fig. 6), it's mostly just silly.

While *G&P* was Gabe's baby, he was always very generous with giving credit to contributors, and increasingly, space for the opinions of others. Issue 6 has a great example of this with the strongly written piece by Kim Nolan returning to the subject of sexism in the straight edge scene. After Gabe's comments on sexism in the previous issue, it's an interesting set up for the perspective of a female on the same topic. Surprisingly Kim says, "[T]he greatest threat to us is not from men, but actually, from other women." Her point seems to be that in a scene already dominated by males, it doesn't help to have girls giving the appearance of only being there to meet guys. This undermines the efforts of those females committed to pushing the scene forward and playing a more significant role. I think Kim would be happy to know how many females are involved in hardcore today; they're standing on the shoulders of giants.

Fig. 6. Illustration accompanying mock interview of Chain Of Strength, *Good and Plenty*, issue 6, p. 52, 1990-1991.

"A zine is a non-musician's band"

The above statement was an interesting thought from issue 7, described as "things I've heard or read that deserve repeating." I'm no zine expert, but I do know bands and any band that can make seven solid records in three years is in an elite class. The Clash couldn't do it, neither could Fugazi. Only bands from the 1960s like The Beatles and The Stones could keep that pace and deliver quality to match. If *Good and Plenty* was a band, Gabe was its lead singer, lead guitarist and main songwriter wrapped into one, so the better comparison is with Prince, who could always count on the Revolution to back him up. That would make issue 7 *G&P*'s *Around The World In A Day*, which was also a departure.

Hardcore Softcore

Nate Pyper

If you ask me what the pit is like at a hardcore show, I'll tell you to find an old copy of a gay porn magazine called *IN TOUCH*. If the pages aren't stuck together, I'll recommend you flip through the March 1983 issue (fig. 1) which describes the pit as "a squirming mass of physical action." It goes on: "The first time you try it, the dancing is a sort of passing through fire; on the other side you'll find a rare unconditional camaraderie. People pull each other up when someone goes down in the fray. They grab you as reinforcement against an oncoming wave of bodies... Our baptism is sweat."

That description comes from an article called "Street Rocking" in issue #77. It marks the beginning of an unusual moment in the publication's history—for several issues, the glistening bodies of punk and hardcore legends like Jello Biafra, Iggy Pop, and Henry Rollins graced the pages of an otherwise uncomplicated and uncontroversial softcore gay porn rag. During this brief period in the early 1980s, *IN TOUCH* introduced the pit to its readers as a sensual body-on-body contact zone. And it explicitly (and *explicitly*) identified how desire factors into the proliferation of subculture.

If you ask me what the pit is like at a hardcore show, I'll also tell you to read *Good and Plenty* where the pit plays prominently. As a zine that published interviews with bands, grainy photos of live shows, and gig reviews, the pit as both a place and an experience is reanimated in printed form. In one issue, zine editor Gabe Rodriguez describes the pit at a show on May 9, 1989: "Everyone was diving, dancing, and having a great time." In an interview with band 411, a band member lists one of the criteria for a successful tour as when "the crowds are just intense body motion." In a grainy black and white image from a Gorilla Biscuits show, a stage-diver's legs sprout up from a rowdy crowded pit, the diver's upper half both submerged and obscured by the mess of limbs and sweat.

Opposite: Detail from paste-up for *Good and Plenty*, issue 5, p. 13, 1990. Photograph of the pit at a Gorilla Biscuits show.

Fig. 1. Peter Belin on the cover of *IN TOUCH for Men*, Number 77, March 1983. Note the "Sex & Men & Rock & Roll" cover line.

Opposite: Detail from paste-up for *Good and Plenty*, issue 7, p. 37, 1992, featuring photos of the band Face Value playing in DeKalb, Illinois. Photo credited to "Eric D."

And because *G&P* largely featured straight edge hardcore bands, the pit isn't something remembered as a hazy memory mediated by the mind-altering effects of drugs and alcohol but as a concrete lived experience that activates all five senses. The pit is worth reproducing because it is worth remembering. The pit is desired, and the pit is desire. But don't get the idea that the pit is just another name for utopia. It's a volatile social space where bodies and ideas clash, often violently, as an interview with fellow zinester, Alyssa Chunx, reminds readers, "I don't know how many times I have had boots in my face, in my nose. I have had the wind knocked out of me." In an earlier zine, Rodriguez recounts an episode of racism. Still, we go back. We desire the disorder.

In many ways, *G&P* is an extension of the pit itself. It is the pit printed, a messy interpersonal site of intense intimacy simulated through text and images. It is a technology for reproducing that same euphoric chaos. *G&P* is the pit for a little longer. It is a place to reflect on the pit, to take note of all the phenomena that surround and saturate the pit. The zine is a pit survivor's support group. It is the pit and everything around it.

In the leadup to an interview with Eye for an Eye in the last issue of *Good and Plenty*, Rodriguez sums up the aspirational transportive nature of the project: "I wish you all could have been there, but that is impossible. I encourage everyone to read on." *Good and Plenty* takes me back to the pit, and *IN TOUCH* reminds me why I stay.

City and Princetown:
Notes on Straight Edge Hardcore
and Youth Crew Vernacular Typography

Kristian Henson

Growing up in the late 1990s/early 2000s-era San Fernando Valley punk scene, I was not really exposed to a lot of straight edge. In our crap corner of Los Angeles, the kind of hardcore my friends were into was a mix of thrash, power violence, grind, and crust. Northern and Central California bands like Capitalist Casualties, Man Is the Bastard, Spazz, and Infest would tour in our area during the height of the scene. California straight edge was more of a thing a million miles away in places like Orange County and San Diego.

My primary interaction with straight edge and youth crew culture would be while digging for records at local shops like Green Hell or Headline Records. You knew when you saw a straight edge album right away: the adoption of minimal design, X symbols, varsity jackets, Champion hoodies, and crewcuts subverted a firmly Northeast American aesthetic. They created a subculture founded on a serious commitment and intensity that projected itself through the design of album art. Their aesthetic was the complete antithesis to my assumed notions of what was punk. Aren't we all trying to live fast and die young? It always made me wonder what created this counter to the counterculture—where do all these design signifiers come from, and what do they mean?

Fig. 1. Cover of SS Decontrol, *The Kids Will Have Their Say*, Dischord/X-Claim!, 1982. Cover photo by Phil-In-Phlash. Album design by Bridget Burpee.

City, designed by Jorge Trump (no relation, thank fuck!) and released by Berthold in 1930 and first used in hardcore on the album *The Kids Will Have Their Say* (fig. 1) by Boston's Society System Decontrol (SSD) in 1982. Part of the first wave of American hardcore, SSD were contemporaries of D.C.'s Minor Threat, L.A.'s Black Flag and N.Y.'s Agnostic Front. Following Minor Threat's 1981 song "Straight Edge," SSD embraced the track as a manifesto of sorts and built on its themes. SSD were part of a larger group of local bands and punks collectively knowns as Boston Crew, who all slowly came to embrace straight edge as well. The design of *The Kids Will Have Their Say* was simple: "S.S. Decontrol" spelled-out in all caps in City on top of a stark photo by Philin Phlash depicting twenty-plus members of Boston Crew storming the Massachusetts State House. Critically, SSD guitarist and X-Claim!

Records founder Al Barile wore a bomber jacket with large hand-painted letters "The Straight Edge" square in the center of the shot. Bridget Collins (also known as Bridget Burpee), the designer of *The Kids Will Have Their Say* as well as five of X-Claim!'s six most influential albums, is considered to be a key part of the design direction of the label. She downplays the importance of her design work to punk history in an interview on the Facebook page for the Boston Hardcore documentary *All Ages*:

> I was just a layout and paste-up monkey. I never did any illustration and most of the bands knew what they wanted the LP covers to look like. I just made them printer format friendly.

Despite her modesty, the design of *The Kids Will Have Their Say* became iconic within the straight edge scene. One proof being how many bands adopted the typeface City for their band logos in homage to SSD. Youth of Today, Gorilla Biscuits, Chain of Strength, Side by Side and Growing Stronger—to name just a few—all use City. The typeface became synonymous with the scene. The pairing of City and straight edge feels perfect in that it captures what the Berlin-based type foundry Berthold describes as being "designed for attention and impact... a rectangular design that evokes a sporty urban feeling." City's industrial style, geometric structure of right angles, opposing round corners, and repeating unified parts fit the intensity and regimentation of straight edge life.

Fig. 2. Typography from cover of Jan Tschichold, *Typographische Gestaltung.* Basel: Benno Schwabe & Co., 1935.

Perhaps poetically City was one of the key typefaces in graphic designer god Jan Tschichold's second book/manifesto *Typographische Gestaltung* (Typographic Design) in 1935. *Typographische Gestaltung* (fig. 2) was a reaction against Tschichold's own seminal and more widely studied *Die Neue Typographie* (New Typography) from 1932. Tschichold, who had escaped Nazi Germany to settle in Basel, Switzerland, now drew parallels between the strict modernist limitations in *Die Neue Typgraphie*, National Socialism, and Goebbels' infamous

29

Gleichschaltung policies. *Typographische Gestaltung* was a rejection of his overly systematic style, achieved by rewriting his design principles to focus on clarity and concern for how design is made. For Tschichold to use a slab serif like City was, in its own way, insane during the tide of popularity that the International Style (Swiss Typography) had during that era. It's interesting to consider that even within the context of graphic design history, City was part of its own counter-revolution, a position akin to straight edge.

Princetown was released in 1981 by British designer Dick Jones for Letraset U.K. and later for International Type Corporation (ITC) in New York City. ITC, a newer foundry established in 1970 by Aaron Burns, Herb Lubalin and Edward Rondthaler, focused on typefaces for film and computer. Princetown was "inspired by college and university sportswear, with its blocky forms and heavy outline." According to ITC, "The Princetown font (fig. 3) is an excellent choice for any work associated with sports or collegiate life." Before Princetown, collegiate lettering came premade with limited size ranges specially designed for jerseys and varsity jackets. Letraset and ITC's wider accessibility made Princetown even more synonymous with high school and college sports in every small town in America.

In 1985 John ("Porcell") Porcelly and Ray Cappo picked up the torch of straight edge hardcore (Minor Threat and SSD disbanded around that same year) and formed Youth of Today. They were from Connecticut and deeply inspired by Boston Crew. Reflecting their lives in suburbia, Youth of Today mixed together skateboard culture, high school athletics (Porcelly played football and Cappo was on the wrestling team) and the harsh urban style of Boston Crew to create youth crew. What started as a small community of straight edge kids all over New England expanded into a nationwide movement without the core youth crew's knowledge or intentions. Varsity jackets instead of leather jackets, Nike hi-tops replacing black boots—it's hard to explain how crazy this was. Youth crew was subverting the punk subculture with everyday suburban culture, and the shift managed to really aggravate the scene, especially when youth crew moved into New York's Lower East Side. Feeding off this "everyone-hates-us" mentality helped crew members feel more tightly woven together.

The album art of Bridget Burpee, Al Barile, and X-Claim! still carried a lot of elements of the original DIY punk aesthetics from the early 80s. Revelation Records was founded in 1987 by Ray Cappo and Jordan Cooper as a hardcore straight edge record label. When Cappo left the business to focus on his band Shelter in 1988, Cooper took over completely. Revelation Records took the original cues of X-Claim! and formalized them into an aesthetic style that was polished but still carried the same rebellious attitude. (The style had a lot more in common with a skateboard company, in my opinion, when you compare the art to what was happening in the thrash and crust punk scene of the same period). From 1988 to 1989 Cooper employed Dave Betts to do design work for Revelation, with strict art direction from Cooper in regards to typography, layout, and photography. It was a minimal recipe: a live black and white photo, the name of the band and the title of the album in capital letters, bold, centered. Done. A clear homage to SSD's *The Kids Will Have Their Say*, the designs were clean, effective, no-frills, and straight to business. People like to say this approach reflects the straight edge hardcore sound and has become the trademark typographic style of youth crew.

Fig. 4. Cover of Judge, *Bringin' It Down*, Revelation Records, REV 015, 1989.

In 1989, Youth of Today members John Porcelly and Mike Ferraro formed Judge (fig. 4). The band's first release, *New York Crew* (fig. 5), was designed by Alex Brown from Gorilla Biscuits. *New York Crew* was the first use of Princetown in hardcore; Brown selected the typeface "to look like some sort of team logo. I was really into the way the first couple of SSD records looked." Much like the situation with City, the typeface Princetown was used by straight edge bands that followed Judge—such as Monster X, Floorpunch, and Face Tomorrow.

Fig. 5. Cover of Judge, *New York Crew*, Schism, SKIZ-2, 1988.

Epilogue

It's interesting seeing the connections between graphic design and straight edge. Later in life, John Porcelly himself became a graphic designer, operating a studio and creating the merch line True Till Death. In an interview on True Till Death's website, Procelly states, "My involvement with the hardcore scene has taught me a lot about design. Don't just create an image—create a mood. Set a tone. Convey what you're feeling through the medium." In another interview for The Hundreds, Porcelly explains that "the band was started by design, not by default."

FACE UP
INNER STRENGTH
STRAIGHT FROM THE HEAR
FREEWILL + TONS MORE!!

RELEASE

ELEASE- THE PAIN INSIDE
Axtion Packed Records 1

NEW JERS.E.Y

X S m E

OUT IN JUNE!

Set You STRAIGHT

A.P. records 1 out June 1st $3⁵⁰

A.P. Issue 1- Wide Awake, Insted,

A.P. ISSUE 2- Release, Turning p
Against the Wall, Gorilla Biscu

RELEASE- 3-sided short,green $9⁰⁰

VINYL

ZINE

SHIRTS

STOP AND THINK MAGAZINE NO.

Featuring interviews with:UNIFORM CHOICE,SLAM DUN

XX FANZINE XX
FREE THOUGHT
XX FANZINE XX

Out now!
Interviews with Blind A-
pproach,Intensity,On-Tra-
ck,and Stumbling Way,Plus
there are zine,record,and
show reviews,and this ti-
me,there are more photos

Alive & Direct‡

COMMON X SENS

XXXXXXXXXXXXXXXXXXXXXXXXXXXXXXXXXXXXXX

POISON×FREE
FANZINE

ISSUE NO.1- Gone!
ISSUE NO.2-Out Now:RAID,CHAIN OF
          STRENGTH,VISUAL DISCRIMINA-
          TION,RISE ABOVE,ONE STEP
          AHEAD,EVEN SCORE,HARDBALL,
          INTENT TO INJURE,GOOD &
          PLENTY,REFUSE TO FALL,
          SPLITLIP,ON GUARD,and
          GAMEFACE. A few words
          on The Straight Edge,
          Flag Desgration,and
          Abortion. Plus:show/
          record/zine reviews.
          90 pages.2 bucks and
          4 stamps.
ISSUE NO.3-Out Soon:FACE
VALUE(Clevo's),SHELTER, A
CHORUS OF DISAPPROVAL,and
          SLAPSHOT. Plus...
          Write for info.Also
PFZ longsleeves t-shirts
out soon.c/o Phil 849
Gramercy Dr.111 LA. CA.
90005 TFTNS!!!!!!!!!!!!

UGLY

XXXXXXXXXXXXXXXXXXXXXXXXXXXXXXXXXXXXXX

Distribution Networks

Ali Qadeer

Warning: In this piece, I risk over-theorizing the most visceral and exciting memories of my youth.

It seems that even the most networked, utopian, and non-hierarchical cultures still require central points of access to flourish. In the case of punk and hardcore scenes in the era before the dominance of the internet, three nodes immediately come to mind: the all-ages show, the print shop, and the post office. Each site performed necessary operations to facilitate a vibrant independent publishing culture of fanzines, a culture that seems diminished or at least radically different today. Did social media kill the fanzine? We can recognize glimmers of the fanzine's particular communicative register within social media today, but punk zines lost their foothold as their material infrastructure fell to digital paradigms of distribution. Without belittling the present (today's DIY punk/hardcore scenes seem more diverse and exciting to me than they have ever been), I'd like to take us through these three essential spaces and the roles they played for the crucial decade from the late 1980s to the late 1990s during which punk fanzines flourished.

From church basements to record store backrooms and union halls, the venues of all-ages shows provide the underlying organizational basis for punk scenes. The DIY ethos expressed itself through an economy of maximum participation: punks played instruments, took photographs, wrote screeds, cooked food, sold records, organized shows, etc. Rarely was one's role summarized by mere attendance. The smell of sweat combined with the waft of bland lentil dishes and spilled beer persists longer than the sound of the bands or even moshpit injuries, though it's not quite as enduring as the tinnitus that rings twenty years later. In the blurred boundaries between performer and audience is where discourses around politics, lifestyle, and ethics grow. Interviews and reviews throughout my fanzine collection document these discourses.

Opposite: Collage of zine ads that appeared in various issues of *Good and Plenty*, 1989-1992.

33

What were the boundaries of one's straight edge practice? What feminism or organizational politic did one ascribe to? These questions were often dictated by genre spectrums that, at the time, seemed insurmountably wide but with a little distance are incredibly proximate. Straight edge, crustpunk, emo, riot grrrl, streetpunk shared more in common than not. The formal qualities which dictate so much of the look and feel of fanzine culture also emerge in these spaces: immediacy, non-expertise, and vernacular tools. They show up in the fills of drummers playing slightly too fast for their own muscles, in record production or album artwork, and, notably, in the fanzines themselves.

A fanzine is a radically independent publication. Another way of understanding the zine is as a genre of publication replete with its own subgenres. Like all genres, zines have recognizable formal tropes that emerge from the conditions of their production. These forms are largely determined by access to limited toolsets. They are intimately connected to the print shop, those commercial entities which barely survive now that paper tasks have been sublimated into purely digital experiences. Photocopy machines, scotch tape, default bond paper all inform the visual form of zine production from a certain era. The print shop served as a de facto design studio, usually in off-hours. Friends working behind the counter offered additional services and ran scams circumventing supply counts. The print shop rarely offered cover stock, color, or even consistent print quality on their machines. This lack of options allowed the paper of zines to take on its buckled character when left in bathroom reading piles. The pages would show black traces where cut-out elements obscured the scanning light of the printer, or the edges of clear tape were picked up on the image. High school photo labs created amateur photographers to document shows, and their pictures underwent a secondary production process when xeroxed. The simplicity of the 8.5" × 11" sheet folded in half and stapled twice creates a wholly recognizable form. Through the conditions of the print shop, skill ceases to be located in craft or typographic mastery but rather lay in the ability to push the capacity of the tools as far from their targeted intent as possible—to drive machines designed for document reproduction to generate new visual forms.

The fanzine is much more than a singled printed artefact. Its metaphysical center rests in its multiplicity and distribution. The fanzine operates within—and builds out—a network of relationships. To send the physical form of the zine across the continent required direct participation with the post office. The connections formed, the records and VHS tapes traded, the tours planned, the whole scriptural discourse activates the form of the fanzine. Every physical form required processing and shipment in a global network of scenes. A photocopied photograph of a band accompanying a show review leads to a mail-order record which leads to a correspondence and eventually a stop on a tour. The fanzine is a channel more than an artefact. For an ur-genre of music which so often emphasizes speed, the pace of communication is notably slow. Between fanzine assembly and production cycles, the pace of mail travel, and even the act of waiting in lines to send packages, the fanzine is fast to make but slow to move.

Nothing remains static and the ways that punk is disseminated changes as technology changes. We shouldn't lament the speed and ease of access to new music and ideas today. When I attend a show, I'm always excited by what I see and hear, and I can easily (and immediately) broadcast my impressions to others through text, image, and even video. The new distribution networks have their advantages over the old ones.

Combing through my collection today, I notice that my fanzines operate as an archive of endeavors to seize the means of cultural production. Whole economies of records, bands, labels, tours, relationships, discourses, and beefs are documented in reviews, essays, and interviews. My fanzines are the public record of what it meant to grow up in and around punk within a given time and place. The scene was written at shows—but designed in the print shop and proliferated via post.

BURN 7/91 PHOTO GREG BROWN

JAWBOX

INSIDE OUT-PHOTO DAVE INDECISION

Good & Plenty

SOFT & CHEWY LICORICE CANDY

NET WT. 1.8 OZ. (51g)

SUDDEN STOP INTERVIEW, BAND ADS, CONCERT REVIEWS, AND A WORD HUNT

ISSUE #1 MARCH '89 ~ FREE!

The cover of the first issue of *Good and Plenty* embodies the spirit of future potential. The hand-drawn group of hardcore youth on the cover are not quite silhouettes. Unlike the classic Side by Side *You're Only Young Once* 7" record (fig. 1) released just a year earlier in 1988, the figures on the cover have enough detail to see that some are wearing hooded sweatshirts, some are wearing t-shirts, some have X'ed up fists, yet the faces are all blank.

Drawing faces would have given each figure an identity, but the decision to not render facial details allows for the group to be inclusive. The rendering is universal, at least as much as it could be in a male-dominated music scene. The youths represent a growing scene that's open and inviting, unified through a shared interest yet still distinct. There are no try-outs, no barriers to making the team; the only thing you need to do to belong is show up. The incomplete drawing also implies a starting point for the zine and for hardcore.

The slapdash design of the cover wears its spontaneity on its sleeve. A small box of Good & Plenty candy is collaged to the top of the zine's cover, presenting the name and logo of the inaugural issue with literal transparency. The candy's net weight and "soft and chewy" tagline on the packaging are unobscured. The irony of labeling hardcore as "soft and chewy" is a beacon of things to come. Together, the appropriated title and the drawing imply that the hardcore scene is good—strong, even—and suggest that this fanzine is a way to engage with this burgeoning scene.

This first issue, given away for free, contains one interview, a handful of show reviews, a couple of playlists, and a few ads. It's all that's needed to get started.

Good and Plenty appears to be the product of someone creating something for the sheer enjoyment of making the thing. It's a fanzine in the most real sense, designed to capture an overflow of genuine excitement and enthusiasm. —C.S/K.S.

Issue 1
March 1989
12 pages
5.5 × 8.5 inches
250 copies
Free

Opposite: Paste-up for cover of *Good and Plenty*, issue 1, 1989.

Fig. 1. Cover of Side by Side. *You're Only Young Once...* Revelation Records, REV 005, 1988, 7" EP.

We here at Good And Plenty 'zine
(all two of us)would like to tell you
what our 'zine is all about before you
go through it. Our 'zines basic purpose
is to give smaller or bigger S.E. or
Positive bands a little recognition.
It may have some personnal parts to it
but not to much. It is also for fun.
Your fun reading it,and our fun making
it. If you have any positive info. to
share with us. Or any bands we didn't
write to. Please send us a letter. Bands
include an ad or something for the next
'zine. We will definitely put any ad in.
And most positive info. Please send it
to- Mike Good
     2120 IIth St. Apt. I4
     Winthrop Harbor Il. 60096

          or

     Gabe Rodriguez
     2II6 Salem Blvd.
     Zion Il. 60099

and please enjoy the reading ahead.

                Thank you,
                Mike and Gabe

G and P would like to Thank:
Paul Aken at LCAVC, Mr. Reijnon,
Tom Lee at Action Printing, Joe
Lopez, Scott Overby, Noth(skin)k,
Jen Bittner, Jeff Fallos, Jason and
Wind of change, Ron + BROTHERHOOD,
Revelation Records, Chi-town SE, Life
Sentence, Soulside, Government Issue,
Napalm Dude, Tommy + Ludichrist, the Plague,
The Outcasts. Only the Strong, and Sudden.
Stop, and anyone who helps make a
better scene.

GOOD AND PLENTY PLAY LIST

MIKE GOOD
No For An Answer-EP
Gorilla Biscuits-EP
Token Entry-Jaybird
Side By Side-EP
Underdog-EP
Bold-Speak Out
Youth Of Today-all
Doxxy Style-Don't Hit Me Up
Hard Stance-EP
Verbal Assault-Trial
Soulside-Trigger

NATHAN R.
Gorilla Biscuits-EP
Uniform Choice-Screaming...
Life Sentence-Demo
Bad Religion-Suffer
Christ On A Crutch-Spread...
No For An Answer-EP
Underdog-EP
Sacred Reich-Surf Nicaragy
MDC-This Bloods,For You
Eazy-E-Eazy Duz It

Jenny B.
Megadeath-Peace Sells...
Metallica-Master of Puppets
Robin Trover-Bridge Of Sighs
Led Zeppelin-4
Anthrax-Among The Living
Iron Maiden-Number Of The Beast
Metallica-Kill 'em All
Crumbsuckers-BOAB
Megadeth-Killing Is My Business
AC/DC-Back In Black

Gabe R.
Men At Work-Business As Usual
NY Hardcore-The Way It Is
Uniform Choice-Screaming...
DRI-Four Of A Kind
Justice League-Think Or Sink
Nuclear Assault-all
Side By Side-EP
No For An Answer-EP
Gorilla Biscuits-EP
Underdog-EP
Life Sentence-Demo

Scott O.
Metallica-And Justice For All
Rush-Exit Stage Left
Slayer-South Of Heaven
Death Angel-Frolic Through Park
Voivod-War And Pain
Joe Satriani-Surfing w/Alien
Black Sabbath-Paranoid
MDC-This Bloods For You

Concert Reviews
Government Issue Soulside Life Sentence March 12

I was very skeptical of the show
from the start because right outside
Club Dreamers was Gwar's Tour Bus. I
thought oh no! We're in for a blood
bath. They didn't play but I could feel
their ghost on my back or was that Mike
with the camera. Anyway Life-Sen-
tence had a short notice to play, but
they ripped. They started with "Problems" and continued with old stuff like
"Punks For Profit" and "Figure It Out"
A few new tunes were played and will
be released on April Fools Day; hardy
har har! They didn't get the croud moving
until Mike Good sang "Men In Blue"
Jeff did a rap for an encore into
"Godzilla" by B.O.C.
   Next was Soulside. They almost
knocked the floor down. You could
feel the ground shake as Bobby sang
War. Bobby Sullivin has a good way of
getting the croud going. They played a
lot of new stuff which will be on a 7"
on april on Dischord. They did "Other
Side" and "Pearl to Stone" from the first
record , but took me to the promise land
during "Baby." Now I know why they
won best new band in Flipside.
   I wasn't very familiar with Government Issue but the crowd was. They
were very tight and together throughout the whole set. As SNFU might
say, "They're not getting older, they're
getting better". John Stabb almost
choked himself with the mic, but that is
nothing new. The only song I knew was
"Where You Live" and it was they're
best. I'm just sorry I didn't know any
others. I gave it 2 thumbs up and you're
at the show.

                Gabe Rodriguez

PHOTO ↑ MIKE

PHOTO ↑ GABE

PHOTOS ↟ Gabe

Concert Reviews
Ludichrist, The Plague, The Outcasts, Decrepit Uth March 5th

Tommy Christ ↓

There was a pretty good size crowd for a Sunday show in Chicago. Before the show I had the pleasure of talking to Tommy Christ of Ludichrist This was going on during Decrepit Uth They were just a cheap thrash band with a bad singer. Nuff said.

The Outcasts were a horse of a different color. I loved them. They were sort of a cross between D.R.I. and Cryptic Slaughter with all the mosh parts in between. They are from the south side and have an lp out. Lookout for them in the near future.

The Plague stole the show; literally. They got everybody going around a brick wall in the middle of the pit. People were playing ring around the rosy like little kids. It was bad. The bass player sang as they did an Iggy Pop cover. They also have a demo for sale. Half the crowd left after The Plague but that was a big mistake.

Ludichrist was next .Even though the new stuff isn't as good, they still had old songs like "Fire at the Firehouse", "Government Kids", and "Down with the Ship", which they mixed old classics in. To top all of that, they did "Earache my Eye" by Cheech and Chong for an encore along with "Green Eggs and Ham" to boot. They didn't have it all together seeing that they have a new bass player each week. It was only a weekend tour of the midwest, but who cares a show is a show. I give it 2 thumbs up and you're at the show.

Gabe Rodriguez

Photos- Gabe   The Plague ↑

INSTED

INSTED

Good & Plenty WORD SEARCH

```
M Y V L N H L T D O O H R E H T O R B X A
N F E C N A T S D R A H S K T I V S L K X
W P R O J E C T X V K F T P U Y B Q B Y R
O C B X A A A F U F F U I S O B F P P O A
D N A Y A D O T F O H T U O Y I A Z E K W
K N L S A E P D F M D D C S L G N S J D D
A K A Y U W G L K E D E S W A Q U S N I E
R C S U T I A C R E G I I N I F O G T C J
K H S N E H D K N H D N B H C Q R O I E L
U C A I O K E S A E H A A B U I D O C J D
U W U T N B T S B E B H L H R C H E Q B U
X N L P D O N Y T I R Q L O C C R D N S O
A A T R P A S I E R Z B I Q M F Z Y A Z R
Q P E I A I Z S T R O A R R E J O M R Q P
M P W D D F G M U Q U N O C S H U D V C K
W I D E A W A K E I L F G O D R E D N U L
M D N E H X L O S K I S B O J H M Q G I A
Y P G Y W S E V E N S E C O N D S M I E W
E J A V P W Q J U S T I C E L E A G U E I
```

ONLYTHESTRONG   UNIFORMCHOICE   GORILLABISCUITS
WINDOFCHANGE   JUSTICELEAGUE   VERBALASSAULT
YOUTHOFTODAY   CRUCIALYOUTH   SEVENSECONDS
HARDSTANCE   BROTHERHOOD   PAGANBABIES
UNITPRIDE   SIDEBYSIDE   SUDDENSTOP
BREAKAWAY   WALKPROUD   WIDEAWAKE
UNDERDOG   KRAKDOWN   PROJECTX
INSTED   RAWDEAL   HALFOFF
      JUDGE

SEND complete word search to: Gabe Rodriguez
       2116 Salem Blvd.
For ONE FREE! box of   ZION IL 60099
Good and PLenty candy.   Don't miss out! FREE

mmm good   LIMIT ONE PLEASE

SUDDEN STOP

Matt Burger - Vocals
Rob Nelson - Drums
Joe Nelson - Guitar
Chris Burger - Guitar
John McMills - Bass

Send 3.00 for Demo to:
Its A Wonderful Life
7764 Woodward
Woodridge IL 60517
(312) 985-6128
check payable to matt burger

G&P - Are you guys a straight edge band?

Matt - No we are not. We're a positive band. With straight edge members. John and Chris dont want to be associated with a straight edge band. We'd rather be what we are right now. Instead of being a S.E. band, and then you get classified by people who say why dont they sound like this or like that.

G&P - How long have you guys been together?

Matt - About 1½ or 2 years now. And he's been with us for about 6 months now John our bass player.

G&P - What are you guys all about?

Matt - We have a very hardstance against racism or least I do. I try to write that in the songs. We all do. (are against racists and nazis.) I stand for homeless people. People shouldn't like beat them up or anything. Yah know give em some money or shit like that. We're trying to stay away from political issues, but stay more on social issues. Like whats going on in society, but not with politics. We're not gonna start singing like down with Bush and stuff like that because thats not immediately whats going against us. And we're positive open minded, being cool to as many people as we can and not like he's got long hair lets go beat him up or he's a skin head what a dope and stuff like that. I mean to me thats what we're all about. We're just trying to be cool being positive, being knowing what youre going to do with your future. We've also got a song about child abuse. About how the kid like learns how to take care of his kids from his father, and his father beats him and stuff like that. Thats a pretty goofy song.

John - I tend to appreciate the kinds of songs we write, I think its important to not be militant, but to expose the kind of social problems that surround us like Matt was talking about. Crackle crunch whurr... I would continue after this. And my apologies to Sudden Stop and you My tape got ate!

GOOD & PLENTY

May '89   FREE   Issue #2
Special expanded version

Only The Strong Interview, Lyric Trivia,
Brotherhood Centerfold, Concert and
Record Reviews, and much more

The Future Is Ours

Two months after the first issue dropped, Rodriguez and his *G&P* collaborators found their foothold with a sophomore effort. Mike Good makes a plea in the editor's letter "for more bands to come through more often and play shows." It's a call for a more prosperous and dynamic scene. That's the utility of a zine like this: to build bridges and make connections, locally and globally.

The symbiotic relationship between local scenes and the larger hardcore band circuit is a critical one. Bands will tour if there are places to play; venues will book bands if there is a community to support them. These alignments of wants and needs ride on the back of discovery. In this period, when the underground was deep underground, zines served the incredibly important role of spreading information. Zines were a flashlight shining a light into a completely dark room.

The half-size pages of issue 2 are filled edge-to-edge with type-written text and black-and-white snapshots. During the interview with local Chicago-based band, Only the Strong, topics included bands pushing vegetarianism, the problem with right-wing bands, choosing record labels and being fairly compensated, and the stylistic evolution of older bands like Uniform Choice and 7 Seconds. The conversation is candid and honest.

Late in the issue, some lyrics trivia appears. The selected verses include: "The future is ours, let's keep it that way," "Always move on, step forward and progress," and "I won't tell you what to do, just how I feel." The sentiments read like omniscient motivations for young zine-makers learning their craft and doing so with the best intentions. —C.S/K.S.

Issue 2
May 1989
24 pages
5.5 × 8.5 inches
250 copies
Free

Opposite: Paste-up for cover of *Good and Plenty*, issue 2, 1989.

G&P would like to thank the following people for their support: Tony, John, Chuck, and Jeremy from Only The Strong, Bruce (Polar-Bear), Ron and Brotherhood, Matt Garcia, Mike Beady, Paul Aken at LCAVC, Nathan(Link) Rodriguez, Mike's Mom and Grandpa for rides and stuff, Gabe's dad for putting up with me, The Accused, Insted, Reason To Believe, Wind Of Change, Russ and Underdog, Life Sentence, Manny Fernandez, Pablo, Dave from Earwaves, Chad, Stringy Hair (nice hair), Poseur Skin, Jeff Nissen, Chris (Franken-wawa) Grooms, Chewawa, the Beaver, Woowoo man, Jah, Stackenstein, Walker, Dykenstein, Pipeye, Waukegan Blueprint, Mr. Slocum and Mr. Reijnen at Horizon, Joe Lopez, Corey Upton, Breakaway, Scott Overbey, Jen Bittner (we still need a ride to Metallica), Sherrie Levick(we forgot you last time) Grease Monkey, Mr. Murphy, Humpback(for letting Mike cheat on the tests in English), a big yahoo to Jimmy Gastapo for diving on me from the speakers, the kids on Degrassie Jr. High, Revelation(thanks for the free stickers), Skate Edge Records, Stepforward Records, Rock 'n Records, and anyone who contributes positively to the scene.
Long-hair, short-hair, Black, White, straight-edge, or not...We are all the same!

Never Again

Never again (4x)
Why do we have to fight
Me and you
Why care who's right
You and me
Why care who's wrong
Me and you
Why can't we just get along
Unsuspecting people see deceiving
In their eyes
Triggered 'til the end
We're gonna fight
Ever again
Ever again
Ever again

(Lyrics by Only The Strong)

THE EDGE

Welcome to the 2nd issue of Good And Plenty magazine.If you have the first issue you can tell this issue is alot bigger and we believe better. We still need contributers of photos,ads,play lists, or anything else we could use for the 'zine.

But now I would like to talk about Chicago.A very presperous scene with open minded people, full of different bands,and always fun shows.The only thing Chicago needs is for more bands to come through more often and play shows.So bands please come to Chicago!

Thats all we have to say for this issue.Please have fun reading the pages and puzzle ahead.Please send stuff for us to use in our 'zine to

Good & Plenty
G&P Hide Out
C/O Mike Good
2120 11th St. Apt.14
Winthrop Harbor Il. 60096

1/100

X ONLY THE STRONG X
Interviewed by G&P on Sat. April. 16th at "ONLY DA'HOUSE". Photos by Gabe at Durty Nellies and Medusas.

Tony-Vocals
John-Bass
Chuck-Guitar
Jeremy-Drums

G&P:First off,what are your views on S.E?
Chuck:John,since you are new you can answer the first one.
John:Uhh,God I hate this question.Well obviously we are a S.E. band,so we have very high standards for S.E. I dont know.
G&P:Do you think pushing vegetarianism is going to far?
John:I dont think its right to all of a sudden be a vege.I dont think its right for people to say "Your not S.E.

John strumming the Bass.

if your not a vege.Thats happening alot on the East Coast.
Chuck:You dont have to be a vege. to be S.E., its just your morals.Whatever you want to achieve in life,go for it.
Tony:I agree in S.E. its just your choice.
G&P:What do you think of bands that are totally right winged,bordrering on fascism?
Tony:We think its totally stupid.
Chuck:We dont want to identify any bands in general, but anybody who has that kind of influence on the scene,does not need to be put in the scene. Theres a lot of stupidity already.The generalization of N.Y. being everybody having to be S.E. should be put aside and just make it a positive movement acro-ss the whole U.S. East,West,and Midwest.

Tony:Right wing isnt that bad but,right right wing I dont agree with at all.Its just a cop out for being a nazi.
G&P:So you say right wing conservative is good?
Tony:Its not bad its just another political belief. You also got your left wing liberals.
G&P:John when you were in Wide Awake,what did you think of the Ct. scene?
John:When I was in Wide Awake it was not big there was only around 5 S.E. bands.It was alright,good shows,had fun.Its different now.I went back last summer and now theres hundreds of S.E. kids at the shows.I saw Verbal Assault and Wide Awake and there were hundreds of kids there.I met so many people.
G&P:Underdog does not consider themselves a S.E. bamd but,do you think they are a major part of the N.Y. scene?
Tony:They are a big N.Y. band a lot of people like them.Everybody can relate to them.They dont single out anything.They talk about broader things that everyone can agree on.Which is good.They dont want to be considered S.E. all the members arent.
G&P:What do you think of the new style of U.C.?
Tony:Uniform Choice decided they wanted to suck. They want to make a lot of money and wear leather and grow their hair long.
Gabe:I like it though.   Chuck with the geetar

Tony:Its like when its one of your favorite records, for a long time,and they go off on another limb. Ian McKaye goes to Fugazi,but if he is still being sincere thats cool.

G&P:How about 7-Seconds?

John:I think that new album rules.Theyre saying the same things as before.

G&P:Do you think they are pushing it musically?

John:They are old though.

Tony:I understand because they are real good musicians.Kevin is a real good singer.They have every right to do what they want.

G&P:How about Dag Nasty?

John:You see thats their thing too. They are out of it.

Tony:Dag Nasty was awesome with Dave Smalley.Then they got these new members and its a different band.

Chuck:Its the cool thing now for old S.E. bands not to be classified as S.E. and make it purposefully known that they are not S.E.

G&P:What are some of the best groups coming up now?

Together:Brotherhood,Chain Of Strength,Beyond, Vision,Underdog.

Tony:Theres so many,you cant even begin to mention them all.

G&P:What do you think of people who make S.E. a joke?

Tony:Thats stupid because its a serious thing.When Crucial Youth does poems its funny,You should have fun with it.I dont know.

John:Its hard to tell is C.Y. making fun of it or are they seriously S.E. kids?Its funny if they are having fun with it,But if they are making fun of it then its going a bit to far.

Tony:They fooled a lot of people.Me also when I first got the 7",and then I kept on looking at it,Then I thought what is this fetish w/ Mr.T(laughter).

John again

G&P:What do you think is one of the most growing scenes in the U.S. today?

Tony:Chicago,the whole midwest is growing.

Together:Minneapolis,Toledo,Detroit,Rockford Il, Cleveland,and Oklahoma.

G&P:Are you guys planning to tour this summer?

Tony:Hopefully,if everything works out.

G&P:Where at?

John:Where ever we can go.

G&P:Any plans to put out any demos or 7"s?

Tony:After a while.We just want to play a lot of shows.

Chuck:We dont want to be a band that has a good demo and then fades away.Its like"oh,well they had a good demo or 7" on Revalation,but they never did anything".

Tony:All of these bands are making people think that they are god-like because they put out a 7" and everybody is like"Oh I got to get it",those bands are not even on the kids level.

Chuck:Its a good way for the small labels to make money,its a good scam like the band from down South No Excuse.They had their little ad in MRR and made it look like they were a S.E. band with a little guy moshing around on the cover with X's on his hands.We were even suckered into it.Alot of people are capitalizing on the X,everyone likes to put X's everywhere that they can.Theres people that we know that put X's on their hands and their not even straight.Its like a fashion statement lately.

Tony:As far as a Demo goes were just going to hang out.When people send us letters,and want us to play shows,we can work something out.Some bands have demos out before they have shows.Thats crazy,we want it to mean something.

G&P:Do you think the X is a dumb tag?

Chuck:I think its a real good tag.

Tony:I only wear them when Im on stage,so people know what we are about.If I go to different towns, I do it.But in Chicago,people know we're S.E. We dont have to prove it.Its something to show.But you shouldnt act like your better or anything.

Chuck:Put the X on your heart,not just on your hand.

Tony:Dont be a dick and put an X on one day and go pound beers the next day.

G&P:When you put out a 7",what label are you going to strive for?

Tony:Probably our own.Labels are monopolizing off it,and its too easy to put out a 7".I dont know why bands just dont do it themselves.I wanna know the people that send in for a record.You get to meet the kids and write them back.If you have a label do it for you they dont care.They will wait too long before they answer the mail.I answer my mail the day I get it,because I love mail.

G&P:In the last Flip Side Mag. No For An Answer said that they got off Revelation Because its a tag and you know their S.E..But they have more to say.Do you think that was a good move?

Tony:I think they did the right thing.They got a big label that was interested.They are gonna help them out,let them do the art work,and get their record around.You just dent have money to do that. I'm sure Revelation was only giving them about $100 dollars for a thousand records pressed thats nothing.If you do have to change do it.

G&P:Do you think that is why bands get off Positive Force and Revelation?

John:See,its a band it takes up your time,and you want to work hard to get it moving.They got Hawker Records.They're going to give them money. Like Y.O.T. they got the band and they are working hard to prove something so Caroline says yeah we will give you money.They said sure we'll take that in a minute.Were working hard and we need this money to live on anyway.I agree with that.Idont

agree with the bands that go on the big labels just to sell out.

G&P:Would you find it offensive if someone starts banging their head to your music?

John:If thats their way,banging their head.Then enjoy the show.Idont care if you spin on your head and break dance in the back because thats their energy through them from us.

Tony:The code word is"Hang Out."

Chuck:As long as they accept us for what we are.

Tony:When we were still called X-Factor,Durty Nellies wanted us to do a show,and we only had 6 or so of our songs.One of these songs was written on a big poster board and it fell down and this crazy metal head picked it up and held it.He was banging his head going nuts.Probably had whiplash but he is a cool kid.He loves us.Every time I see him hes asking about us,thats awesome.He likes other things,but if he likes us thats cool.

Chuck:The only thing is that I'm not into the division of Metal & Hardcore.Alot of people who are into the metal scene try to put a negative attitude with us.The band had problems at Cubby

Bear,the Murphys Law concert with metal heads.They were like"Who the fuck are you?"and this and that.It was like a contraversy over whos scene it was.That is one thing we dont want to have. The division of scenes,where it has to be cut and dry.

Tony:Hardcore is supposed to be fun not for people smoking pot and stuff here.You dont do that at shows.

Tony(a little wet)

Chuck:It makes everything bad.I personally dont see people who are cut and dry metal heads being involved with the Hradcore scene.If they're going take such a negative stand.The same with punks. They shouldnt be into what we are about if they are gonna be so negative towards us.

Tony:If you like the music then you go.

Chuck:We dont hold grudges against anybody.There are so many times when people crack on us for living the lifestyle that we wanna live.When we were skins,when I was a skater,now I'm S.E. and I still gotta hear it.People have enough balls to come up to us and say that we are putting pressure on their lifestyle which is total bull,because we never slagged anyones lifestyle.Everyone jokes around about us like "Oh nice Champion your wearing,or nice blonde hair."Certain people take jokes to far,They cant have a good time.

Tony:Everybody's got to be a philosopher.

Chuck:Everybodys got to be so serious about everything.Tony made a little joke at a metal show,he goes "Mortar"and right away people gotta talk like "dont you like this or that".

Tony:The code word is "Hang Out".

Chuck:We dont want to be seperated from anyone else.Just Hang Out.

G&P:As a band what are your values?

John:S.E. we are vegetarians.

Chuck:Dont let your body over power your minds actions

Tony:Be yourself,Hang Out

G&P:What are some good bands coming out of the Illinois area?

Tony:Full On Straight,Insight.

Chuck:Los Cause has been real coolote us.I know they had their problems when they dipped down and then they came back up.

Tony:Chicago does not have alot and Joe Kelley hung in there.They are not S.E. but they are cool. Joe Kelley is a cool guy to us.How could I be a dick to somebody that has been cool to me.

Mike:I just didn't like his dives a Murphy's Law,I got a knee to the chops.(Ha,Ha,)

G&P:Do you think he is a major part of the Chicago scene?

Chuck:They go on tour with Murphys Law and represent Chicago.When he goes to the East Coast.

G&P-What was your best show?

Tony:The last Durty Nellies show Feb 26.A lot of people were there. Punks,skins,metalers,SE kids,and there wasnt any fights.

G&P:That dude from NJ was there.

Tony:Brother Ted.Dancing with style in 89. Him and the Polar Bear are going on a USA tour. Theyll be on Dance Party USA.(It rules by the way)

G&P:So there is a little Chicago SE posse?

Chuck:Yeah there is!

G&P:John,being from Cn. what are the pits like compared to here?

John:They blow away Chicago.They have big pits. Its different everywhere depending on the kids.Stagediving is big there.

Tony:This girl I met in Toledo said she never saw a circle pit.She said they are crazy.I agree.When I first started going to shows,everybody was running in circles.But now you dont run in a circle.

Chuck:You put miles on your shoes.(laughter)

G&P:What do you think about stagediving?

John:That rules.Its the best part of the show. But it gets out of hand sometimes.I was at a show and Im sitting on the stage and people were jumping off of me.

G&P:Sitting on the stage still.This man is the stage potato.(a burst of laughter).

Together:We would like to thank all of our friends Especially all of the Choago skinheads,Peter for the van,Perry for being the coolest guy,everybody we write to,the Oakbrook Posse,The Polar Bear,Ness, Rob, Alice.(The phone rings and guess who it is... The Polar Bear.)He then tells us his story.

Polar Bear:One day at an Only The Strong show,I was really exhausted and "Chicago",my favorite song came up.Suddenly this big Polar Bear appeared in front of me,tapped me on the shoulder,and I felt infused with new energy and I cleared the floor and it ended with a good time head by all.

Jeremy on drums

State of Emergency/Only The Strong/ and International Jet Set
April 23rd,1989   Durty Nellies

What a combonation!Two ska bands and a Chicago straight edge band. How much more could you ask for? Sta of Emergency was first. They are a 3 piece ska group from the windy city. These guys can funk it up. They had a definite something that made me tap my toe so to speak. It's a different kind of mosh, but it still rules.Next was Only the Strong. If you have'nt heard these guys yet check'em out. They are straight edge but they don't have a typical sound. They are probably the best thing to come out of Chicago lately.(I'm not just saying that cause I know them.)They did have technical problems with the bass,so John(ex Wide-Awake)moshed it up a while.Look out for these guys. Last was International Jet Set. I didn't see much with these guys but the crowd did.Ok I admit it: I was only there for Only the Strong, but it was well worth the 6 bucks cover.I give it 2 thumbs up and your'e at the show.

Brotherhood/Only The Strong/Impulse Manslaughter
The Accused   May,9th 1989   Stars Inn

Brotherhood,a S.E. band out of Seattle started this night of havokful fun.These guys really ripped. Unlike the demo tape the lead singers voice is very clean live.They played old ones and new ones.These guys have a message to be heard.
   Then next comes a band that wasnt on the bill Chicagos own Only The Strong!They only played around six songs but they tore it up.They ended their short set with a cover of Youth Of Todays "Youth Crew". Everyone was on stage singing along,it was awesome.
   Impulse Manslaughter,another hometown Chicago band,played next.They played from the gut and it sounded like it came out of the gut.They crossed over Hardcore and Thrash with a touch of mosh to keep it going.
   Last but not least was The Accused.These guys get intense with their unique style of mosh and thrash.Everyone was diving,dancing,and having a great time.They played a somewhat short set,but they jammed out fully.They ended their set with the song "Baracudda".The crowd was going nuts.
   This was the funnest show I have been to in a long time.This is what in my opinion Chicago is all about!

RECORD REVIEWS...

Insted-LP: This 12" which we finally got was well worth the wait.Kevinsted's voice is awesome as well as fabulous music and to the point lyrics.A must for all S.E. hooligans.

No For An Answer-LP: Calling this slab of vinyl,album of the year would be an under statement.This album is great!I love it more every time I listen to it. Dans lyrics are superbly written and the music matches.2 thumbs up to Dan and his crew.

Hardstance-EP: Hardstance is taking a hardstance against racism and other issues on this one.His voice is harsh,the mosh parts rule,and its on blue vinyl.These 3 things make this one of my favorite EP's.

Madball-EP: Second generation Agnostic Frenter Freddy alias Rogers lil bro.Takes a shot at the spot light.Vocalizing this new breed of N.Y.H.C. as well as A.F. members playing the instruments.Too Cool.

O.P.I.V.-LP: If you liked the EP you will love the album.A combination of SKA and if you want to call it "punk" make this album too good.As well as a Ska cover of"These Boots Are Made For Walking".

Judge-EP: The old school returneth on this one. Break out the construction gloves,crank the volume up,and relive the old days with this one,Judge & Porcell are more than a band.

Reason To Believe-EP: Sounds like a Sammich Records Band,but its not.These guys are melodic,Heavy,and sometimes fast.Reminds me of Minor Threat but much better.They definitely have something going for them.

Sudden Stop-Demo: This one starts out melodic,I like that.Then comes this speed with young vocals. Lyrics deal with homeless people,caring,and friendship.Potential here."I think"so"&"Rage"highlights.

M.D.C.-Live in the Rhineland: This is heaven for you M.D.C. freaks.25 live tracks from all of their releases.A little rough on the vocals,but you cant blame Dave.They still got it.Why Berlin?

Agnostic Front-Live at CBGB'S:I cannot tell you how much I love this one.Anyone who has not heard these guys,get this one.Something for everybody. They do old songs galore.My favorite being "Last Warning"with Rogers little brother Freddie singing.

In Effect Sampler: You cant go wrong for 2 buck$. Check this out:24-7 Spyz,Raw Deal,Prong,Madball, Sick Of It All,and Agnostic Front.Everything here kicks.Stuff from old Demos.Dont miss out.Mail order only!

Christ On A Crutch-EP: These guys have something to say.Great artwork and great production.This is the best non-Straight Edge 7" all year.I cant wait to see these guys.

Crucial Youth-Crucial Yule: Can you believe these guys?This is best as of yet from C.Y.They cover "Crucified"but change it to Christmas time for the skins.OI!

Wind Of Change-Rain EP: You have to like something that comes in the mail in less than a week.Only 2 songs but it still has a lot to offer.These guys are not typical S.E.Dont miss them on their "Rain On The Nation Tour".

Wide Awake-Ct. Hardcore: What can I say I'm blown away.I have not heard something this good since Gorilla Biscuits.S.E. lyrics definitely,but I give these guys credit.Good Job Boyees.

Chain of Strength-Ep:I knew this would be good.The newest release from Revalation and I wasn't let down.These guys are harsh,heavy,and great.Low vocals,but they make up for it with mega-crucial moshes

MAXIMUM ROCKNROLL
Issue

INSTED
INSTED
INSTED
INSTED
INSTED

Interviews with-*Insted*, *Youth Of Today*,
Only The Strong, *No For An Answer*,
Hardstance, and *Underdog*. Plus Scene
Reports, and other Straight or Positive info.

GOOD AND PLENTY LIST

Polar Bear
Wind Of Change-All
U.C.-Screaming For Change
Crippled Youth-Join The Fight
YOT-Cant Close My Eyes Ep
? Seconds-Skins bootleg
Fugazi-All
Turning Point-EP
SSD-The Kids Will Have Ther Say
Degrassi Jr. High Theme Song
The Zit Remedy-Everybody Wants.

Tony
Upfront-Spirit
No for an answer-Lp
Underdog-Lp
Brotherhood-Ep
Revalation-everything
Raw Deal-Demo
Unit Pride-?"
YOT-Were not in this
Project X-7"
Breakdown-anything

Gabe R.
No For An Answer-LP
Bold-LP
Brotherhood-Demo
Chain Of Strength-EP
Agnostic Front-Live LP
Life Sentence-LP
Breakaway-EP
Insted-LP
D.R.I.-4 of a Kind
Wide Awake-EP
Nuclear Assault-All

Chuck
Underdog-Tape
Blast-Its in my Blood
Cro-mags-Age Of Quarrel
Raw Deal -Demo
Verbal Assault-Trial
Beyond-Demo
YOT-Breakdown the walls
Abused-BFY ?"
Marginal Man-New Release
Chain of Strength-Ep

Mike G.
Brotherhood-Demo
Side By Side-All
Septic Death-Kichigai
Agnostic Front-Live LP
Hardstance-EP
No For An Answer-All
Gorilla Biscuits-All
O.P.I.V.-Energy
Underdog-EP
Doggy Style-Last Laugh

Matt G.
7-Seconds-All
Side By Side-EP
Gorilla Biscuits-EP
Wind Of Change-Rain EP
Bold-Speak Out
Wide Awake-EP
Y.O.T.-Breakdown
Token Entry-From Beneath...
Pagan Babies-Next
D-Vision -No Laughing Matter

Mike B.
REM-Green
7 Seconds-Ourselves
Public Enemy-All
Gorilla Biscuits-EP
Bob Marley-All
MDC-Live Lp
Replasements-Dont Tell..
KMFMD-Dont Blow Your Top
Fugazi-LP
Soulside-Trigger

INSTED

ARK•II CANADA
542 MOUNT PLEASANT RD., SUITE 104
TORONTO, ONTARIO M4S 2M7
(416)487-4681

If Slaughterhouses Had Glass Walls . . .

The black-and-white steer waiting outside the slaughterhouse is called an Angus, which is the name of the Celtic god of love. It weighs about 1,100 pounds and has lived its entire life of 19 months on a Canadian farm. As the slaughterhouse approaches, it is moving left and right on its front legs, and if its facial expression were translated into human terms, it would be called uneasy. The slaughterer places a round stun gun at a point between and three inches above the steer's blinking eyes and fires a black cartridge. Bullets are not used because the steer's brain will be sold for consumption. The steer drops immediately and soundlessly to the floor. The metamorphosis of living animal to cellophaned meat has begun.

The steer's two rear legs are brought together and fastened to a chain hoist. This is done with considerable difficulty, for the steer, though silent and glassy-eyed, is kicking and thrashing. Once the chain is attached the animal is hauled into the slaughterhouse and upward so that it is hanging head first over a six-foot-square concrete pit. The slaughterer vomits into the pit. The slaughterer sharpens a long knife and then, in one quick pull, slits the animals throat. Blood pours into the pit as water from a huge bag. The steer does not react, save for three spasmodic twitches of its head. The blood pours in a steady stream for several minutes and fills the pit to about three inches. At some point the steer bleeds to death. There is no sound except for a radio, which is playing gospel music, and the air is varnished with the sweet smell of blood.

The slaughterer wears high rubber boots and

a rubber apron, which are frequently hosed off to remove blood. Blood covers his hands and arms, and it is spattered on his neck and face. He steps into the steaming pool of warm blood and beheads the steer. Holding it by one of its horns, he carries the dripping head to a barrel, where he deposits it with other heads. The headless carcass is removed to a low-lying metal block, called a cradle, where two other workers lay it on its back. Its legs, which are sticking upward, are removed and the steer is neatly skinned, rear to front.

The animal is eviscerated and its unsalable entrails are removed and hung separately—livers with livers, hearts with hearts, tails with tails, tongues with tongues. The men work quickly and with the same indifference that munitions workers develop to dynamite. They frequently stop to hose themselves and their work area. Meanwhile, the original slaughterer is using a squeeze mop to push the blood in the concrete pit down a small drain.

The skinless, headless carcass is again hoisted up on a mechanical pulley and, beginning between the rear legs, a worker with a huge power saw cuts it in half. The resulting two sides of beef are hosed clean of blood and hung in a refrigerated room. Later, the halves will be butchered and given names like brisket, sirloin, prime rib, rump, round, shank, flank and chuck. The 1,100 pound animal will yield about 600 pounds of meat. Each piece will be weighed, priced, placed on a styrofoam tray and wrapped in cellophane. People will buy them, cook them, garnish them and eat them.

...The Whole World Would Be Vegetarian!

Lyric Trivia

How well do you know your lyrics? Try these for size. These are all taken from stuff you should know.

1. On to greener pastures, the core has gotten soft.
2. The future is ours, let's keep it that way.
3. How come I keep feeling the kiss of the whip?
4. It's safest, it's smartest to live poison free.
5. To you it was just music, but to us it was so much more.
6. If you were smart, you would lose that f**king joint.
7. The knowing is real, it's how I feel.
8. Always move on, stepforward and progress.
9. Takes more strength to put down your hands.
10. Friendship- To you it means nothing.
11. You're welcome to join the crew.
12. It's hard to hold, when the world is spinning.
13. For there are none as blind as those who will not see.
14. More than music, it's a way of life!
15. Trying to do hard constantly, sometimes it may be hard to see.
16. I'll do better than try, I'll give a 110 percent.
17. I'm not convinced enough to think the world is through.
18. With a mind, with a heart, fight to the finish, fight from the start.
19. We must be together, fight the good fight.
20. I won't tell you what to do, just how I feel.

WANTED!!!

The following is a list of stuff that the staff of Good and Plenty are looking for. If you want to sell or know someone who does, contact the person who is looking for it. Thank You.

Mike Good
2110 11th St. Apt 14
Winthrop Harbor Il. 60096

Youth Of Today-Crucial Times 7", Underdog 7", Last Option 7", Project X 7" w/zine, X Marks The Spot 7" w/zine, Walk Proud 7", Unity 7", Turning Point 7", Justice League "Think or Sink", any Dag Nasty live tapes, 7 Seconds Skins, Brains, and Guts bootleg, Thanks-Lunchmeat /Mission Impossible(Sammich), or any Straight Edge videos (Side By Side, Bold, Gorilla Biscuits, Token Entry, etc...)

Gabe Rodriguez
2116 Salem Blvd.
Zion Il. 60099

Reason To Believe(1st pressing on Soulforce), Token Entry 7" and From Beneath The Streets lyric sheet, Raw Deal demo, Last Option 7", Wide Awake 7", Project X 7",Wind Of Change- A Promise Kept, Again/Keep in Mind split ep, Hard Stance 7' (red or black vinyl), Halfoff Lp (red cover or vinyl), any Justice League Lp.,Sacred Reich-Draining You of Life demo, Unity 7', Misfits- Beware 12"or Wolfsblood, NYC Hardcore-The Way It Is 7",AOD-Let's BBQ 7" or AOD/Bedlam split 7", Uniform Choice demo, or any live videos from Chicago '86-'89.

Matt Garcia
1111 Rt. 41 Apt. 2
Gurnee Il. 60031

Walk Proud 7", Token Entry-From Beneath the Streets w/insert, 7 Seconds- Commited For Life (1st pressing w/both inserts), Justice League Lp.(Positive Force), 7 Seconds- Walk together Rock Together (yellow or purple), Outcry 12" (Positive Force), any old 7 Seconds, Minor Threat T-shirts in good condition, or any audio or video tapes of 7 Seconds except Aug 17 '86 Metro, Chicago.

GOOD & PLENTY

#3 SEPT. 89   .75¢   DA 'ZINE

GORILLA BISCUITS
BROTHERHOOD
JUDGE

INSTED
BOLD

Gameplay

Chess is a two-player strategy board game played on a checkered board with 64 squares arranged in an eight by eight grid. Despite its clean and straightforward design, the game did not originate in Switzerland.

Issue 3
September 1989
44 pages
5.5 × 8.5 inches
500 copies
75¢

Swiss Style, also called the International Typographic Style, developed in the 1940s and 1950s and utilized sans-serif typography, grids, and asymmetrical layouts. Swiss designer Josef Müller-Brockmann stated that "one must learn how to use the grid; it is an art that requires practice." *Good and Plenty* wasn't designed on a strict grid, but it was grid-adjacent. There was a tendency to favor order over disorder. Straight lines did the job fine, so why fuss with complicated angles? The whole point of a fanzine was to communicate and share ideas.

At the time *G&P* 3 was being folded and stapled, it would still be another three years until the first issue of *Ray Gun* magazine hit shelves. Designed by David Carson, *Ray Gun* exemplified a chaotic approach to design and published articles intended to be purposely obscured or unreadable. Carson explained, "Just because something's legible doesn't mean it communicates." Content is just a pawn in the game of design.

The Bauhaus school in Germany certainly loved the square. But that was a polyamorous affair—there were other shapes to be loved too: the circle and the triangle. Dutch graphic designer Wim Crouwel—"Mr. Gridnik"—used the grid to create some of the most iconic graphic design of the 20th century; he's probably played some chess. We imagine he must be great at it. His 1968 poster, *Vormgevers* ("form givers"), uses an underlying grid from edge to edge, not unlike a chessboard; the top half of the design is black while the bottom half is white. The grid forms letters: light squares become dark, letters become words, and meaning emerges block by block. Crouwel once said, "You can play a great game in the grid or a lousy game. But the goal is to play a really fine game."

Opposite: Paste-up for cover of *Good and Plenty*, issue 3, 1989.

51

The artist Marcel Duchamp opined, "I have come to the personal conclusion that while all artists are not chess players, all chess players are artists." Similarly, while all designers are not zine-makers, all zine-makers are designers. In 1940, Russ Chauvenet—a competitive American chess player and an avid fan of science fiction—helped produce the science fiction publication *Detours*. Sources credit him as the first person to coin the term fanzine. *Detours'* first issue was completely handwritten with colored markers (green, purple, blue, and yellow), with paragraphs alternating hues throughout. Chauvenet and his collaborators were thoughtful about design. It was amateur, and that reason was exactly why Chauvenet preferred the term *fanzine* over *prozine*. "Pro" implied professionalism, and this was more passion than polish. There were other contenders for a moniker—among them "fanac," "fanmag," and "fanag"—that last a word the writers of *Detours* declared "un-euphonious." In bright purple ink, neatly printed in the premiere issue, they announced their "intention to plug fanzine as the best short form of fan-magazine." Checkmate. —C.S./K.S.

Welcome to the 3rd issue of G&P. It has been a while since the last one but I think the content will make up for it. I want to thank all of the bands who were kind enough to do interviews with us, and all the people who write us. If you would like to place an ad, send it to the G&P hide-out. Also, send scene reports from your area, or whatever will ad to this publication.

GOOD & PLENTY #3
C/O Gabe Rodriguez
2116 Salem Blvd.
Zion Il.60099

#1,2 sold out/sorry
photo credits:Mike B,Gabe, Matt G,Insted 7",Brotherhood,and "Ness"

Gabriel Rodriguez   Mike Good

Together we built this we have all done our part:Ron (Brotherhood),Underdog(We still need an interview), Gorilla Biscuits,Insted, Bold,Judge(Stay Heavy), Up-Front,Billings Gate, Target,Only The Strong-Thanks for getting the ball rolling in Chicago, MRR,Flipside,Open Your-Eyes,Kiersten(Straight Up), Mike from New Age,Comisky Park Crew(Mary,Greg,Martine,Pablo), Mary and Judy,(New York next Summer),Polar Bear,Steve G.(Gear), Seth,G&P Pen Pals(Carl & Mike,Tim, Craig C,James H,Jason H,Aaron, Pinky,Lisa(Hope its thick enuf 4 u), Megan(Thanks for trusting me),John-B.(RTB),Rudy O(Happy Birthday Bro hope you like the video)Mike Nike,John The Bastard,Chris K & Sherie T(Restless),and the Waukegan crew:Ruiz,Tom, Steve(Katz),Chad,Mark,Masada,Big Mike,Edwin,Tom T. Nathan(stand tall bro).Thanks to Mike B.for pics, and extra special thanks to Matt Garcia for all the help on this issue.

STRAIGHT EDGE-TREND OR WAY OF LIFE

You've heard people say,"Straight edge is just a trend,it will fade like everything else."I don't think so.It is true,for some people it is a trend, but fo me it is a way of life.It doesn't make me any better than anyone else,it is just what I chose,and it works for me.I have seen what drugs and booze can do and I ask myself,"Is it really worth it?No way! I hear these people saying,"Yeah man,I got so wasted last night.Got my ass whipped,got laid,and passed out in a sewer.It was great."Sure,til you find out you need stitches and you got a girl pregnant.Nope, I dont need those kind of hassles.Im glad I've got Stright Edge because I have a little brother who takes it seriously,and I dont want to have to find him wrapped around a telephone pole dead somewhere. I have nothing against people who drink,but if you think you need it to have a good time,I know a lot of people who can tell you different.As one smart man said,"Its safest,its smartest to live poison free."
Gabe Rodriguez

VERBAL ASSAULT-CHICAGO

This is a compilation of playlists from the staff of G&P and some of our friends.In no particular order.

TODAY	YESTERDAY...
Underdog-Live in Mil.	7 Seconds-all
Insted-Ep	Insted-Bonds of Friend.
Judge-WNYU radio	Brotherhood-Demo
Sick of it All-Lp	Soulside-all
Free for All-Comp.	Underdog-all
Upfront-Spirit	Big Daddy Cane-all
Wide Awake-Ep	Turning Point-Ep
Noise Forest-Comp.	Uniform Choice-Lp
New Breed-Comp.	Side By Side-Ep
In-Effect-Sampler Cassete	DRI-all
2 Live Crew-Double Lp.	Suicidal Tendencies-all
Beastie Boys-Hey Ladies	Token Entry-all
Dag Nasty-Live in Chicago	Dag Nasty-all!
Death Angel-Frolic...	Misfits-all
Destruction-Eternal...	Samhain-all
Bold-Speak Out	Doggy Style-all
Gorilla Biscuits-all	Iron Maiden-all
Youth Of Today-all	Life Sentence-Lp
Wind Of Change-Rain Ep	Slayer-all
OPIV-Energy	Nuclear Assault-All
	NYC Hardcore-comp.

John-Only the Strong

Tony-OTS

GORILLA BISCUITS

LUKE-DRUMS
MARK-BASS
ALEX-GUITAR
WALLY-GUITAR
CIV-VOCALS

G&P interviewed GB in Milwaukee on July 20 in their van.This was my first running with da'Biscuits and I was suprised at what I saw.I expected them to be upbeat,hyper people,but they were the total opposite.As a matter fact,they were laid back and mild guys.Join me as I shoot the breeze with one of the best bands tocome out of The Big Apple.

G&P:So how's the tour going.
Alex:Good so far.The last few shows were a little small but thats ok considering we dont have a major record out.All we have is our 7"so we are just going on our reputation.
G&P:What about the new lp.?
Walter:It should have been out by now.
Luke:It probobly isn't.Its supposed to be out in Europe now.It should be here in a few weeks.
Alex:You wanna know our best shows?Jersey was great.Miami was cool.DC,Boston,all the East coast.
G&P:Is this your first time in the Midwest?
Alex:I live here.
Luke:You mean as a band?Yeah.
G&P:Ive always wondered,how did you get your name?
Walter:When we had our first show,we needed a name and it was like a funny thing.So we made it ours and we never changed it.There's nothing really important about it.It works good and bad sometimes.
G&P:My friend has a video of you guys with Ernie from Token Entry on drums.
Alex:Uh-Oh they got a hold of it!

Walter and Civ

Walter:That was our first show.Civ and me were in it back then.
G&P:I have this tape of Judge at this radio station in NY(WNYU),and they dedicate"In My Way" to you guys.What is up with that?
Walter:A lot of people misunderstood that.He just said it. We'll do a song and say "This goes out to Judge,its called Big Mouth."
Alex:Its just for the sake of dedication.-Whoa,that sounded really cool.You could put that on a shirt or something."The Sake Of Dedication".
Walter:That will be the name of the next Insted tour.
Alex:We're real good friends with Judge though.We'll be touring with them after California.
G&P:Tell me a little bit about the song GM2.You did that one with lyrics on the video.Why not now?
Walter:That was the name of our first drummer.George M.We did an abbrevieted version of it.It was pretty silly,so we did it and called it GM2.It was the first song we ever wrote.We haven't played it since.
Alex:We tried it once at Irving Plaza.
G&P:How about another Bad Religion cover?
Walter:We haven't done that since then either.
G&P:Your EP has gone through many pressings,can you give me the lowdown on it as of now?
Walter:The yellow is cool to have,but there are 3 pressings each of 2000.The first one has a different mix and labels.The others have a poorer mix.
G&P:All right Civ,how did you get your voice to crack so much on the EP?Can you control it?
Civ:It just happens.Sometimes I do it and sometimes it just happens.
G&P:Whats the meaning behind the song "Better Than You?People come up to me and say better than who?
Walter:Its just a song saying you are better off not getting involved with fights and all that stuff.It is sort of misleading.You just have to look at it from our point of view.

Milwaukee at its best

Walter:Is Al's Diner around here somewhere?You know from Happy Days.We all dreamed about going there.
G&P:I think that was only for the show.Do you guys eat meat?
Alex:We are all vegetarians.
G&P:What do you think about the band Grudge?Did they get permission to do the Big Mouth thing?
Alex:They paid us.
Walter:Everytime its played on the radio we recieve royalties.No just kidding.There's nothing we can do.
Marc:I think its annoying.Imean I live closest to them and Ihear it most.
Civ:Im pretty sorry when bands have to exist off of other bands for popularity.
G&P:What do you think of some of the earlier positive bands that have taken a new direction.Like 7Seconds.
Walter:I dont like the new stuff.The old stuff is great though.
Mark:They are good.I just dont like them as much as bands that are doing the same thing.
Walter:I know ? Seconds didnt do this,but a lot of hardcore groups say that they were just kids having a little fun.They still got paid though.
Luke:How come it smells like eggs in Milwaukee?
G&P:I think it smells like French toast.I dont know. Does GB have any kind of a metal following you think?
Walter:A lot of metalers bought the Revalation sampler.They are interested in hardcore.
Civ:But we dont have a big metal following.
Walter:You might say Agnostic Front do but not us. Its mostly SE kids and people into plain hardcore.

Hit it Walter!

Mark & Alex

Alex

For info write:
Darin
11433 CR 137
Flint,Texas
75762

G&P:What do you think of these people who sell their records for outragous prices?
Walter:I should have brought my stuff.
Alex:If you owned a store, that could be your business selling old records .
Walter:It sucks,but the prices wouldn't be so high if there weren't people to buy it. It would be nice to get them now for 3 bucks.
G&P:Do you still have shirts through Revalation?
Walter:They got a new shirt now that is superspectacular with 5 colors.They dont sell the old ones.
G&P:A lot of people say they dont like them.
Walter:The Revalation one?
Alex:Show us who they are!
G&P:Its the fit of it that is out of proportion.
Civ:Maybe their bodies are weird.
Luke:We didn't get specially molded t-shirts.
G&P:You want to say anything at the end here?
Alex:Milwaukee smells like rotten eggs.
Civ:Good luck with the fanzine. Check out the new record.
(Sorry,Luke your pictures didnt turn out.)

INSTED

FROM SOUTHERN CALIFORNIA

KEVIN and Steve of the O.C.powerhouse INSTED were interviewed before their show in Rockford Il.July 22.

Insted is:
Rich-Bass
Steve-Drums
Barret-Guitar
Kevin-Vocals

G&P:Are you happy with the new 7" on Nemisis?
Steve:Yeah,we like it.We could have brought up the guitars a little bit.But you know it happens.Its hardcore.
Kevin:We like the layout.Its cool.Lots of pics.
G&P:How many were pressed?
Kevin:We're not sure.Probably a couple thousand. We'll keep pressing them.Maybe some colored vinyl.
Steve:The first press is on black.
G&P:How did you get on Nemisis?
Kevin:We talked to Frank.The guy who runs Nemisis. He also works at Zed Records in Long Beach.
G&P:It sounds like they are getting a lot of good bands on that label.
Kevin:Yes they are.He's keeping the buisiness aspect of it real low.He deals with the bands more direct.Its like a friendship label.
Steve:Plus,we gave him the stuff on June 14,and our 7" was out July 17.
Kevin:He's on the ball.He doesnt dilly dally around.
G&P:What ever happened to Wishingwell?
Kevin:They folded.They are no more.They owe some$$. Its just,whenever you get into big labels,see,W.W is Giant,and Giant is big,things dont go the way you want them to.Whenever I would call them for things,they'd give me the runaround.I dont mean Pat, I mean Giant.
G&P:I never saw Bonds of Friendship in the stores, Is it still being pressed?

Kevin:Yeah.That's another thing with Giant,some places get it and some places don't.
G&P:What do you think of the Midwest?
Kevin:Hardcore in general is unpredictable.Chicago is cool.Green Bay has always been cool.I like everywhere.
G&P:You just like to play?
Steve:Yeah,like the Midwest scenes are smaller than what we are used to because LA has such a big scene. But as a whole,its almost better for the fact that everyone knows one another.Theres a lot more unity.
Kevin:You can't really segregate the scenes like East,West,or whatever.That's what a lot of people do We just like to play.As long as there are people there and things run smoothly,we're happy.
G&P:What are some of your influences?I hear a little bit of 7 Seconds and Uniform Choice in you.
Kevin:OLD UC!

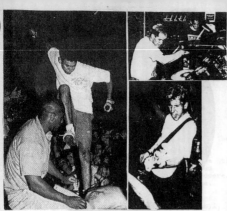

Steve:I'd say 7 Seconds is a big influence.We all listen to old stuff like Antidote and stuff like that. The new 7" is a bit different though.

Kevin:Yeah,it's a lot different than the lp.Its a lot harder and straightforward.The music is crunchier. More powerful I would say.

G&P:On the lp,you left out the lyrics to the song "At Last",why ?

Kevin:I dont know.It was just something we did.

Steve:It was something YOU did(Kevin).Its your song.

Kevin:We dont play that song live.Its a personal thing I did.

G&P:Are you guys vegetarians?

Steve:The whole band is and we're all straight.

Kevin:We have a song on the new ep.called "Feel Thier Pain"about vegetarianism.It is something new,not just in hardcore but with people in general.We stand behind it and I just want more people open their eyes and realise what they are doing to themselves and the animals and the environment.

Kevin:We dont condemn people who eat meat.Just as if you drink beer,we dont say youre bad or youre good.Its just what we believe in.

Steve:Insted is a straight edge band yeah,and Kevin and I wear X's on our hands,but we can't expect people to live their lives the way we do.We just accept people for what they are.If someone doesn't want to listen to us because we wear X's,then that is them condemning us,not us condemning them.I could care less if they wear X's or are posi-youth or whatever.If you are a good person then that is all that matters.

Kevin:It doesn't matter if you are a skin or if you have a mohawk.We are not out to separate people.We are just trying to open some eyes.We say,"This workes for us,maybe it will for you.I think a lot of problems in todays society is if people would take the time to think about what they are doing.You know killing animals,it breeds a lot of hate and violence in society.

Next page →

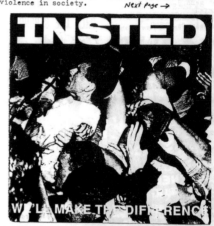

INSTED

WE'LL MAKE THE DIFFERENCE

G&P:What do you think of bands like Grudge?

Steve:Greudge was a SE band who didn't make it. They had a different name.They turned on SE cause they weren't accepted.They put out a zine and said some pretty bad stuff about Insted.I could really care lessabout them.They are nothing.

Kevin:Crucial Youth are cool guys.They just dont do anything for me.If I want to laugh,I'll turn on Carsen or Letterman.

Steve:I dont want anybody making fun of what I believe in or what is truly in my heart.When I see Grudge cracking on SE it brings me down,but then again, it pushes me a little harder.

The interview was cut off there because Upfront started their set. If you would like to order the Insted 7""We'll Make The Difference," just send 3.50$PPD.to:

Insted
658 S.Scout Trail
Aneheim Ca.92807

ONLY THE STRONG

CHICAGO

belief
straightedge

s OK
OT T
DRINK!

DON'T
NEED
RUGS

DON'T
NEED
RUGS

Joe-
ATW

Mike-
Freewill

George-
PPP

STRAIGHT EDGE

ONLY THE STRONG
T-SHIRTS · 8.00
STICKERS · 3-FOR A DOLLAR
CHICAGO S.E. T-SHIRTS·8.00

SEND TO:
JEREMY STRAMAGLIO
1376 WAUCHOPE ELGIN
ILL 60123

PHONE: 697·4135

BOLD

Bold:Matt-Vocals
Tom-Guitar
Howie-Bass
Sammy-Drums

This was the line-up for the show in Chicago on Aug.13.Matt was interviewed by G&P after the show.

G&P:So what did you think of Chicago?
Matt:I thought it was really cool.I was really impressed.I didn't know what to expect.It is a good show anywhere you go if the energy level is high or if the kids know the words.It doesnt matter if you are in Memphis,Chicago,or New York.As long as the kids are into it is all that really counts.

G&P:I saw some new faces in the band.
Matt:Yeah,Tom.ourguitar player now,joined the band about a year ago as our second guitarist.The other guitarist,John,couldnt tour cause he had to work. Drew and Tim toured for the first half of the tour but for various reasons,they had to go back home.So we got Howie our roadie to fill in on bass and we got Sammy from Judge on drums.

G&P:You sound pretty good,have you been practicing?
Matt:We're trying the best we can with the new members.We're doing all right.

SPEAKIN OUT IN '87

G&P:Is this your first U.S. tour?
Matt:Yes.
G&P:How old are you guys?
Matt:I'm 17,Tom is 19,Howie is 20,and Sammy is 16.
G&P:Are you getting ready to go back to school?
Matt:I'm starting college Sept. 3rd,and I don't know what I'm majoring in yet maybe communications.

G&P:So what about the new 7"?
Matt:It should be out any day now on Revelation. It has four songs and it looks pretty good.I saw the cover and lyric sheet and I'm pretty happy with the finished product.

G&P:Are you happy with Revelation?
Matt:Yeah, because we know them as people, and I know I can trust them.I'm glad I know them because it makes it alot easier.Now its Jordan but, Porcell is going to help.Ray is doing other things.

G&P:Is there any link between Crippled Youth and Bold?
Matt:We were the same band but we changed the name in 1986.For awhile we played some Crippled Youth songs.We had the same members.

G&P:So how do you like touring the U.S.?
Matt:It's cool, it has its ups and downs. Its better than staying home and working. Its definitely worth while.

G&P:Did you like the West Coast?
Matt:Yeah we stayed there for 2 weeks.We hung out ans played 2 shows.

Chillin in Chicago HOWIE

G&P:Are you all vegetarians?
Matt:Yeah.
G&P:Are you gonna startwriting songs about it?
Matt:As far as the band goes, I dont know. Since we are all doing different things nextt year. I dont know what the bands future is. Who knows. If the band ever breaks up, hopefully I'll do something with a band.

G&P:Has Bold taken a new direction with this 7"?
Matt:Yeah, its more melodic,more intricate.Were really happy with it. Its still powerful. Pretty intense . We all wrote it, but Tom wrote most of the riffs.

G&P:You have been been playing music for how long?
Matt:I've been in the band since I was 13.When we first started, I played guitar and sang.

G&P:Do you want to say anything to anybody?
Matt:Check out the 7",read the lyrics.The songs on this one I cant really say it's about this or that, It's more personal and wide open to interpratation. I think they are cooler cause you can take it different ways.

G&P:Are you still straight?
Matt:I dont know if you could call the band as a whole a straihgt edge band.Personally,I am.Most of us are.I dont know if we call ourselves a SE band anymore..

G&P:Do you think people are growing out of it?
Matt:For the people that it was a trend for they are gonna get out. But ,for the people who were S.E. who really meant it, they will remain.

G&P:Are you seeing different kinds of people at shows, like long hairs?
Matt:Yeah its cool to play for different types of people. We have a following and its cool, and kids are great, but its also cool to play for people who dont know us. Maybe we could turn them on to us.

G&P:I've been playing the Lp to my long hair friends and they really get into it.I mean you do have a crunchy metallic sound.

G&P:Do you see yourself slowing down, like some of the older straight bands?
Matt:NO,but most kids get bummed out when bands change.Some bands do it because they want to do it.It is better that they do what they wnat to do,than just play the same old stuff and not be into it. Kids cant help it if bands want to play softer or more commercial stuff.

G&P:Has there been much fighting at the shows at all?
Matt:There has been some on this tour.In Berkely after the show was done there was some tension and a couple of punches were thrown, also in Boston.

G&P:What do you do to try and stop it?
Matt:A lot of times people bring it to us,and were really not going to back down. We don't go looking for fights, but being from New York,alot of people like to start stuff.It was just a few instances.It makes it more exciting.

The Bold Ep should be out by the time you read this interview and is available through Revelation records for 3 dollars and fifty cents post.paid.

BOLD

REVELATION RECORDS
P.O. Box 1454
New Haven, CT 06506-1454

G&P PHOTOS

RUSS UNDERDOG

7 SECONDS-MADISON

SUPERTOUCH

GORILLA BISCUITS

UNIFORM CHOICE

911-MILWAUKEE

RICHIE-UNDERDOG

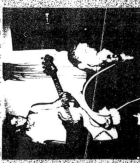

BROTHERHOOD

Gilman St.

June 18
Interviewed
by mail with
the help of
Kierston Han-
son.Ron had a
lot on his
mind that day.

Brotherhood
RON
VIC
EVAN
DARRIN

G&P: Who is this guy Lenny who puts on free shows?
Ron: Lenny is this guy who livis in Bremerton Wa.He
plays guitar for a band called I Wish I.He used to
put on big shows,I guess he's gonna start Natashas
again.He lets us play at his house.He's had us two
times,Big Drill Card just played there,and he also
had the Dough Boys once.He's just a real cool guy.
G&P: What is the Seattle scene like?
Ron: Lots of punk rock.People here dont really know
about the newer hardcore bands because they are into
the old stuff.They're content with their Crass,Con-
flict,and DK.They dont go out of their way to search
new material which is unfortunate cause the newer
good bands like Raw Deal,Bold,YOT dont really have
a following here.People dont even know who Underdog
is and they are one of the most popular bands in
the country.The scene here is really big though.
We'll find out on July 8,which is probably the biggest local show of the year;The Accused,Brotherhood
and somebody else.That should draw everybody who is
into hardcore or metal.Id say about 800 people.
G&P: Name off some Seattle bands.
Ron: Some real cool bands are:Christ on a Crutch,Sub
vert,Gesters of Chaos,and some S.E.bands popping up
likeRefuse,Feeding the Cause,First Step,Better Off,
Take Charge,Hateful Youth.We also have the Accused.
G&P: Is there a problem with racists in Seattle?
Ron: Its unfortunate that you ask me cause I havent
been to a show in Seattle in about 8 months.We've
been on tour and play weekend shows a while.I guess
we'll find out at this show coming up.

G&P: How are you trying to prevent racism in Seattle?
Ron: By saying what we say and feel.We put out records and play shows.People see us and say,"Hey,if
these guys can take a stand,so can I",thats what we
are doing.We're calling them out,letting them know
that we are here.Now more people are joining us and
saying,"Fuck those assholes.We're not going to let
them mess up what we have!"
G&P: What is the deal with your EP?
Ron: Its out now.The second pressing just came out,
and it rules!You can get it for $3.50 ppd.from-Skate
Edge Records 9862 E.Pinewood ave.Englewood Co 80111
M.o.payable to Rich Jacobs.It got an ok review from
Tim Yo at MRR.It has 6 songs(4 from the demo and 2
new ones),the first 500 were on blue vinyl,then we
just did 1000 on red and we'll see were we go from
there,either black or green.
G&P: You've seen a lot of the US on your recent tour,
    what do you think of the S.E.movement nationwide
Ron: We hung out with SE kids in every town almost,
but we really didn't see any bands or local shows.
Its small,some people say its a trend,but if it was
you'd think there would be more people into it.I
mean,everywhere we went there were people contrib-
uting to the scene.In Buffalo,the promotor is a SE
guy and has a radio show.We met a lot of kids who
had zines,put on shows,or just went to the shows.
Its cool to have a scene like SE where you really
are pressured to get involved.The straight edge
movement is small,but it is making a large contrib-
ution

Chris & Greg-Chicago

G&P: You have some pretty harsh lyrics, why don't
you expand on some.
RON: Don't be an asshole to people. There is so much
hate and anger and violence in this world and we
just say don't be a part of it. We are an equal
rights band. Not just color but heterosexuals,
homosexuals,punk rockers,skin-heads,metalers. We
are all just people trying to make a living in
this world. Its bad enough we got so much B.S.
around, Exxon oil spills,homelessness,high unem-
ployment,government supporting war and bringing
drugs into the country. We should be helping each
other not hating. Don't let people walk all over you
because they will. I f you have people starting
trouble at your shows, get together and tell them
they are not welcome. I'm sure there are more
people that will see your side. People don't go to
shows to get beat up and pushed around. They go to
to have fun. Stop it. I know that doesn't happen in
Chicago because they don't take that kind of shit.
We played other places where people would sit back
and let drunken fools come in and put people down
in some cases we had to say something to stop the
B.S.. If Joe Schmoo is getting pushed around and
you don't know Joe,don't let him down, help him
out. Maybe in the future he'll do the same for you.

Look for Brotherhood shirts
in MRR classifieds.Also you
can write Brotherhood at:
PO Box 20224
Seattle Wa.98102
(At the time of the interview,Greg and Chris were
no longer in the band.

Ron

BROTHERHOOD
FUCK RACISM
NO TOLERANCE.

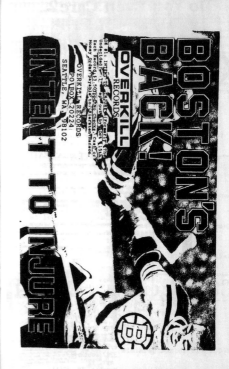

Do You Even Care?

GO VEGETARIAN

FRONT

HUMANS AREN'T MEAT EATERS!

OUR TEETH AREN'T DESIGNED FOR TEARING FLESH!

MEAT EATERS HAVE STOMACH ACID 20 TIMES THE STRENGTH OF HUMANS

MEAT EATERS INTESTINES ARE ONLY 3 TIMES THE LENGTH OF THEIR BODY FOR QUICK EXPULSION OF MEAT

HUMANS INTESTINES ARE 12 TIMES THE LENGTH OF OUR BODY – MEAT LITERALLY ROTS IN OUR INTESTINES

IT'S UNHEALTHY

IT HAS BEEN KNOWN TO CAUSE CANCER OF THE COLON

WE DON'T EAT MEAT TO GET ALL OF THE NUTRITION WE NEED

HUMANS ARE CAPABLE OF FINDING OTHER WAYS OF NUTRITION WITHOUT KILLING ANIMALS

BACK

Contact

SLEVE

1) Who says "Ye Sucker,You get a big mouth!"?
2) Who plays horns on Murphy's Laws album Back With A bong?
3) Who runs Workshed records?
4) What label was Reason To Beleive's 7" on first?
5) What direction does Token Entries arrow point?
6) What was Soul Sides former name?
7) Who is Chicagoes Only S.E. Band?
8) Whos baby is on the cover of New Wind?
9) Who originally stated "Its OK NOT TO DRINK"?
10) What was Underdogs original name?
11) Who wrote "The Bitch"on Pagan Babies Next Lp?
12) Who is pictured on the Gorilla Biscuits 7" itself?
13) What is etched on side 2 of the Judge Ep?
14) Who drew the Screaming For Change Cover?
15) What is Mike Judges real name?
16) What label is Justice Leagues "Think Or Sink"on?
17) How old is Matt on Bold's Speak Out Lp?
18) How many Project-X Eps were pressed?
19) What color vinyl is Crucial Yule on?
20) Who played the father on The Courtship of Eddies Father?

Answer 5 correctly and you will recieve free Good+Plenty stickers. All correct will recieve a free Box of Good and Plenty candy. Send answers to:→

CHICAGO AREA HARDCORE
BILL...

G&P Hide out
c/o Mike Good
2120 11th st. Apt.14
Winthrop Harbor Il. 60096

BIG MIKE

JUDGE

MIKE-VOCALS
SAMMY-DRUMS
MATT-BASS
JOHN-GUITAR

Judge was interviewed on Aug.13 after their show in the windy city of Chicago.When I think of Judge,Ithink harsh,hard,and just plain heavy.They were very friendly and had high hopes for the band's future.Come with me and face sentencing from the allmighty JUDGE!

G&P:Mike,how did you get such a wimpy voice,but when you sing it's heavy?
Mike:Come en guys,you think my normal voice is wimpy?
Porcell:It is new that I think about it.
Mike:I cant help it,I learned from Negative Approach.
Porcell:He went to the John Branden school of vocals.
G&P:So is Judge a full time band now?
Mike:For me it is.Its MY only band.
Porcell:Shut up.Yeah,we're going strong.
G&P:Youre on tour with Bold across the counrty.
Porcell:We started in Cal.and we're on our way back.

G&P:Mike, is your real name Judge or is that a joke
Mike:It is no joke.My real name is Mike Ferraro,Bu everybody calls me Mike Judge.
Porcell:This guy who went to pick up Mike at the airport in Cal.couldnt find him,so he paged him as Mike Judge.He was even looking up reservations.Its like look under J.
G&P:How were the shows out there?
Porcell:La.was great.We played 2 shows there and they were both awesome.
Mike:Ther wasnt one fight in La.There was a minor one at Gilman.
G&P:Mike, didnt you play drums with Youth of Today
Mike:Yes,I played drums with YOT.,Death Before Dis honor,and Supertouch.I had my set ripped off on the last YOT.tour.That was teh last time since the EP.
G&P:Whats the scoop on the Schism breakdown?
Porcell:Me and Alex just couldnt do it.We are both in bands and touring for 4 months didnt help.We wer not to serious about it.We were just putting out a fanzine and Project X as a freebee inside.Then we did the Judge record.We put an ad in MRR and then the nextedthing we knew we were getting like 25 let ters a day and we couldnt handle it,We had to stop. We just didn't do it well.
G&P:Are you ever gonna try it again?
Porcell:I might work with Revalation when I get back.It is just Jordan and his friends doing the mailorder.He is in over his head.I went to his hous and he has got boxes everywhere of mail.
G&P:How did you get the name Judge?
Mike:When I quit YOT. I guess I was just in a bad mood.I was looking for a name that would piss peo ple off.
G&P:I read a review of the EP and it said that it had gang related lyrics.
Mike:Thats bullshit.We dont eat gangs.Its just made up because of one song,"New York Crew".That was back in '82.and this is '89.It doesnt make any sense.

SAMMY IN EFFECT

THE DYNAMIC DUO OF CRUNCH
MATT | PORCELL

G&P:Any knew Judge record soon?
Porcell:Yeah,we got an album coming out in 2 weeks on Revalation.Its got 9 songs.Its a lot heavier than the EP.
G&P:I heard some from that thing you did on WNYU radio and I heard an advanced tape.It is heavy.
Mike:I remember that.That was fun on WNYU.
G&P:What are the members now?
Porcell:We finally got a full line-up now.We got Sammy on drums,and this guy Matt on bass.
G&P:Do you plan on staying on Revalation a while?
Porcell:We dont know what we're gonna do.
Mike:We are definitely gonna record a new album.
G&P:Are you still straight?
Porcell:OF COURSE!
G&P:For some reason I think it has grown out of a lot of people.It was going good for a while.
Porcell:I dont know why.I think its happening also. I dont get it.
G&P:What do you think of bands like 7 Seconds or Uniform Choice that take a new direction musically?
Porcell:I think its cool.It is their band.Nobody has the right to tell themwhat to play.7 Seconds still have good lyrics.No matter how wimpy you think it is,they still have the same massage.
G&P:Did the group Grudge ask you to do that song "Drinking's Great?"
Mike:Obiously,they didn't ask us.
Porcell:I'm not mad at them,I just dont think its funny.Crucial Youth was Funny.
Mike:If you read the reviews,noone is taking them

seriously..They are definitely a joke.
G&P:What did happen with We're Not In This Alone?
Porcell:When we were in the studio,we were leaving to California the next day and we had to mix the whole thing in like a half an hour.The drums were al messed up because of the engineer.We redid it and it sounds pretty good.
G&P:How old are you guys?
Mike:We're both 22.
G&P:Do you see yourselves doingthe same thing 5 or 10 years from now?
Mike:I know Judge is going on for a ways longer. We got too many ideas to stop.
G&P:Thats good because you really have got somethin good going with Judge.I hope you keep it up.You want to say something to finish it up?
Porcell:Lookout for our record cause we are pretty psyched about it.
Mike:And our tour for our new record.

SHOW REVIEWS

July 20,Odd Rock Cafe-Gorilla Biscuits and Orchestra
This was the first show in months for the area.We had 4 carloads from Illinois and only a handful from Milwaukee. Orchestra started out and I did the inter view with G.B..They sounded sort of like a college crowd band.They weren't to bad,but I was psyched for G.B..They are now a five piece and sounded pretty good all things considered.They now have Mark from Hardstance on bass and Alex (ex Side By Side) on 2nd guitar. The new stuff kills.They let me tape it and it jams.They did stuff from the Ep as well as Posit- ive Outlook by Y.O.T.. They don't monkey around.I had high hopes for a show like this and it will nev- er be forgotten.Nice tattoo Civerelly.

Gorilla Biscuits singalong Milwaukee

June 24,Alpine Valley-Metallica with The Cult
I would first like to say that yes,I did pay $30 for floor seats to see Metallica.They were fairly de- cent seats(even though I scammed about 15 rows)Any- way,The Cult opened with a good attempt to warm up the crowd,which wasn't easy considering the audience was mostly metalers.Metallica hit the stage with a fairly long set.They did a little something from all of their Lps.They even tried The Wait & Breadfan. They did a few encores including Whiplash(which fit the theme of the evening).They did all right but if you've seen them oncebefore,you know how it is.

July 24,The Elks Lodge(Rockford)Full On Straight,Up- front,Insted,Gorilla Biscuits,Underdog.
It took 2 hours to get there but it was worth it. First up was a band from Rockford,Full On Straight, no comment.Then Upfront came upfront.They have a new singer but they still jammed.They did some new stuff that sounded heavy.Can't wait for the new Ep.Next was Insted.They have new members,but they were still tight.The new stuff off the Ep rules.Gorilla Biscuits followed with a short but powerful set.The new Lp wasn't out yet but it sounds good live.Last was a band I've been waiting a lifetime see again,or so it seemed.Underdog.They fucking rocked!They did stuff off the Ep as well as the Lp.The reggae sounds great live.Richie lighted up the stage with his presence. Give this place a better stage and a good p.a.and it would have been the best show of my life.

August 26,Chemical People,Only The Strong,and Verbal Assault,at Club Dreamerz.
Its been a long time since I've been to a good show, and this was it. The Chemical People opened up for the nights presentation filling in for a band that didn't show up.They were loud.Too loud. Then came Only The Strong Chicago's only S.E. band They've been out of commision for about 2 months due to illnesses:down but definitely not out.They hit the stage and the mosh'in began.They ended their set with Youth Of Todays "Youth Crew",and it turned into a dive fest.There's nothing better than diving off of the speakers.Last to play were Verbal Assault.They played lots of good stuff.New and old(look for the 5 song Ep).If it is as good as it is live it will prove to be a great slab of vinyl.The show was a steal for 8 bucks.

YOUTH OF TODAY
LAST L.A. APPEARANCE

BOLD
GORILLA BISCUITS
UNDER DOG
INSTED
JUDGE
CHAIN OF STRENGTH

X X X

FRIDAY AUGUST 4TH
8:00 PM
Fender's

Aug 4 Fenders Ballroom-Bold,Judge,Gorilla Biscuits,
Underdog,Insted,Chain Of Strength,Youth Of Today
  The night was set and I was there to make it hap-
pen.It started with a whopping 13.50s to get in Fenders to see seven bands that gathered here to play.
I missed the first 2 bands because I had to get shir
and stuff.Then Judge went on.I never heard them before but they really got off.The crowd really enjoyed
them alot.Bold was up next.I've been waiting to see
these guys since the Crippled Youth days and I was
not disappointed at all.They played a shitload of
new tunes as well as the old ones.Gorilla Biscuits
was up and they were intense.Words can't explain how
good they were,and the crowd went bananas.Insted hit
the stage next.Kevinsted's first words were"Let's
show NY how it is done!"The crowd went apeshit for
the whole set.They hit the last song "Proud Youth",
and pandemonium struck Fenders.Up last was Youth of
Today.Since I'm not a big fan of theirs and I was
breathless,I left after the first song.Sorry.
                                          Rudy O.

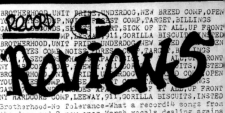

Aug.13,Bold,Judge,and Gorilla
Biscuits at Club Dreamerz.
  Holy Cow where do I begin. I
get there and Judge has already
started.As I make my way to the
front, I feel my feet moving to
the beat of Sammy's drum.These
guys are the heaviest band alive.
With Porcells crunchy guitar and
Mike Judges harsh lyrics combined
you can't stop these guys.Look
out for the 12" on Revelation.
Next was Bold.They had a few new
members,but who doesn't.They
really stun me as actually playing well.The new stuff was melodi
but heavy. Check out the new Ep
it could be the last.Gorilla
Biscuits kicked in last,but they
were definitely at their best.
Everybody knew the new stuff,and
they went Ape shit.It was all for one at Dreamerz
for a change, and as I kneeled down on the stage
I feel Porcell dive off my back. When N.Y. meets
Chicago all hell breaks loose.

July 24 Odd Rock Cafe-Urban Renewal,Supertouch, and
Underdog.
  I missed the first band and as I arrived I hear
Supertouch playing the only song I know "Searchin
For the Light" from the comp. NYC Hardcore.They are
like no other band I've heard before.It was their
first show for this
tour and thay had
it together.Under-
dog was up next
and I knew they
were gonna be he-
avy.Richie has a
stage presence
like you wouldn't
believe.When he
says"As One We
Fight And We Win"
you better believe
it.They played old
stuff"Say It In My
Face,"with a rap at
the end.This was
the 2nd time I saw
'em and Chuck broke
a string both times
Ain't that right MC
Shredder my man?
They also funked it up with"Without Fear" and"No
Matter What".For the last number they did "Get
Together by ??This is definitely a highlight of
this summer.

Underdog in Milwaukee

RECORD
Reviews

BROTHERHOOD,UNIT PRIDE,UNDERDOG,NEW BREED COMP,OPEN
YOUR EYES COMP,NOISE FOREST COMP,TARGET, BILLINGS
GATE,SHOUNDS,SHEER TERROR,SICK OF IT ALL,UP FRONT
HARDCORE COMP,LEEWAY,911,GORILLA BISCUITS,INSTED

Brotherhood-No Tolerance-What a record!4 songs from
the demo and 2 new ones.Harsh vocals dealing agains
racism,sexism,and apathy.Heavy on the bass.Get this
one while you can.   Skate Edge(adress in interview

Unit Pride-Ep-This one is already a classic 7".Alot
of bass(which as you can see I like)with a very
heavy approach.Simple lyrics,but they get the point
across.   Stepforward Records

Underdog-The Vanishing Point-This album is music to
move the soul.I knew the new album would be good
but this sucker is great.It has something to offer
to everyone.Reggae,Mosh,and Heavy as hell.   Carolin

New Breed Comp.-This is probably the 2nd best N.Y.
compilation I've ever heard.The sound level is good
Also good stuff by Absolution,Pressure Release,Raw
Deal,Abombination,and other really good N.Y. are
bands.Nice Magazine included too!   Urban Style

Noise Forest Comp-When its compiled by Pushead you
know its going to be good.The Sound quality rules!
Includes soon to be classic material by Insted,
Underdog,Brotherhood,Unity, and Uniform Choice.
                                            Pusmor
Open Your Eyes Comp #2-O.Y.E. does it again with
another quality compilation.Nice Layout too.Good
stuff by Brotherhood,Turning Point,Implement, and
Antidote live at CBGB'S.   Open Your Eyes

Target-Demo-An upcoming band from Woodridge Il.
They sound pretty good, sort of a DC sound to it.
Write them at Target c/o Mike Welsch, 6024 Tyler,
Woodridge Illinois 60517.

Billings Gate-Demo-These guys are to good.When its
fast its fast and when its heavy its heavy.Good
lyrics and a Ska song to boot.Look out for them in
the future.(See ad for info)   Polar Records

7 Seconds-Soulforce Revolution-Well,after a few
phone calls and a lot of patience,we finally got an
advanced copy of their new album,and it is well worth
the wait.(for us anyway)Great music,strong vocals,&
powerful lyrics show that 7 Seconds are taking their
musical talents a step further.This is not HC,but if
you liked the last few albums,you'll love this one.
Songs to look for are:Satya,I Can Sympothise,& Moth-
ers Day.A must for true 7 Seconds fans.Available:
Sept.25 on Restless Records.

Shades Apart-12"-This an ok album,but not one of
WishingWells greatest.Sounds like a cross between
Sociol D.and Husker Du.After a while,songs start to
sound the same.

Sick Of It All-Blood,Sweat & Tears-This album rips.
Good packaging and even better production.12 great
new songs and 7 old ones.One bad point,you have to
send for a lyric sheet. In Effect

NY Hardcore Comp.-Where the Wild Things Are-Little
variety here.All hard and heavy,but if you are into
NYHC,tou'll love this one.High points are,GB,Out-
burst,Breakdown,& unknown band at the end of side B.

Upfront-Spirit-One time is all it takes for these
guys.This record has great packaging and 16 heavy
songs that make it one of the best.Deliverence,&
Decisions are my favorites.   Smogasbord

Leeway-Born To Expire-I got this tape on a hunch &
I wasn't let down.Sort of like Anthrax but with a
lot of bass.A must for you crossover freaks. Profile

911-Demo-Look out for these guys if you are into
stuff like Cryptic Slaughter or DRI and all the mosh
that your brain can handle.14 song demo available:
911-9166 70th St.Milwaukee Wi.53223

Gorilla Biscuits-Start Today-Holy Cow!11 new songs
from GB.What more could a person want?The Biscuits
really deliver with this one.Civ holds nothing back
on this one with great lyrics dealing with,vegetar-
ianism,couch potatoes,and wasting your life.An all'
around classic album.I hope you see it the same way.
                         Revalation
Insted-We'll Make The Difference-What a difference.
Insted is heavier than ever.Great production by
Nemisis.One song about vegetariarianism,Feel Their
Pain.There's nothing like this one. Nemisis

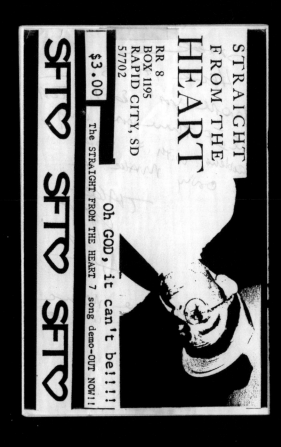

Veterans of Foreign Wars

Ian Lynam

Opposite: Detail from paste-up for *Good and Plenty*, issue 4, p. 17, 1990, featuring Youth of Today in Providence, Rhode Island. Photo credited to "Brian B."

I thought the era of the Champion sweatshirt was long over. Walking around Tokyo today, this is not the case—the kids are decked out in Champion gear in a way never foreseen, other than by the denizens of hardcore fans that read and were featured in *Good and Plenty*.

The aesthetics of *Good and Plenty* issue 4 mirrored any number of the relatively aesthetically stripped-down hardcore-oriented zines that cropped up in the late 1980s and early 1990s. Nearly all were typeset with early word processors, bits of Letraset distorted due to the process of photocopier enlargement, and hand lettering for one-off features. Reproduced band logos accompanied interviews, and there was an insistent reliance on the photography of live hardcore shows.

The photography in *G&P* 4 is dynamic, either shot from the audience's point of view angled upward or from the side of the stage, with captions typed-out and then roughly cut and pasted on top of the images, with a handful of the photography pages overlaid on concentric line-work backgrounds. Most of the photographs were just pasted into the layout and photocopied, yet some incorporated halftone-screening, what must have been a technological breakthrough for Gabe and company.

Interestingly, the aforementioned photos in *G&P* 4 come from all over the U.S. and Europe, a testament to the organic DIY networks that sprang up between scenes in different cities. These photos allowed readers to seemingly teleport into situations where the frenetic music they listened to on cassette tapes and vinyl was performed live. They capture the possibility of imagination in a way that video never could.

The fourth issue of *Good and Plenty* featured interviews with bands such as Inner Strength, Up Front, 7 Seconds,[1] Refuse, and Even Score.

Beyond the content generated by the writers and photographers, there are elements which could easily be overlooked: the abundance of advertisements for other zines, indubitably traded

1. Years later, I would move into a weird-smelling carpeted apartment that I hastily rented in Oakland, California. Shortly thereafter I began working at the Berkeley Kinko's with a former member of 7 Seconds, Joe Bansuelo. It turned out that he'd lived in the same apartment years prior and he'd had a pet duck who pooped everywhere. In lieu of cleaning it, the landlord covered the duck-feces spattered floor with carpet when they moved out, hence the smell.

NG X EDGE

#1 $1.50

POWERHOUSE
FORTHRIGHT
SAY NO MORE
FED*UP · RELEASE
UP FRONT · REFUSE

ZINES: SEND AN AD AND COPY
FOR TRADE.
TAPE TRADERS: YOUR LIST FOR
MINE!
EVERYONE: WRITE TO ME!!

CARING x EDGE
c/o Mike Karban
15749 Highview Dr.
Apple Valley, MN 55124

/ A NEW DIRECTION

STEP UP!

FANZINE
#1: BROTHERHOOD,
SOCKEYE, RELEASE &
FORTHRIGHT.

RYAN P.O.BOX 284 BEECHGROVE, IN
46107

Link of Weakness

for ad space in the respective advertised zines. Having been entrenched in zine-making myself at that time, I know firsthand the importance of this form of communal advertising.[2] Within the issue, zines from Connecticut, California, New Jersey, Indiana, Minnesota, Ohio, Texas, and London have ads, as do record labels from elsewhere. (As *G&P* was also involved in record-making, trading ads with other music labels must have been incredibly helpful, though I will stick to the zine-making aspect here.)

ZINES: SEND AN AD AND COPY FOR TRADE

Nationally, the lone DIY punk/hardcore clearinghouse with massive distribution was *Maximumrockroll (MRR)*. The newsprint zine, *HeartattaCk*, which focused on straight edge and emo-oriented hardcore music and culture, would not emerge for another four years after the publication of this issue of *Good and Plenty. MRR* focused more on the non-straight edge side of the contemporary hardcore scene (though the editors were more than happy to take money from labels and zines for advertising). It made sense that zines like *G&P* would cultivate organic networks of like-minded publications. Zines had the hardest time surviving without networks like this—ad-trading and zine-trading produced stimulating content, an enhanced readership, an awareness of hardcore on an international scale, and most of all, nascent friendships.

Writing is a lonely business, and zine-writing even more so, as the audience is so small. The act of sourcing photography, designing and trading ads, and receiving other zines in the mail must have filled the *G&P* crew's hearts with joy. It did mine when I received zines in trade in the mail—especially the good ones.

Then, when you got to travel and meet the exciting people who made them, or when they'd come to your town, and you'd hang out, and on not-so-rare occasions, collaborate—well, writing and drawing and photographing and photocopying and cutting and pasting and photocopying again became much less of a lonely business. One met others who understood the magic: the heat and the sweat of being up front in a VFW hall and trying to relate that to others via the most seemingly incongruous method possible— photocopied paper. Yes, somehow it worked. And still works.

Opposite: Detail from paste-up for *Good and Plenty*, issue 4, p. 9, 1990, featuring ads for *Caring X Edge* and *Step Up!* fanzines.

2. I am writing this while on vacation in the U.S., visiting my parents with my wife and her parents. This morning I asked my mom if she remembered any change that happened other than changed tastes in music and an increased focus on subculture when I started going to hardcore shows and making zines in the late 1980s. She said that it somehow cultivated a sense of agency in me that I hadn't had prior, and that she didn't see amongst other kids my age in our podunk town. My love for BMX and skateboarding didn't diminish, but all of a sudden I had realized that there was a whole world out there to communicate with. I started thinking more globally, and hardcore opened my eyes up to so much more. Direct quote circa 2019: "Ian, I never thought I'd say this, but I am so happy that you got into hardcore. It changed your life."

GOOD & PLENTY

THEZINETHEZINETHEZINETHEZINETHEZINETHEZINETHEZINETHEZINETHEZINETHEZINE

#4

$1.25

JAN. 90

INTERVIEWS WITH: REFUSE, EVEN SCORE,
INNER STRENGTH, UP FRONT, 7SECONDS.
ALSO: SHOW REVIEWS, LYRIC TRIVIA,
AND TONS OF PHOTOGRAPHS!

Unconventional Uniformity

Christopher Sleboda
Kathleen Sleboda

The fourth issue presents a modernist, default cover design. Simplicity and efficiency are favored over brazen and ostentatious forms, and a sans-serif clarity replaces hand-drawn and graffiti-inspired letterforms. Rodriguez employed Helvetica—typeset in all-caps, purchased as an alphabet sticker set from a local chain store—and applied the letterforms one by one to a slip of white rectangular paper. Notice the wavering baseline, a subtle kinetic detail. Like the boxed-in title (which stems from an inability to knock out type easily), it's an artifact of technical limitation. The boxed title also echoes the famous rectangle logo of *Life* magazine (fig. 1), later appropriated by *File Megazine* (fig. 2), the arts and culture journal published by General Idea in the 1970s and 80s.

Issue number, cover price, and date are all set in the same point type as the masthead. It feels fresh and self-assured but is the practical result of only one size being available to Rodriguez. The uniformity is unconventional, a move that rejects unruliness as it simultaneously embraces order.

The margins of the titling box, however, are purposeful. Consider how the white paper around the other cover typography is carefully cut around the words and numerals, effecting a closer representation of knocked-out text. Just a few flourishes persist: a cut-out thought bubble listing the issue's contents; a line of repeating text ("THEZINE" over and over, without word spacing, the letters set in a continuous stream) running beneath the masthead. The cover's combination of text and image is raw and immediate.

Previous *Good and Plenty* covers used smaller photos or illustrations. Issue 4 took advantage of a larger trim size (7.5 × 9.6 inches instead of the 5.5 × 8.5 inches of the first three publications) and featured a single large photo: the guitarist for Say No More frozen in mid-air against a backdrop of blackness. The elements and forms in play are similar to those utilized by Swiss designer Armin Hofmann in the Giselle poster he designed for Basler Freilichtspiele in 1959 (fig. 3)—though a flying guitarist has traded places with the spinning ballerina.

Issue 4
January 1990
44 pages
7.5 × 9.6 inches
1,500 copies
$1.25

Opposite: Paste-up for cover of *Good and Plenty*, issue 4, 1990.

Fig. 1. Marta Toren on the cover of *Life*, 1949 June 13 issue. The cover features the red rectangle logo used for issues published after Henry Luce's purchase of the magazine in 1936.

Fig. 2. General Idea, *File Megazine*, vol. 3, no.1, 1974.

Fig. 3. Armin Hofmann, *Giselle, Basler Freilichtspiele*, photolithograph, 1959.

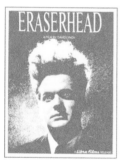

Fig. 4. Steve Samioff and Melanie Nissen, *Slash*, vol. 1, issue 5, 1977 October.

Fig. 5. Ben Barenholtz and David Lynch, *Eraserhead* poster, 1977.

The starkness of the black and white photo, produced in super high contrast with blown-out areas of white and large areas of solid black ink, is framed by a white margin on all four sides. It's reminiscent of early *Slash* magazine covers—like Debbie Harry's from 1977 (fig. 4)—designed by Steve Samioff and Melanie Nissen. The composition, a departure from previous issues, also echoes the poster for David Lynch's *Eraserhead*, produced in 1977 and designed by Ben Barenholtz and David Lynch (fig. 5). The quality of these images was likely achieved or inspired by the technical possibilities of photocopying machines. Xerox explains on their website, that contrast control "enhances the tonal separation, especially in the midtones. Increasing contrast moves midtones (gray) toward black or white. Decreasing contrast makes blacks and whites appear gray."

In 1990, photocopying machines offered limited means for photo manipulation. Adjustment of light and dark tones was manual, done via a horizontal bar with five or so "stops." Users could adjust an indicator left or right depending on the effect they hoped to achieve.

To do something more extreme involved multiple rounds of copying. A copy made of a copy could degrade the image as the machine produced successive copies. Today, with Adobe Photoshop, the high contrast effect can be achieved by dragging a digital slider under a histogram of luminance levels; the slider offers 255 discrete stops.

The year *G&P* 4 was released, 1990, Xerox released their first DocuTech system. Based on a 135 page-per-minute black & white 600 dpi xerographic print engine with attached scanner and finisher modules, the copier was arguably the first affordable 'print-on-demand' publishing system. And so the revolution truly began. —C.S/K.S.

Gabe Kotter-Air born in Milwaukee

There has been a lot of people who have helped put this zine where it is today, and these are the people who I want to personally say thanks.
Mike Good(R.I. here we go), American Speedy Printing, Casaver at Jobs Printing & Mailing,Marc,Tony, Chuck,Mike(Even Score)Kelley,Bob,Jeff,Todd,(Say No More).Jeff(Up Front),Joel & Mark(Refuse).Brent(Inner Strength),7 Seconds,Mike(Caring Edge),Carl(Altered Reality),Anji(Positive Influence),Becky(Contax One),Mike T.(Restore)Edward(Outraged),David-(Comin Correct).Mike(New Age).Phil,Josh,Jeff B., Chad,Nathan(Bro),Tom T.,the Jobs Mail Crew,(Tom, Ruiz,Steve,Paul,)Don Majkowski and the Green Bay Packers,Masada.Grant(911),Dan(Stop & Think),Tim Brick.Megan Luther,Damon & Carlos(Outright Prod.) Brani(Pure Thoughts).Joe Lopez.J.B.,Sandy(my college pen pal),the back up choir Rhonda & Jerry,Casandra, American Outfiters.Kerry and the Milwaukee Crew, and most of all Matt Garcia for putting all of the time and effort in this zine.

Issue 1,2,3-these were very limited. write to me if you would like some copies. I will reprint if enough people want them

Good & Plenty t-shirts- We did 3 sided shirts and if you hurry, we do have some left. $8.oo xl only

I need pictures for future issues. Anyone who helps out will receive a G&P shirt. B/W or color.

I do trade heavily. I have a list of demos, live shows, 7's and lp's. Please send your list if you are interested.
I do trade records also- so if you have stuff to trade write me.
GABE RODRIGUEZ
2116 SALEM BLVD.
ZION IL.60099
Cover shot-Say No More

GOOD AND PLENTY #4 WINTER 89 $1.25

Welcome to the third issue of Good and Plenty the zine. It has been a while since the last issue but I can explain. As far as the Chicago area has been lately, their has been no shows. I had to do all of the interviews via mail this time, and some of these never made it back. There has been a lot of cool stuff happening recently around here. We have 3 new 7"s coming out.Even Score(Auction Packed), Billingsgate(Victory) and Say No More(G&P Productions), all of which should be out soon. Victory Records is doing a split 7" with us which should be out also. I would like to say thanks for that. Good & Plenty Productions is a project that my partner Mike Good has. We sort of split duties;I got the zine-he does the label. For more info check out the ad. Now, I'd like to say thanks to everyone who did their part in helping out put this publication. I'm sorry I could not put the photo credits on the shots, but so many people sent in shots. And if I forgot any, I'm sorry.Thanks.

Mike and I built this zine from scrap, and to those who saw the first 3 issues, you know what I'm talking about. But I'd like this zine to be remembered for it's open views, cheap prices,and quick mail response. Enjoy!

PHOTO CREDITS: Martin, Mike B, Casandra, Dave Jaworak(New Ideas Photography), Mike Thain, Timmy Brick, Terry Brennon,Matt G., and Gabe.-If I didn't mention you,I didn't have any reference.

INNER STRENGTH

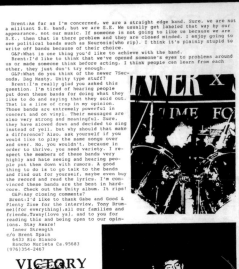

Brent-Drums   Steve-Bass
Jaymz-Guitar   Shaun-Vocals

This interview was done by mail with the drummer Brent. I had just gotten the 7" from Victory Records. Inner Strength have a unique style that I think will set these guys apart from the usual bands. Don't take my word for it though, get their 7" before they are all gone.

G&P:How did the band hook up with Victory Records?
Brent:The whole thing was pretty unexpected in reality. Tony (Victory) had ordered one of our demos and from there we started to write each other. I remember mentioning that we had hoped to release a 7" in late summer. We asked if he knew anyone who could help. He said he would and the rest is history.
G&P:Why didn't you hook up with a label from California?
Brent:We basically didn't because we didn't have any offers til after we signed to Victory. I'm not saying we would rather be on a Cali. label. To us it really didn't matter.
G&P:Do you have any plans to tour?
Brent:We hope to soon. We're working with people from So. Cali. with hopes of getting some shows there in December. If I had to predict, a tour of some sort would probably come late next summer. By then, we hope to have our album, so the time would be appropriate.
G&P:It seems a lot of bands lately have been putting out records then breaking up. Do you see Inner Strength doing that?
Brent:Right now I would say no. I can't say what will take place in a year or so, but now we're fine.We've had our hard times, but so does every other band. You just have to learn to stick it out when things get rough. I think our music will keep driving us.
G&P:I.S. has a different sound musically than most straight edge bands, do you consider Inner Strength a S.E. band? Do you get labeled as a S.E. band?

Brent:As far as I'm concerned, we are a straight edge band. Sure, we are not a militant S.E. band, but we are S.E. We usually get labeled that way by our appearance, not our music. If someone is not going to like us because we are S.E., then that is there problem and they are closed minded. I enjoy going to see political bands such as Neurosis(who rip). I think it's plainly stupid to write off bands because of their choice.
G&P:What is one thing you'd like to achieve with the band.
Brent:I'd like to think that we've opened someone's eyes to problems around us or made someone think before acting. I think people can learn from each other, they just don't try enough.
G&P:What do you think of the newer 7Seconds, Dag Nasty. Unity type stuff?
Brent:I'm really glad you asked this question. I'm tired of hearing people put down these bands for doing what they like to do and saying that they sold out. That is a line of crap in my opinion. Those bands are extremely powerful in concert and on vinyl. Their messages are also very strong and meaningful. Sure, they have slowed down and decided to play instead of yell, but why should that make a difference? Also, ask yourself if you would like to play the same songs over and over. No, you wouldn't, because in order to thrive, you need variety. I respect the members of these bands very highly and hate seeing and hearing people put them down with rumors. A good thing to do is to go talk to the bands and find out for yourself, maybe even buy the record and read the lyrics. I'm convinced these bands are the best in hardcore. Check out the Unity album. It rips!
G&P:Any closing comments?
Brent:I'd like to thank Gabe and Good & Plenty Zine for the interview, Tony Brummel(for everything),all our families and friends,Tawny(love ya), and to you for reading this and being open to our opinions. Stay Aware!
Inner Strength
c/o Brent Spain
6433 Rio Blanco
Rancho Murieta Ca.95683
(976)354-2467

VICTORY RECORDS

In the previous issues of Good and Plenty, we came up with some kind of quiz for you to answer and send in for free stickers, candy, or whatever. We got a good response from the lyric trivia so we decided to do it again. Any reply with a few correct answers will get some stickers, and if any of you are really hip to lyrics, and get all correct, you will get a free G&P 3 sided shirt. I have to warn you, I threw in a few tricky ones for the metallers out there.

GOOD LUCK

1. Fighting doesn't solve problems-Creates a new blockade...
2. Push for change, only the help supress it.
3. I always thought you were my friend, but it seems that in the end, you're a backstabbing fool!
4. Help each other strive for more, so a better future will be in store.
5. Equality between us all, is what I fucking dream.
6. Why do you always fuck with people that you don't even know?
7. The future is our burden, we cannot stand and watch.
8. Look for what's inside before you make up your mind.
9. They say that the shadow is the reflection of your soul.
10. One more quarter for the Dragons Lair.
11. You better change your ways before I strike back.
12. I've had friends that pass like the breeze.
13. I see right through the shield you hold.
14. I'm standing tall and I still have my pride.
15. We're trying to do all that we can, we're always aware.
16. Don't push me too far, I might forget what I stand for.
17. The tradition of killing is the downfall of man.
18. Do you remember when we used to hang out,and we knew what we were all about?
19. We never know who to blame, why wouldn't they stay the same.
20. Loyalty is never certain except from one man.You'll find him in the mirror, he's the best friend you have.

Well, after their Spirit Summer 89 tour of the US, Up Front have gone through some changes. I guess I can say that I'm glad I didn't interview them then because it would probably be outdated by now. If you don't have their already classic Spirit lp, by now, I'd advise taping it or try and catch it in its 3rd pressing with a blue cover & vinyl. Thanks to Jeff for taking time out to do this for me.

G&P:Who are the present members and how long have you been together?
Jeff:Me,Jeff, on bass and Jon on guitar- we are presently looking for a new singer and a drummer.
G&P:How did you hook up with your second singer Roger, and how was the response with him?
Jeff:Well, we got Roger through a long friendship. He was always a big fan of Up Front and we needed a new singer. He was there to fill the spot. When he was with us we got a great response and people loved him.
G&P:How did the tour go?
Jeff:The tour was awesome. We had so much fun, I couldn't describe it in words. We didn't have any real problems-only once we got a flat in the middle of the desert somewhere. There was nothing around us but sand dunes and cactus.
G&P:Now that you have a little time, what is next?
Jeff:To find new members, do a 7" on New Age Records and a second tour this coming summer.
G&P:I saw a picture of you in a zine where you had these cool New Balance shoes. I have a pair just like them.
Jeff:I had bought them because I liked the color. They were black and green and white. Now I don't wear leather, so I wear vans. I can't say I'm a New Balance fanatic or something, I just liked them at the time.
G&P:I have heard your demo, the X Marks the Spot comp., and the Spirit lp., and you seem to get a lot better on each occasion. Do you think the next thing will follow the same pattern?
Jeff:Well-the demo was horrible, the comp. was all right, and the lp. is great. But the new material is going to be even better yet.
G&P:Are you happy with the way Smorgasbord has treated you?
Jeff: Smorgasbord has treated us great and we have no problems at all with Chris. But change is essential and it's time for us to move on and change.
G&P:Have you played any shows recently?
Jeff: No- not since August 27 at city Gardens.
G&P:On the song Foolhearted, after Steve says,"You never even gave yourself a chance," you do this nanny-nanny- booboo thing on bass. The first time I heard

that I cracked up. I love that.
Jeff:Foolheartd was one of our first songs ever written and it is kind of a joke song. The bass fill fit so I used it.
G&P:Up Front seems to have a metal influence from what I can hear. Do you?
Jeff:Jon, Steve, and myself 5 years ago were metalheads. We evolved into straight edge hardcore. So we might have a tinge of metal in our songs.
G&P:How old are you and are you vegetarians?
Jeff:Up Front as a band this day is not. I am and have been for a year now. Also, Steve, Roger, and Ari(no longer in the band) are vegetarians. Jon is not.He is 21. and I am 20.
G&P:Any closing comments?
Jeff:Thanks for the interview. G&P is awesome! Look for a 4 song"Face"Up 7" out soon on Smorgasbord Records. Also,3rd press-Up Front Spirit lp with a blue cover and blue vinyl.

PHOTO BY: CHRIS KRUPA / A NEW DIRECTION

GET UP AND CHECK THIS OUT!

Link of Weakness

GB-in Florida

REFUSE

Refuse is a young straight edge band out of Seattle.The singer,Joel,was kind enough to answer a few questions for me.Read on.

REFUSE
Joel-vocals Jason-guitar
Mark-guitar Josh-bass
Ryan-drums

G&P:Give me a little history of the band.

Joel:Well,me,Mark and Ryan originally started with a couple punk-core bands which lasted about 3 weeks.We had a few names before Refuse,but they were lame.We don't play any of the songs from back then.We've been together for about a year. We went through a few bassists before we got Josh, but we are happy with the line-up now.

G&P: What are some of the bands influences?

Joel: My main influences are from Brotherhood,(Greg and Ron), they got me into straight-edge. As far as bands, Youth of Today, Inner Strength, Bold, and most S.E. bands. The list is too long to mention.

G&P:How does the band find time to practice and play shows while still in High School?

Joel: It's hard. Mark is gone every other weekend so we practice at least one day each weekend that he is here. Also our school has a ½ day every Tuesday, so we have those 2 days. As for shows, we've only played 2 so far. We work it out.

G&P:What do the people at your school say about Refuse? Do they take the band seriously?

Joel: A lot of kids at school ask,"How's the band" just to make conversation.I don't know if they really care, but a lot of friends bought the demo and weren't even into hardcore. I think our friends take us seriously.

G&P:Do you have any plans to record or tour?

Joel:We are doing a 7".We may go with Victory Records. We are playing a show with 7 Seconds soon. There is always plans to tour but there is never enough time or money or permission by our parents. We sure would like to. at least around here.(Wa.,Or,Ca.,etc...)

G&P:Is the band straight edge? Vegetarian?

Joel:Yes, we all are definitely straight edge.Mark and Jason are vege. I'm trying to, but my parents are making me eat meat.I think vegetarianism is a great thing.

G&P:What is your opinion on hard edge?

Joel:I think that people going around arguing about who is harder is stupid. I like to mosh, but when it comes to people trying to hurt each other to prove who is harder just makes it no fun.

G&P:I have seen bands come and go lately.How long do you see Refuse staying together?

Joel:I see Refuse staying together a while longer.Maybe not the same members.I can see some people leaving on account of too many arguments.I'm sticking with it..

REFUSE

G&P:You guys are kind of young to be playing in a band. What do your parents say about this? Are they supportive of you guys, or do they not like what you are doing?

Joel:Our parents back us morally... I think. They like the fact that we are not into drugs and all of that. My dad lent us money before but I think they use the band to blackmail us.They say,"If you don't act right, you won't be practicing for two weeks.

Mark and Joel also do a zine called Mario Brothers.#1 has Insted, Powerhouse, Amenity, & Inner Strength.It is 1 dollar and well worth it.write to:

Joel Decraff
1800 NE 172
Seattle Wa. 98155
$1
Mark Holcomb
3551 NE 166 st.
Seattle Wa. 98155

RESTORE MAGAZINE

RESTORE FANZINE #5 out now with interviews of Token Entry, Underdog, Murphys Law, Lost Cause, Screeching Weasel, Images, Knifedance, The Bag Men, Die Hard, and Heads Up, plus show, fanzine, record, and tape reviews, opinions, eye-grabbing layouts, art and comics by Ace Backwords, Sheridan, Carrie, FaDaDaDa, and lotsa other zany stuff. Each is new clean 9" size with 40 pages. The cost is $1($2 foreign. Contributors get a free copy. 10 copies are $6. Send your zine, record, etc. for trade.

RESTORE c/o Allen
621 Bassett Rd.
Bay Village OH 44140
USA

SICK 'N' TIRED DISTRIBUTION

Send S.A.E. (or else letter if you live outside the U.K. - I.R.C.s are a ripoff) for list of Punk/H.C. records, tapes, and patch printing stuff - all profit-making prices low:
SICK 'N' TIRED, 50 Tom, 43 WARNER RD., HORNSEY, LONDON N8 7HB. U.K.
If anyone wants anything distributed, PLEASE GET IN TOUCH!!!!

---

7 SECONDS

It is not every day that 7Seconds comes and plays a show in your home town. well this became a reality on Nov. 8,in Waukegan Il. We couldn't let them stroll through town without interviewing them. Kevin and Chris were questioned after the show by Matt Garcia.

G&P:How is the tour going compared to the Ourselves tour?

Kevin:Great, much better than the last tour in my opinion its cooler.

G&P:What have been some standout shows of this tour?

Kevin:Salt Lake City, San Jose, Hollywood,The Whiskey in L.A.This show tonight was really cool. It was hard to get sound together at first, but tonight was a lot of fun Chris:I had a blast tonight!

Kevin:Minneapolis would have been a lot of fun if it wasn't so packed.but those were some good ones.

G&P:Why are the shirt prices as high as they are?

Kevin:The shirt prices are high, and it mostly has to do with the deal we signed with the company. because we don't have the cash to print our own shirts.So we went to a company that would do it for us. They set the prices,and they wanted to charge a lot more, but we said no more than $15.We're hoping that they see we could sell far more shirts for $10 or $12. None of us are happy with the prices.

G&P:What is going on with the $$ owed by Positive Force Records?

Kevin:Little by little with what money that I can get from whoever owes P.F.R. money.as far as people that have screwed us with record pressing or distribution. It is just a lot of shit. I want to try and refund the money, or if we can, press the records or keep them in press and get the records to the people who still want them. If they want refunds,then I'll try to get them their money because a

lot of people have waited. I'm not happy about it at all.

G&P:Why did Bobby leave and how did you get Chris?

Chris:I'm having fun and I don't know why he left.

Kevin:It was sort of a mutual thing with us and Bobby. He knew there was a certain commitment he had to make to the band. A lot of it is hard work. You just don't come into it and think your going to be a rockstar, and that's what Bobby wanted to do. So we basically gave him the option.you straighten out your attitude and work with us as a team or we can't work with you. His attitude with other people was just terrible. You guys know, you saw him on the last tour. We came through, and he didn't like anybody, and I don't think he likes himself...

G&P:When you first started as a band, you had a very dedicated following,but now that your music has become more accessable, do that dedication is fading. How do you feel about that?

Kevin:I think it faded for a while but now I think it is just as strong as it ever was. After New Wind, Praise, and Ourselves came out, there were a lot of questions about what we were doing. More than ½ the people who rejected the new stuff at first, now they went back and listened to it and liked it. and wrote letters to us saying,"Wow,we didn't get it at first. we thought you were just wimping out, but I really like it. "They also came to see us live and said the same. Judging from the record sales and people at shows,there are a lot of people still willing to give us a chance. That is great for us. The more the merrier

Chris:I've seen so many kids singing along with the new record, it is almost like the old stuff.

G&P:I heard you guys are #180 on Billboard's charts (nov 165).

Kevin:We are really pretty happy about that. That is an accomplishment. We never thought we'd be on Billboard's charts. It's pretty neat. I don't know what it means, but it's sort of cool to see your name up there with a little bullet or whatever.

G&P:Chris, now that you are in 7Seconds, what's happening with D-vision?

Chris:Nothing really. Eric has been mentioning little side projects and my friend Lint from Operation Ivy has mentioned a little ska thing maybe. It depends on how much time I have between things.Which I don't think will be for years maybe. Things seem to be going really good now. Jeff, the old guitarist, is now a plumber and plays in a band. Ben is going to college, and I'm here.

G&P:What kind of music have you been listening to lately?

Chris:A lot of Operation Ivy. Soulside, All, stuff like that. Sometimes Jane's Addiction. Mind Over 4.

Kevin:I'm into like the Soundgarden album, the new Fetchin' Bones, Janes Addiction, there are a lot.

Chris:We've also been listening to a lot of Public Enemy and the new Beastie Boys lp.

Kevin:Not by choice nesaccarialy.(laughter).I don't mind P.E.

G&P:Have you been playing any over 21 shows lately?

Chris:Not really.

Kevin:We have done one and I think it is pointless for us to do them.

G&P:What do you see in the band's musical future?

Kevin:Finishing up this tour. Hopefully doing the best we can. I'd like to see the album go as far as it can. because I think it is a good record. We want to go to Europe. That's our big plan because we have yet to go there.

G&P:Do you have any plans to do another live album or 7"?

Kevin:Yeah, we're talking about this live thing Restless puts out called the performance series and they want to do a live one with us. which I think would be fun with the new line-up with Chris. Hopefully, we'll do it when we get back to the west coast.

G&P:Have you given any thought to re-releasing any of the older stuff?

Kevin:There has been talk. but I don't know if it would be worth it. People who haven't heard the early stuff, it is very raw and harsh. I know a lot of old 7Seconds fans would like to have them and I wouldn't mind seeing them get it, It is just one of those things that wouldn't be easy to master and put on vinyl. I don't think it would sound very good. It's possible. You never know. (Since the interview, Kevin has re-released the Skins, Brains, & Guts ep. on Pazzafist Records.red or black vinyl.)

G&P:What are some of your favorite new songs?

Kevin:Tickets to a Better Place, Soul to Keep, Satya...

Chris:I like the whole album.

Kevin:Usually after every record we do, I get bored with it. But I still like this one. It's a good record. It was fun to make.

G&P:Have you written any new material?

Kevin:We kinda invented one tonight. We did another one in L.A. during the soundcheck.

G&P:How have the people been at the shows?

Chris:I haven't run into much violence on this tour.

Kevin:It has been great.

G&P:What do you think of the breed of positive and straight-edge bands today?

Kevin:I really like the energy. I still love to see bands go out on stage and really go for it. Musically, it's less interesting to me these days. Not to take anything away from any one band, but most of the bands coming out aren't very original and it's recorded badly. God, people probably thought that way about us though. I try to listen to it. I just bought the Inner Strength 7" tonight. I'm listening to it and trying to keep an open mind to it. One thing I don't like is anybody that shoves anything down your throat! I don't drink or smoke, but I don't go around saying,"If you do, I'm gonna..."or just preach & preach. I've been at a point and I've done it. It just turns people off. They don't listen. All of a sudden there is a wall there you don't reach them.It's like "Screaming at a Wall"

G&P:Do you think the music needs to move in a different direction?

Kevin:It's possible.But just when you think you've reached a dead and, someone comes up with something new and crazy. So it's very possible someone can turn it around and bring in a new influence. We see it first hand touring because you're not involved in the scene. Like, we come here and obviously there is organization with you guys. You are doing a lot of stuff, and you can tell the difference between the people who come to shows to have fun, and the people who are the movers and the shakers. AS far as the scene goes, I think there needs to be new blood, new influences,and inspirations. It gets stale.

Chris:It's really too bad because a lot of bands that are doing that are good.I'd like to see them do something different.

Kevin:To me, one band stands out. INSTED. They are real tight & have a lot of energy. There are influences you can hear from other bands, but they come across as sincere.

Insted are good, and are fun to watch. I'd seen them in N.Y. and I had just about given up because they had all of these hardcore matinee shows on Sunday at CBGBs Most of them were the big S.E. bands and they sounded the same. Then I saw Insted, and they really stood out.

G&P:Are you guys vegetarians?

Chris:I'm not.

Kevin:I don't eat red meat. I eat chicken occasionaly, and fish. I don't eat things that look bloody.

Chris:I was,but I wasn't eating healthy. So I figured I'd better eat what's in front of me.

G&P:What are your feelings on animal rights?

Kevin:I love animals and support their rights completely. But then there is a selfish element of me that would like to wear a leather jacket.

Chris:I tend to watch cosmetics that are tested on animals. That is not right. Stuff like veil I try to stay away from.

G&P:Any closing comments?

Chris:I thought Target ruled.

Kevin:I had a great time. I wish our bass amp was not so messed up. Thanks to you, Matt & Positive Force Midwest for putting this show together and the food, and the interview. It is obvious that you put a lot of work into this stuff. You did a good job. Thanks.

For more 7Seconds info: send a SASE to Family Tree 1442 A Walnut Street Berkely Ca. 94709

or try to get the re-release of Skins, Brains, and Guts ep, now on:

PAZZAFIST RECORDS

2014 J St. #122 SACRAMENTO,CA. 95816

Token Entry

Demand

I WOULD LIKE TO THANK EVERYONE WHO SENT IN PHOTOS.I'M SORRY IF I DID NOT GIVE THE CREDIT TO ALL,BUT I WAS PRESSED FOR TIME AND SPACE.

GB-in Chicago

Mark-GB in Italy

Walter

Civ GB

Underdog

Mystery man with a flip

Youth Of Today-Providence RI.   photo:Brian B.

Under Construction fanzine   no. 2

WITH:

INSTED
UPPERCUT
KILLING TIME
DISCIPLINE
BROTHERHOOD
and more...

2.00 ppd.
84 HILLARY LA.
PENFIELD, NY
14526

Youth Of Today-The Living Room

Judge-Bringin it down

photo:Brian B.

Beyond-Anthrax

photo:Brian B.

Outburst

Vision

Only The Strong-Chicago

photo:Mike B.

GB-Chicago

Even Score-Indiana

As you can tell,I like Gorilla biscuits

GB-Chicago

One more GB-Italy

Bold-Buffalo

H.R.-Living Room 89

Photo-Jen Kuisman

Chris-7Seconds

Haywire

Vision

Say No More-w/M Good

Vision

Release-on the line?

Matt-Judge

Insted-The Anthrax

photo)Brian Boog

Youth of Today

Release

No For An Answer-Anthrax

photo:Brian B.

Beyond-Anthrax

photo:Brian B.

Dean-Underdog

Eddie from Leeway

photo:Brian b.

A Crowd Shot From The Anthrax-88

Ray Cappo-The Living Room RI.

photo:Jen K.

Arthur-old GB

Inasted-89

photo:Brian B.

photo:Brian B.

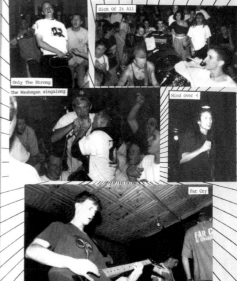

Sick Of It All

Only The Strong

The Waukegan singalong

Mind over 4

Far Cry

Say No More-in Milwaukee

Bottom Line

Token Entry

Hardware

Die Hard

Sick Of It All

Underdog-a shot from the Blindside

Judge

Bold

Sammy on the percussions!

Intensity

Bold-Chicago

Intensity

Brotherhood

Confront

Turning Point

Judge

Chuck Treece

This word search was taken from the very first issue of G&P. Since it was very limited, I decided to reprint it.

```
M Y V L N H L T D O O H R E H T O R B X A
N F E C N A T S D R A H S K T I V S L K X
W P R O J E C T X V K F T P U Y B Q B Y R
O C B X A A A F U F F U I S O B F P P O A
D N A Y A D O T F O H T U O Y I A Z E K W
K N L S A E P D F M D D C S L G N S J D D
A K A Y U W G L K E D E S W A Q U S N I E
R C S U T I A C R E G I I N I F O G T C A
K H S N E H D K N H D N B H C Q R O J E L
U C A I O K E S A E H A A B U I D O C J D
U W U T N B T S B E B H L H R C H E Q B U
X N L P D O N Y T I R Q L O C C R D N S Q
A A T R P A S I E R Z B I Q M F Z Y A Z R
Q P E I A I Z S T R O A R R E J O M R Q P
M P W D D F G M U Q U N O C S H U D V C K
W I D E A N A K E I L F G O D R E D N U L
M D N E H X L O S K I S B O J H M Q G I A
Y P G Y W S E V E N S E C O N D S M I E W
E J A V P W Q J U S T I C E L E A G U E I
```

Token Entry

ONLY THE STRONG	UNIFORM CHOICE	GORILLA BISCUITS
WIND OF CHANGE	JUSTICE LEAGUE	VERBAL ASSAULT
YOUTH OF TODAY	CRUCIAL YOUTH	SEVEN SECONDS
HARD STANCE	BROTHERHOOD	PAGAN BABIES
UNIT PRIDE	SIDE BY SIDE	SUDDEN STOP
BREAKAWAY	WALK PROUD	WIDE AWAKE
UNDERDOG	KRAKDOWN	PROJECT X
INSTED	RAW DEAL	HALFOFF
		JUDGE

Pushed Aside

Judge-Takin it away

PhilMac
Live
record reviews
Sonyanshit

Although I am heavily into tape trading, I really haven't gotten a lot of new stuff. As a result, I've asked some friends to help out. Also I don't like giving bad reviews to anything. So if it is not reviewed, it is possible that I don't like it or I don't have it. Here are some cool releases that I feel deserve some recognition.

COOL C- I GOTTA HABIT- When I heard the cut The Glamorous Life off this album, I thought the whole album would be cool. It turned out to be false. It is just regular rap with a lot of bass. Sorry Cool. Mike

DOC- NO ONE CAN DO IT BETTER- This is the new NWA counterpart, The DOC. I gotta say he is bad! Maybe even better than NWA. This has a lot of funky beats and powerful rapping to boot. All together it's funky enough. Ruthless Records Mike

INTEGRITY- PRE-RELEASE- This is in my opinion the hardest band ever! 2 times harder than Judge. I might even say sorta like Venom. You really have to pick this up when available, and play it loud, because it will tear you limb from limb. Soon on Victory Rec. Mike

INNER STRENGTH- TIME FOR REALITY- This is the first release from Victory records, with many more to come. Inner Strength hail from Cali. and come with a quick, melodic beat, with melodic vocals. Already in it's 2nd pressing, you better get it while you can. Victory Mike

EVEN SCORE- PRE-RELEASE- Formerly Only the Strong, this band from the Chicago area have a unique style of music that should take you by storm. Now with a new drummer and bassist, this should be one of the heaviest releases in a while. Get it soon on Action Packed Records. Gabe

AWAKE- EP- Awake is a band that I can compare to a band like All. It is melodic, with early Dag Nasty type vocals. It has a touch of reggae, along with rap. I like this ep. but if you are hoping to hear heavy stuff, this isn't it. Can't wait to see the cover. Skene/Victory Records Mike

VICTORY
RECORDS

BILLINGSGATE- REACH OUT- This is the premier 7" from a band out of Evanston Il. They have a style that can blow anyone away after one listen. Positive lyrics and great vocals. If you like tight, crunchy music with perfect time changes, I recommend this one for all. Victory Rec. Gabe

BOOGIE DOWN PRODUCTIONS- GHETTO MUSIC...THE BLUEPRINT OF HIP HOP- I almost gave up on rap music before I heard this one. BDP are not your typical self centered, foul rap groups you hear today. These guys have a message to their listeners, and I can respect a group that try to get a point across. Give this one a listen, and you may learn something. RCA REC. Gabe

VISION- IN THE BLINK OF AN EYE- Lp. I can't say enough about this band out of New Jersey. This is in my opinion, the best record of 1989. If you like tight music with a lot of bass, then you better make it to the store or order this one. Nemisis Records Gabe

WHICH WAY COMP.-A GENERATION OF HOPE- Finally, after a long delay, I finally got this one. I'm disappointed with the packaging, But it is Includes; Against the Wall, Full On Straight, Chain of Strength, Confront, & Brotherhood. Good luck getting one. WWR. Gabe

Billingsgate & Crew in the studio

MASADA- WITNESS THIS GENOCIDE demo- Are you sick of all of those cheap thrash bands that all sound the same? I am too. But wait, before you go and cut all of your hair, check out this band Masada. This 5 piece from Waukegan Il. really got it together on this one. Sorta like old Slayer. I recommend this for anyone who has ½ a brain. Edge Entertainment Gabe

SOCIAL JUSTICE- UNITY IS STRENGTH- I got a hot tip from a friend that this was a cool lp so I picked it up. This is sort of like a cross between Suicidal and Up Front. If you like either of these bands, I'd say check this one out. Safe Side Records Gabe

D-VISION- THAT WAS THEN-EP- This is by far one of the better 7"s I've heard in a long time. It is kind of a reminiscent of the Descendants. Don't pass this one up. Pazzifest Records. Matt

RELEASE- THE PAIN INSIDE-EP- This 7" is harsh and by all means to the point. There are some really cool songs like Drug Free Youth and The Pain Inside. I think it is still available so try and get it for yourself. Not bad for a debut 7". Action Packed Records. Matt

WALK PROUD- FIRST IMPRESSION TAPE- This is not available as of yet but when it is, you better be ready for a lot of bass and the usual WP touch. Definitely better than the ep. Gabe

SOUNDGARDEN- LOUDER THAN LOVE LP.- When I first heard these guys, I thought Oh No, not another college type noise band. After giving it a listen, I thought differently. This reminds me of Led Zeppelin, But don't let that stop you. (I hate LZ.) Some standout songs are Hands All Over, and Loud Love. Matt

FAR CRY
DC STRAIGHT EDGE

FAR CRY-DEMO- This is weird, a SE. band out of D.C. Is that hard believe? Well I am glad that D.C. has more to offer than that stuff on Dischord. This demo is heavy and tight. I'm not sure if it is still available but get it somehow. Far Cry- 10104 Donegal Ct. Potomac Md. 20854 Gabe

MIND OVER 4 LP.- This is an lp. that is hard to classify, but still rocks out all the same. I would have to say this is Metal, but with more to offer. Don't miss them live. Matt

POSITIVE APPROACH- JUST HANG ON ep.- This is not the most original records today, but it works. Nothing really grabs me, sorry. Conversion Records Matt

INSIDE OUT- ABOVE ALL ep- Well, well. This is another New York release and I have to admit, this is heavy. If you want to hear something that will definitely move you, than pick this up. 4 songs. Noiseville Records po box 124 Yonkers NY. 10710 Gabe

CRUEL
FLYER
issue #6 out now with:
LEEWAY, FALSE JUSTICE,
and INTENSITY interviews,
pics, reviews, and much more!
$1.00 CASH or equilivent
trade to: CRUEL FLYER
12 white oak way
trenton nj 08618

INSIDE OUT

SAY NO MORE-pre-release ep- I first got to hear this after I decided to help put this out with Mike G. and Mike F. so it better be good. I was pleased when to hear this tape. 4 great songs that blew me away from the start. Lyrics dealing w/ awareness and ignorance. Out some time in Feb. on G&P Productions. Gabe

JUDGE- BRINGING IT DOWN-lp.-After hearing the other recording and the NYU tape I knew this would be a killer record. 9 songs from the heaviest band to date. My picks: Hear Me, Give It Up, and Like You. Another great package from Revelation. #1 on my playlist. Gabe

Even Score

Only the Strong

When someone thinks about the Chicago area, they normally say Bears or Cubs, Bulls or Blackhawks. Well I think that there is a band that is going to put a stop to that. I'm talking about Even Score. I have had the privelage of seeing these guys play a few times and after hearing the pre-release of the 7", I seriously think they can put the wind back into the Windy City. I just wish they had more support locally. Since a few line-up changes and the changing of the name, there is nothing stopping them. Tony and Mark were interviewed at the house and we covered all sorts of stuff.

EVEN SCORE
MIKE-DRUMS
MARK-BASS
CHUCK-GUITAR
TONY-VOCALS

G&P; How long has this line-up been together?
Tony: We have been together since November 16, 1989.
G&P: So is 1990 the year of the Even Score?
Mark: Most definitely...For the next few years.
G&P: How did you guys hook up with Action Packed Records?
Tony: Well, they first wanted to put out a &" with Only The Strong, (Chuck and my first band). Then they wanted to do this one. We said ok.
G&P: Have you kept any of the old Only the Strong stuff?
Tony: No. No way. Not at all.
G&P: Do you think it was fun while it lasted?
Tony: Yeah, it was ok I guess. Two of us carried the burden of other people. They are doing what they want now.
G&P: Do you think that the Chicago Straight Edge is back on track?
Tony: Yes. The fools have been...
Marc: ...Eliminated.
G&P: It seems that you have taken a different direction musically from OTS, who writes the music?
Tony: It is still the same thing. Chuck writes the music and I write the lyrics.
Mark: Yeah, and me and Mike put in where we can.
G&P: Do you plan to tour any time soon?
Mark: Yeah, the East Coast over the Summer.
G&P: Do you have anything lined up yet?
Tony: No, not yet. As soon as the 7" is out we will have something. Hopefully we'll hook up with a big band. Maybe Integrity from Cleveland. They are gonna be on Victory.

G&P: Give me the scoop on Victory.
Tony: A lot has been happening. Inner Strength's first pressing is sold out. The second pressing is now out. Billingsgate have a 7" coming out by the end of January. It is a 6 song 7" called Reach Out. Integrity has a 7" called Contrast Of Sin that should be out at the end of January. 5 songs. Victory shirts are (out now). Hopefully by the end of Jan. we'll have Integrity and Billingsgate shirts. Ep's are 4 bucks and shirts are 9 bucks ppd.
G&P: This is sort of a cheap question, but what are some your influences.
Tony: I try not to listen to the same bands. I don't listen to that much. The only things I do listen to are bands on my label. Inner Strength, Billingsgate, & Integrity. I also like Killing Time, Judge, Bad Brains, American Standard, 4 Walls Falling. I try not to listen to HC all the time so we don't sound like other bands. We try to get our own sound.
G&P: Do you think a lot of bands are starting to sound alike?
Tony: Yeah, everything is getting so generic. That's why all the bands on my label don't sound the same. I try not to pick generic bands.
G&P: Is Even Score a non meat eating band?
Mark: Yeah, it is actually as a band.
Tony: Noone in the band eats meat. I'd say some of our lyrics are militant, vegetarianism.
G&P: As far as the Chicago area is concerned, there has been a few record labels popping up. One of them is giving the area a bad name. Do you think...
Josh: (Josh lives at the house and steps in)...Do you think Ness should have bootlegged the Project X 7"?
Tony: No I don't Gabe, lets go with this.
G&P: Which Way Records has a reputation for bad mail order, and I have had first hand experience. You probably know more about this than me. Tell me what's up.
Tony: All he is is a rich kid who is trying to buy his way into hardcore and he realizes that it is not working because he can't run a label. So now he's trying to buy his way out. Hopefully, kids will get their records. There are a lot of other labels like that around the country, but Which Way is really bad. It is false advertising. "Sorry the 7" isn't out yet, but we are trying to get the covers made."
Mark: He put out flyers in the summer. (It wasn't until Winter that the 7" was out.)
Tony: "It is January, and the record is still not out yet. Maybe I'll get the covers made. Maybe I'll lay it out. Maybe I'll realize my life is a joke"
G&P: What do you think of the Bold Ep?

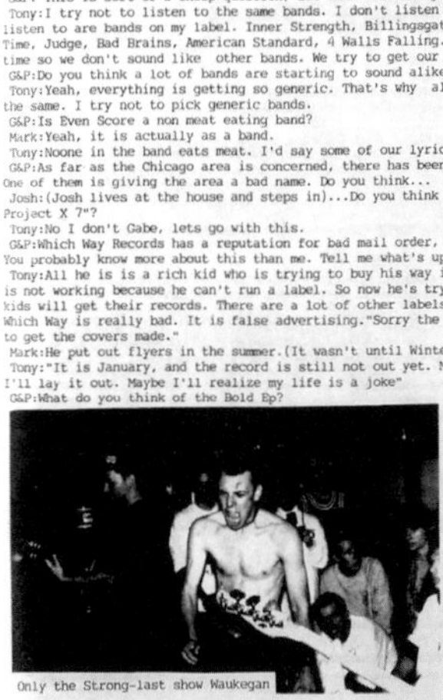

Only the Strong-last show Waukegan

Tony: It is not Bold. It is Matt and Drew. I don't know, I can't speak for them. It is really Matt and Tom's stuff. I thought it was ok. It is kind of a let down though. It is definitely riff sampling by Iron Maiden and Metallica. The image they portray doesn't work. I like the music, but it isn't Bold. They should have made it a project band and changed the name. If that's the way they wanted to go out, then fine. It is their band and they can do what they want. If it worked for them then fine.
G&P: Do you like comic books?
Tony: Yeah, all the rare Victory stuff we are gonna trade for comics.

Tony:Inner Strength had 100 on colored vinyl.(orange)And 100 with a limited cover.Billingsgate will have some white vinyl. The Integrity 7" will have some colored also. If people don't have comic books, then they can get them from their brother or whatever. Just like Revalation. People went out and found GI Joe stuff. There is a way to do it. I trade for lots of things.
G&P:Have you seen some Only the Strong stuff on comps. Are you happy with that?
Tony:It's fine. At least the music will be used for something. I really don't care. If I didn't have a new band I would. I think it is kind of generic now. All it was was naive positiveness. It was based on greed and that doesn't work in the real world. It was a little game. I didn't feel that way at first, but other people in the band didn't take a stand for this.
G&P:What are your views on record collecting?
Tony:It is ok if you are into it. It is greedy. I don't know how addicting it is, but you can be totally stuck with it. You get obsessed with it.I stopped collecting when I started my label. It's cool unless you're trying to find ways to scam people.
G&P:Would you care if you saw the Even Score 7" going for 50 bucks in a few years?
Tony:It would probably get on my nerves. I guess it would be kind of cool, it would mean that people really like your band.
G&P:There has been a Project X bootleg around. What do you think of bootlegs?
Tony:I like bootlegs. There are some cool boots like The Seige or The Cromags 10" of their demo. Those are cool because the band has been established. It can get out of hand.For most parts it's wrong. If I was in the band, I'd be pretty upset.
G&P:Do you know of any good bands coming up that deserve mentioning?
Tony:Yeah, Billingsgate, Integrity, Refuse from Wa.are getting better and better.Raid from Memphis. A lot of the other bands have generic names and have the same message.It's been said.
G&P:Nowadays, what do you think is taboo?
Tony:I really don't know because everything is so liberal. To me I think that if you don't eat meat, do drugs or drink it seems you are in the wrong. Everyone looks down on you. It is not taboo. It is reverse taboo.
G&P:Whatever happened to Chain of Strength? They fooled a lot of people.
Tony:I think so. They disappointed me. All I know is I met one guy and he was the biggest dickhead I had ever met. All they are is a fashion statement. I think people finally see them as they really are.Ass kissers. They are cool one minute, but stabbing you in the back the next.
G&P:What are your religious beliefs?
Tony:I grew up Catholic. I went to Catholic school for 8 years, but I don't go to church anymore. I think it is corrupt. I do my own thing. Somewhere the translation got screwed up. I think there has got to be an after world.
G&P:What subjects do you cover in your lyrics?
Tony:They are a little harder. Vegetarianism. More personal and far more intelligent. I think the record will speak for itself. It will be out at the end of Jan. for sure.
G&P:What else is new?
Tony:Well, Socrates, this guy Josh and me are starting another label. It's gonna have all bizzare people from the Chicago scene like ex-skinheads. People with weird outlooks. It is going to be very limited. The first will be 200 pressed.
G&P:Why are you doing this?
Tony:Well, certain people have something to say.
G&P:What do you expect to get out of this?
Tony: Just fun. See, Victory is totally serious. Now we can have some fun. This other thing is a joke. It should be pretty humorous.
G&P: Is Victory making any money?
Tony:Not yet. It takes time.
(The interview gets cut. You can get in touch wit Tony and Victory Records at:
Po Box 197 Clarendon Hills Illinois 60514)

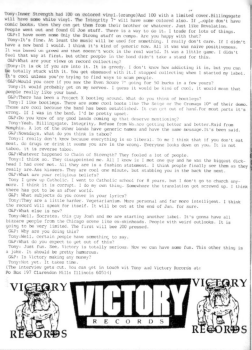

VICTORY RECORDS

SHOW X REVIEWS

Dec.1-Fiesta Palace Waukegan- Ordained Fate, Necromancy, Not-Us, and Masada

Yes, this is a local metal show, but these are the kind of shows were anything goes.Ordained Fate were first. They were a female Queensryche type project. They did a few covers, but seemed to just fill time.

Necromacy was up next, and they weren't too bad. they were fast, and got some feet moving, but if you know the area, that isn't very hard.

Not-Us was next and they are the local HC band that always tend to get a little pep in the audience. They did "Rest for You" by Bad Religion to finish off a long set.

Masada broke out with a heavy approach to what I think is the best in the area. If you like ,our music fast,heavy and with killer mosh parts than you better look into this 5 piece from Waukegan. They are pretty tight live, and deserve a lot more credit than they get.I hope that these guys go somewhere cause I'm proud to have a band like Masada representing the local scene.

Masada-Waukegan Il.

The Waukegan Youth Crew

Nov.8-Goodfellow Hall-Target. Only the Strong, and 7 Seconds

This was Waukegan's first real show and it was a great one. Target off the night with a melodic style to ease up the crowd. They sounded sorta like a cheap Soulside.

Only the Strong was due up next, and this was to the there last show. They were kind of loose, considering they didn't practice, but it was going to turn into a dive-fest anyway. They ended it with the classic "Youth Crew" and that was all she wrote for Only the Strong.

7 Seconds hit the stage and put no doubt in my mind that they can still play as powerful as ever. It was a very personal show, as they did tons of stuff from the latest lp. You can bet they did old classics like,"Walk Together",and "99 Red Balloons". My favorite was "Young Until I Die". If you ever get the chance, and you want to see a great band live, I'd go see these guys.

Dec. 9 Tear Jerker, Even
December 9-Tear Jerker, Even Score

This show was in a basement so it wasn't a lively show. Tear Jerker was a local band that was called at the last minute. It sounded like they've been together for a short time.

Even Score was up next and it sounded like they have been practicing up for this one.(unlike the last OTS show).They take a sorta different approach than the old OTS stuff.This was definitely for real (as opposed to weak). From what I've heard, this band is gonna be a hot outfit and you better pick up the 7" while you can. They played a short set, but it was a sweet debut from what seems to be the future for the Chicago area scene.

Even Score-The Basement

March 18- Anthrax Norwalk Ct.- Crossface, Blind Approach, Vision, Insted and Slapshot

This was a benefit for Roger Merit of AF. First up was Crossface from Boston. They did a really hard set, but all they did was complain because they got a weak response.

Blind Approach was good as I expected.

Vision was no awesome. I can't even describe it. Insted wasn't as good as I hoped them to be. They were kind of sloppy but they are still one of the best.

Slapshot were next. They completely ripped the place apart and played the hardest set I had ever seen live. They did so many songs.new ones included. They got a killer response from the enthused crowd. See them!   Tim Brick

October 13- U of Conn.- Ant Farm, Vision, Supertouch, and Underdog.

It was a 3½ hour drive to get there, but hey, I'll do anything to see a show. Sad to say, Ant Farm opened and did nothing for me,or anyone else in the crowd for that matter.

I had never seen or heard Vision before so I didn't know what to expect. Me and a friend had talked to the singer before the show and he seemed pretty psyched about it. Most of their music had a fast steady beat that rocked. The crowd moved those chairs (why chairs?) out of the pit in a mad frenzy. I bought their album after and I hope to see them again soon.

Vision

People were finally starting to show up and Supertouch went on next. I had seen them before and I was psyched to see them again. Of course,the whole crowd went nuts during Searching for the Light, which anyone must know.

Underdog started at about 11o'clock and no one showed any signs of being tired. Recently the band got rid of their guitarist,so they are playing as a 3 piece,with Ritchie playing guitar. The pit was so crazy that a few fights broke out which sucked cause they called off the show early. The weird part of it is that Underdog talks a lot about non-violence at shows. Everyone gave the band a huge applause as we were shoved out. They still played lots of the 12" songs and a few 7" stuff. It was a great show in spite of all the fights.
Sandi Ajjala

Underdog

Metal Fest 2- Central Park Milwaukee- Dec. 2
Mortar, Tyrants Reign, 911, Gothic Slam, Morbid
Saint, Zoetrope, Indestroy, Old Skull, Sick of
it All, Ludichrist, Mordred, Acrophet, Evildead,
Autopsy, Obituary, Nuclear Assault, Death !!!!!

This was a metallers dream show. This was the
longest show I had ever seen and I'd do it again. There were a lot of good bands and some
crap. Diving was allowed, but someone forgot
to tell the dickhead bouncers. The band I went
to see, Sick Of It All, couldn't make it. Some
outstanding bands were: Mordred, Ludichrist,
Autopsy, 911,and Nuclear Assault. My only gripe
was the battle royale going on in the pit. I
wish someone would tell the scummy metalers
to join the wrestling team, instead of taking
it out in the pit.

Nuclear Assault-Metalfest 89-Milwaukee

GET IN TOUCH WITH SOME OF THE MOST
ENERGETIC HARDCORE-THRASH-PUNK
MATERIAL TO HIT THE UNDERGROUND!
IF YOU LIKE IT FAST AND HEAVY,
CHECK THIS OUT!

911

FOR A 14-SONG DEMO SEND:
$5.00 U.S.
$6.00 FOREIGN

FOR A 2-SIDED T-SHIRT (WHITE WITH
RED & BLACK LOGO ON FRONT,TAPE
COVER ON BACK)

$10.00 U.S.
$12.00 FOREIGN

TO: 9-1-1
c/o GRANT KNULL
8140 W. HOWARD AVE.
MILWAUKEE, WI 53220

ANY RADIO STATIONS OR 'ZINES
PLEASE SEND US A BLANK TAPE WITH
RETURN POSTAGE.

March 17- Anthrax Norwalk Ct.
Face Up, Turning Point, and Up Front

The original bill was Up Front, Beyond, and
Bold. Beyond and Bold cancelled so the other 2
filled in. Face Up was first, and I never heard
them before. They played quite well, but didn't
get a great response cause no one knew them.
Next up was Turning Point who were great.
They played with a lot of energy and the crowd
responded the same. If you ever get the chance
to see them, don't miss it!
Finally there was Up Front. They opened with
a really cool intro and continued with great
songs from the lp. such as "Deliverance","Our
Best", and "What We Need".This was the first
time I had seen them with the new singer Roger,
and I wasn't let down at all. Keep the spirit
alive!.
Tim Brick

Turning Point

THE FALL BRAWL- Nov.4 Wust Hall Wa.DC.- Battered
citizens, Mad Dog, Initial Reaction, Release, 4
Walls Falling, Gut Instinct, Turning point, Outburst, Icemen, & Token Entry.
Besides the fact that the show was billed with
more bands than actually showed, it went well.
Battered Citizens from Pitt. started it all off with
a short set that met a good response.Mad
dog, was next and the small portion of the
set I saw was alright. Initial Reaction
got the crowd moving. They were followed
by Release, Gut Instinct, and 4 Walls,
who have sorta a Raw Deal sound played
all having 800 people dancing and singing
along to their sets. Turning Point did an
equally exciting set and did some new
stuff that was good. The last 3 bands,
from NY played hard sets and the crowd
Outburst, the Icemen, and Token Entry,all
totally went off. The show went well,ex
cept Token Entry got cut cause the club
had to close.
Mick Colabrese

Free Thought Fanzines

KILLING TIME

ZINE #1: Interviews with Inner Strength, Face Up, Implement,
Straight From the Heart, PowerHouse and Stomping Ground.
Also included are reviews, a few pages of photos - some in
full color, an editorial concerning vegetarianism/animal
rights and more. $1.50

ZINE #2: Interviews with Sick of it All, Killing Time, Up
Front, 4 Walls Falling, Anti-Racist Action, Say No More,
Burn Scare and Forthright. Also included are reviews, tons
of photos - most in full color, poems, cartoons, skating
stuff, editorials on various topics and more. Twice as big
as issue #1. $2.25

Free Thought T-Shirts

T-SHIRTS: High-quality shirts of the Free Thought design.
All shirts are double sided, 2 color, on colored shirts.
Shirts come in XL only and are $8.00

All items include postage & handling.
Make all checks & money orders payable
to 'Eric Smith' and send to the address
below:
FREE THOUGHT FANZINE
5219 Wyoming Rd.
Bethesda, MD 20816

H.R.-The Living Room 89   Photo:Jen Kulawas

GOOD & PLENTY ZINE
C/O GABE RODRIGUEZ
2116 SALEM BLVD.
ZION IL. 60099

Maximum Volume

Gabe Melcher

G&P 5 is a perfect clash of constants and variables, reflecting an economy of means and speedy DIY production. The layout is dense and efficient, packing in as much content as possible over its 48 pages with very little breathing room and few moments of pause. Structural and logical typographic treatments over a consistent grid are paired with a cut-and-paste approach to hierarchy and an idiosyncratic editorial approach.

The contradictions position the zine at the intersection of DIY and mechanical production; underground and legitimate; refined and immediate. The speed of production stands with the ephemerality of performance and against any notions of the permanence, or preciousness, of print. The design is as unrelenting as the music it represents.

The entire zine, aside from titles and some specific treatments, is typeset in Courier at a single type size. Variation—from the introduction to interviews to captions to show reviews—are created through changes in column structure and the more aggressive interruptions of hand-drawn titles and photographic collages. Interviews sit across the page in a single column, while editorial elements and concert reviews sit in two-column layouts. Images, ads, and captions move around the page more dynamically over a 3-column grid, often interrupting or splitting the main content. The typewritten text sets an unrelenting tempo across the pages, and its consistency creates an atmosphere of noise. The shift from one- to two- to three- columns signal a variation in pace, but not in volume or density.

Whether intentionally or not, *G&P*'s embrace of the typographic limitation of a single font for all of the primary texts creates a structure that lets the idiosyncrasies of Rodriguez's editorial voice and the complexity of his illustrated titles and advertisements exist in harmony. From page one there's an unexpected level of typographic complexity as the fanzine ads and titles lock-in to the column-set texts, and it all works because of the drone of Courier and the understanding of flow from page to page.

MURPHY'S LAW

INTEGRITY

SOMETHING TO SAY

RESO

REFUSE T

Upon surveying the landscape of other punk fanzines of the time, the pure "utilitarian" appearance of the Courier presents as more raw than if the entirety of the contents was collaged and illustrated. The use and then departure from conventional typesetting bears perhaps more resemblance to the Dadaist expressive "misuse" of printing methods in the 1920s and 1930s than to the pure anarchic xerography and collage of many other punk zines of the 1980s and 1990s. It's a legible cacophony that telegraphs perfectly the feeling of the scene.

Using the conventions of magazines and books, *G&P* 5 creates a baseline for more aggressive gestures (both visual and editorial, and perhaps, and perhaps conscious as well as unconscious). All the parts of a formal publication are present, but the approach is raw and immediate, with elements slightly too tight or misaligned. Unintentional artifacts like the visible tape securing the pieces of the layout on the back cover add a level of abrasive contrast to the regimented results of the typewriter. The rules are there, but they don't stop the continuous flow of content from front cover to back cover. As soon as a subject changes, or a caption or band credit is needed, the layout shifts gears without wasting space.

I love that the layout feels almost like a stream of consciousness. The elimination of whitespace acts as a guiding design and editorial methodology. Typos and errors are left in, content is made to fit snugly, and pull quotes, lyrics, drawings, logos, photos, ads, and even blocks of noise texture fills space that would otherwise be left empty. There's a single direction of movement—forward—and the process of making the zine is a visible part of the publication. Looking through the issue, it's evident from the very first page that the writer, editor, and designer of the zine are all the same person. The result is immediacy, and it's as if the zine was designed as it was written, in a straight line, from start to finish.

Opposite: Detail from paste-up for *Good and Plenty*, issue 5, p. 14, 1990, featuring photos (clockwise) of Murphy's Law, Integrity, Resolution, Refuse to Fall, Youth of Today, and Something to Say.

GOOD AND PLENTY

$1.25

THE zine

#5

SPECIAL ONE YEAR ISSUE
EXPANDED PHOTO SECTION
GOOD AND PLENTY...
NOT JUST A CANDY ANYMORE

CARRY NATION, VISION
TURNING POINT, BILLINGSGATE
SAY NO MORE

MAY 1990

Pegasus is a mythical winged horse, and one of the most recognized creatures in Greek mythology. Its name, when traced back to its roots, roughly means thunder and lightning. The NYHC band Judge have a song called "The Storm" with lyrics that state, "The storm is gonna wipe away, wipe away the insincere. There's no more white, no more black, no more barriers, no more traps."

By the time issue 5 was released in May of 1990, *Good and Plenty* was only a year old. Five issues in twelve months indicates a period of tremendous productivity, especially considering that two of the first five issues were offset-printed.

Rodriguez began taking on more responsibility with the zine. His former partner, Mike Good, had departed, and he was now undertaking the publishing alone, though buoyed by a full slate of contributors. He frequently mentions the zine is a "combined effort." He notes in the introduction, "[t]his zine is 90% done by females. For those of you who think there is no place for girls in the scene, screw you, because there would be no zine without their help."

The changing scope of what kind of music the zine is intended to cover is also addressed: "I'd like to take this space to make it clear that this zine is not restricted to any particular type of music. I hate labels as a means to identify things and especially me." Rodriguez pointedly drew comparisons between the limitations of labels and the danger of stereotypes.

Rodriguez is asserting his intentions and laying the groundwork for where he hopes to take the publication. Even in this pre-internet feedback loop, Rodriguez knew it was vital that he not be confined by, or constrained to, a narrow, close-minded outlook. Growth relies on the ability to be expansive. "I have to warn you that I do like a lot of metal..." he quips, knowing he'd draw the disapproval of some of his hardcore readers.

The large drawing of a rising pegasus (fig. 1) featured on the first page of issue 5 is fitting. At first, it might seem out of place when considered against the youth crew figures who appeared throughout previous issues. But this winged horse, who can strike

Issue 5
May 1990
48 pages
7.5 × 10.6 inches
2,000 copies
$1.25

Opposite: Paste-up for cover of *Good and Plenty*, issue 5, 1990.

Fig. 1. Pegasus drawing from *Good and Plenty*, issue 5, p. 2, 1990.

the earth with its hoof and bring forth water, is a hybrid of creatures that live on land and in the air. Is this signaling the evolution of the fan and the zine—breaking down barriers and avoiding traps?

The issue also marks an evolution in production—issue 5 delivers the first cover printed in two colors, black and purple. The cover photo, of the band Carry Nation photographed by Sean Higgins, is printed as a duotone.

The cover claims an expanded photo section and the zine devotes almost twenty pages to 110 photos of live performances. There are photos of stage dives; Civ from the Gorilla Biscuits in Europe; New York's Judge playing California in 1990; Insted playing at 924 Gilman Street; a pile-on singalong with Project X; Bad Trip playing at the Safari Club in D.C.; Zack de la Rocha in Inside Out; Fugazi playing the Anthrax in Connecticut, and lots of images of Youth of Today. Rodriguez was able to amass an extensive collection of hardcore photography from contributors around the world. He printed *G&P* shirts and would send a free shirt to anyone who submitted a photo. "I am also heavily into trading tapes, records, and videos. Write to me for a list," he notes in the zine's intro. This network of equally committed and enthusiastic fans unequivocally allowed zines like *Good and Plenty*, and many others, to prosper and thrive. —C.S/K.S.

GOOD AND PLENTY

GOOD & PLENTY #5 SPRING '90
$1.25 ppd.This is a special issue
for me because 1.it is now a year
since G&P was formed.2.This was the
first issue done entirely by me.
But I had lots of contributers.
This is not just my zine,it is all
of us working together.

I always forget someone here so please
forgive me if I do.These are all the people who have helped in any way to put this
publication where it is today:In no order.
Megan Luther,Matt Garcia,Chad A.,Mike B.,
Dan(Stop & Think),Mick,Scott Viera,Joel and
Mark(Refuse),Ken Flavel(Turning Point),Gear,
Tom Turner,Nathan Rodriguez(bro),Mike Ruiz,
my dad Manny R.and Scott L.for printing this
on their spare time,Caesar Fontana John,Steve,
Tom R.(bro),Trash American Style,Big Frank,
Billingsgate,Say No More,Vision,Jeff Johns,
the whole state of Texas and everyone who I
write to there:Damon,Carlos,Audrey,Bram,Dave,
Alejandrina,the Witchita crew:Jon,Andy and
Carrie,Mike Karban(Caring Edge),Carl Skildum,
Ken Salerno,Jen Kulawas,Brian Boog,Phil,Josh,
Tony B.,Kim(Molly),Colin,Eric Ramos,Johnny L.,
Kerry Pries,Sandi Aijala,Becky(Contax One),
Jeff(Up Front),Todd(Far Cry,Hands Up),Hard Pat,
Mrs.Luther,Pat Costello,Grant(911),Jason McGill
Ron(Resolution),Dave Pudney,Eric Fortner,Paul,
Mike Thain,Cara Longo,Dave(Comin Correct),Badd-
Repp,Jesse Keenan,Frontside Chad,and the guy
who started this zine with me a year ago 4/89,
Mike Good.

GOOD & PLENTY T-SHIRTS:Yes,I finally have
a new design.2-sided.100% cotton.XL
$8.00 ppd.The design is on the back cover
and upper left corner of this page.
I do trade shirts for good photos,but,
please write first.

Good And Plenty back issues:
#1-Sudden Stop,word search,show
reviews.   #printed-50 free
SOLD OUT!
#2-Only The Strong,show reviews,lyric
trivia. #printed-105-$.25
SOLD OUT!
#3-Gorilla Biscuits,Brotherhood,
Insted,Bold,Judge,show reviews,
& much more. #printed-130$.75
SOLD OUT!
#4-Refuse,Seven Seconds,Up Front,
Inner Strength,show reviews,
lyric trivia,& much more.
#printed-475-$1.25 some left.

Good & Plenty Playlist
Suicidal Tendencies-all Gorilla Biscuits-all
Death Angel-Act 3   Outspoken(Ca.)-all
Moondog-tape   Alone in a Crowd-Ep
Far Cry-Story Of Life   Inside Out(Ca.)-demo
Billingsgate-Reach out   Bent In Pieces-sampler
Excel-anything   Social Distortion-Lp.
Beyond-Lp.   No Mercy-Lp.

Photo credits:Many people sent shots in,
here is the ones that I know.You people
made this zine happen:Tony B.,Gabe R.,
Mike Thain,Cam,Cara Longo,Tim Owen,Micha,
Ken Salerno,Colin,Mike B.,Tim Duggan,
Kerry Pries,Dave(C.C)Pete.Jason McGill,
Chris Mohan,H.Zurcher,Mario Schranz,Igby,
Van Drom,Bram,Eric Fortner,Scott Viera,
Becky Perrone,Erik Szantai,Tim Brick,
Mark,and lots more I don't know.

Cover photo:Carry Nation.by: Sean Higgens

This is the hardest part of the zine
for me because this is where I have to
be totally creative and have to attract
the reader.I could write about many
things,but I will focus on a few.

First,you may notice that there are
no record or zine reviews in this iss-
ue.It is very hard to give something a
bad review if you get it for free from
one of the band members or the editors.
Everything has faults somewhere and I
don't feel I have the authority to pick
at any of them.What I may find to be bad,
someone else may find good.That is why
I refrained from reviewing records and
zines.I will say thanks to Big Frank,
Soda Can,Counter Punch,Reaction,Overkill,
Crivits,and everyone who sent in stuff.
I'm not saying these are bad,actually
you might want to look into all of these,
but as I stated,I won't review stuff for
a while.

Second,you may see one persons name for
this zine,but it is a combined effort
from many people.I sent free shirts to
a lot of people for pictures.and some I
didn't because I ran out.But now I do
have some again with a different design
and if you write first stating what you
can trade,I will do it.

I am also heavily into trading tapes,
records,and videos.Write to me for my
list.It is hard to do trading with people when you do a zine,but I do the best
I can.I am especially looking for live
stuff from:Dag Nasty from Field Day,
Sacred Reich demo,any live Gorilla B.,
live Judge,just about anything from Beyond,
and lots more.Some Records I am looking for
are:D.R.I 22 song 7",Underdog 7"(blue),
Judge Chung King,Youth of Today We're Not
In This Alone(German,Yellow)Iron Maiden
Running Free first press,and Sound House
Tapes,and that is about it.I do sell records also so check with me on that.

And finally,I'd like to take this space
to make it clear that this zine is not
restricted to any particular type of music.
I hate labels as a means to identify things
and especially me.You may never know it is
going to pop up in here next.I have to warn
you that I do like a lot of metal,so don't
be surprised to see Suicidal or D.R.I. in
a future issue.One major goal of mine is to
interview the best band to ever form...
Iron Maiden.(strictly opinion of course).

Oh yeah,I almost forgot,there is one
more thing I'd like to get off my chest.
This stupid sexism thing.This zine is 90%
done by females.For those of you who still
think there is no place for girls in the
scene,screw you because there would be no
zine here without their help.There is one

There is one person in particular that
really made me think about myself,other people and the world around me.This person I
met through the mail and became friends with
very easily.I was thinking about quitting
this zine because the scene here was so depressing,but after seeing a real scene at
a glance,I didn't.And I have this person to
thank.This person taught me to "Cease the
day" and"Grab the moment" so to speak.
They are a true friend,and those are hard to
come by these days.Thanks.You know who you
are.

NEMESIS KNOWS HARDCORE!

Nemesis Live #1
Features unreleased songs by
No For An Answer, and Hard
Stance plus Slapshot and
Pushed Aside.

Special Nemesis notice:
Nemesis will not be manufacturing or
distributing the new Chain Of Strength
single.

Nemesis Live #2
Haywire needs to be seen live
to be truely appreciated. This
performance was captured the
night of the massive earthquake
in San Francisco and features
unreleased material.

You know where to get these
records, if you don't, ask a
friend.

Nemesis #9
Long awaited 7 inch by one of
California's best hardcore
bands. Heavy duty and ready
to explode!

Special Nemesis notice #2:
We will, however, be releasing a
live single featuring Bad Religion,
Insted, Visual Discrimination and
Carry Nation and a gatefold double
7 inch by Uniform Choice.

BILLINGSGATE

I don't know how many people have heard of Billingsgate before,but soon that will be a household name in
the hardcore scene. Just to have them as a part of the
Chicago scene is definitely a plus for the few people
that acknowledge them.This 5 piece outfit from the Chi-
town area is the most promising band I think nationwide.
They do have a 7" out on Victory Records
and you can hear for yourself why I say
that.They do plan to tour,and I expect
anyone who has this zine to see them if they
play near you.This interview was done after
a show they did at Club Blitz.(a show where
2 bands cancelled for reasons unknown.) Erik
and Steve were interrogated,so to speak.Come
with me as I recollect that night.

ERIK-LEAD GUITAR
STEVE-RHYTHM GUITAR
JASON-DRUMS
CHRIS-BASS
SQUIRREL-VOCALS

all photos by:Kerry P.
Tony B.
& Gabe R.

G&P:How long has this line-up been together?
Steve:About 2 months.Since New Years.It was cool
cause Chris came in knowing all of the songs off
the 7".We only had to teach him the newer songs.
G&P:Is it a pretty solid 5 piece now?
Erik:Yeah.Billingsgate has been together for 2½
years now.We all dig
Chris.We had never met
him until he came to our
practice.He is a nut.We
are having trouble with
work and shows,but we
will work it out.
We need a van. 
G&P:You have been
around for a bit
what are your
main objectives
now,and have they
changed since you
first started?

Steve:It used to be just to go out and play and maybe get on vinyl.Now we have a 7"
and we play shows.I don't know.
Erik:The objectives have changed a lot.Right now,materially we want to get a van so
we can play more shows.
Steve:We want to go on tour this summer.That is a short term goal.
Erik:We definitely want to go out to New York and places out East.We may hook up
with Say No More.We also want to do an lp. in the Fall and find a label to do it.
G&P:Speaking of Say No More,how was that last weekend with them.I got their views,
now do you feel about Indiana?
Erik:The metalheads were dumb at the rink.I never knew anyone who was willing to
defend Motley Crue.I know a lot of metalheads,and I've considered myself one for a
long time.Everyone knows,if you like Motley Crue,it is not cool anymore.
Steve:Motley Crue isn't a band that you would fight to defend.
Erik:And these guys were willing to do it...Also,the livest thing was Gabe's dive
on old boy's head.That will stick with me for life...Say No More was cool.I had talked to Bob on the phone a few times and by the end of the weekend,we were cool with
everyone.I got their 7"and I think I totally like it.Milwaukee ruled.
G&P:Gorilla Biscuits played there and there was about 15 people from Milwaukee
there and 20 from the Chicago area.But it was a cool show.
Erik:Milwaukee was great.They are a young scene which is great because I know a lot
of kids 7th grade-freshmen out here.They don't go to shows.They don't even know if
there are shows.They only go to the $15 Henry Rollins shows.
Steve:Butt Ugly Zine sucks!
Erik:It was a good zine,but they could have refrained from things like the drawing
of Mike G.They drew him with brass knuckles saying,"Hey,limited edition numbered
copies".I don't know what he did to them,but they didn't have to do that.
Steve:At one of the shows in Waukesha,some band did an Only the Strong cover and
Mike sang the whole song.
Erik:Everyone knew it was a joke so it shouldn't have been a big deal.
G&P:There was more to it than that,but let's not get into that.Let's just say that
Mike isn't too fond of them and vice-versa....Now,can you give me a little insight
on some of your lyrics?
Erik:Our lyrics are positively geared.I think Squirrel is pretty good with words.
We mostly talk about the big guy who is out to get the little guy.Now,though we're
gonna get more political.Most of the positive bands in the past few years have been
more socially orientated.The old HC bands were more political.And Squirrel has very
strong political stands to say the least.
(Tony B. steps in and the subject changes)
G&P:Are you happy with Victory Records?
Tony:All except the stalling.
Erik:There were reasons for that. We didn't have any pictures and stuff.Everything
else went well though.We got the recording done,we got the records,and shirts done.
Steve:We got Pat Costello on the flipside.
Erik:Tony has been doing a great job with this.He's been dishing out some serious
money.We are talking gatefold,4 sided shirts,Tony has been doing THE JOB.

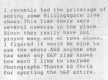

Steve:If anyone out there owns a record label,and they want to do an Lp,get a hold of us.

Erik:We have new material every day.We do want to do a good job with a 12".esp. do the recording.We don't want a $20 an hour thing. We're gonna go to the same place where the 7" was recorded.

Steve:Jaff Murphy is a great engineer.

Erik:We want to put out a great product. Something that rivals the Judge or GB lp. We needed a label that van help with that.

G&P:Who writes the music?

Erik:During the time of the 7",I wrote most of it.Squirrel started writing later. He did 2 songs from the 7"-Holdstrong and Reach Out.He also wrote a new song called Outlet that everyone seems to like.He used to play bass.Steve is also busting some new riffs.I write.But we have little time.

G&P:I think that there is a whole lot of Metal influence in most HC.Do you think so?

Erik:Oh yes.If it doesn't contain any metal sounding riff,it sounds like that old 3 chord punk.When I write,I try to use all the aspects of metal and HC that I like. Another thing,I love Slipknot.They are a- long the thrash lines,and the way that guy sings is insane.If they had long hair,they would be an all thrash band.

G&P:I asked Say No More this,do you ever plan to make money with this band?

Erik:Actually we are making more money now than we had ever did.

Steve:We never really made money before.

Erik:If we go out of town we would like to get some because we have to rent vans.But there is no such thing as profit.Everything we make goes back into the band.

Steve:We have a band account.Whatever the band needs,that is what it is there for.

Erik:and when it comes to pricing things like our shirts,we are gonna try and keep the prices down.We want to do like the Dischord thing where you put the price on the record.That place in Milwaukee is sel- ling the SNM 7" for $6.It just came out. I guess a record is worth as much as one will pay for it.Trading is cool though.

G&P:To change to a different subject,what is your stand on abortion?

Erik:I'm strongly pro-choice.So is every- one else.But I don't know about Chris,I never really asked him.I don't know many pro-lifers that can let things be.

Steve:I was on an airplane once and I read an article that had 30 womens views on it. That made me decide to be pro-choice.

G&P:What about meat?

Steve:I like it.

Erik:Squirrel is a vege.I am also.I only eat shrimp.I have trouble thinking that shrimp is an animal.Chris is a vegetarian.

I recently had the privelage of seeing some Billingsgate live shows.This time there were several cameras in the place. Since they really have not played many out of town shows. I figured it would be nice to use the shots.And anyone who has seen any G&P zine knows how much I like to include Photographs.Thanks to Chris for sporting the G&P attire.

"TOO IDEALISTIC SOME MAY SAY, BUT SOME MAY NEVER ACHIEVE"

Steve:It was a lot different 4 or 5 years ago.The Metro used to do shows every weekend.

Erik:I went to Rollins last night and I hung out outside.I saw so many people.Why don't I see these people regularly.They won't go to the local shows for $5, but they will dish out 15 for the big bands.

G&P:How about the Chicago SE scene?

Erik:What do I think about looking at it and hanging around it,I think it is good. A lot of people give Tony B. shit cause they think he's Mr.SE and people have to follow up to him.He doesn't see it that way and neither do the kids.The SE scene is the best thing working in Chicago.Esp. the shows here.(Club Blitz.)

G&P:Have you ever gotten ripped off from mailorder?(I had to ask)

Erik:Oh boy.Do you wanna see what I have right here?My check that I made out to Ryan Hoffman(Chain Of Shit).It is signed by him and was cashed in Nov.89. As of now March 23 I have received nothing.Not even a letter.Ryan,if you happen to get this zine,I did not send you $14 cause I thought you needed it.I didn't think you'd be hungry one night and get a pizza.I don't know if I'm mad or glad you guys didn't show up tonight.I'm glad cause it may have been a bad scene.But it would have been fun to watch.

G&P:I feel bad because I ran the ad that ripped people off.He scammed $24 of mine.

G&P:How did your singer get the nickname Squirrel?

Steve:He used to have bangs that went into his face back in the mod days.Basically, he looked like a squirrel.

Erik:Pat,our old singer looked at him one morning and said that he was gonna call him Squirrel from now on.He asked him to put his arms up and act like it,and he did it.Next time you see him ask him to do the squirrel.We toss him a few nuts once in a while to keep him happy.

G&P:What was the best show you ever played?

Erik:Milwaukee.Chicago is lame.Unless you are an out of town band,people won't dance.Except at Club Blitz.In Milwaukee,the club was great.They had a Mexican Rest- araunt upstairs.Check it out if you ever play the Unicorn.It is very rare that you get people moving for your intro.They danced from note one to the endtro.

G&P:Do you have anything definite for the tour yet?

Steve:Oh,if anyone out East or on the way out there wants to book a show with us, get a hold of us.

Erik:We were talking about hooking up with Say No More and Refuse To Fall in the middle of June.Actually what we wanted to do .We had this idea when Upfront was looking for a drummer and Underdog didn't really have a guitar player.We would open, I'd go play drums for Upfront.(I used to play drums).Then I'd play guitar for Under- dog.Then Squirrel would play 2nd guitar for Judge.They are his favorite band.

G&P:Do you wanna wrap things up.Normally people just say thanks for the interview.I hate that.Spice it up.

Erik:Ok...Thanks to Gabe for the interview.(haha)Thanks to the people here at Club Blitz.Mike Bonner.Pat Costello. Thanks to the people who get this zine for helping Gabe and us both.Peace to the nation of Islam.

Write Billingsgate c/oJosh Flaherty
610 Forest Ave
Evanston Il 60202

Chris and Steve are killers.Just kid- ding,they eat meat.

G&P:Lets talk about the Chicago scene.

Steve:I think it is on a comeback.

Erik:I thought that about 6 months ago promised to put in this zine.If you like shows now though in reality,the only HC bands here are us and Even Score.Even just a year ago if there was a show,people would come out.Recently we advertised a show with us,Even Score and another band for $15.Only 50 people showed up. Back then it was incredible.The Metro

VICTORY RECORDS

THE LEGENDARY CARRY NATION

The band Carry Nation is not just some project band that got together as a joke.To the contrary,they have been around since 1985 and has just recently put out their debut Ep on Workshed Records.Anyone who has heard it may agree with me when I say it is a very powerful 7" and could stand up to any other release to date.But what exactly is Carry Nation?Why did it take 5 years to surface?Come "Face The Nation" with me and learn what makes this O.C. 4-piece tick.A "Big" thank you to Big Frank who sent this interview back in one week to barely make it in this issue.
Band photo:Sean Higgens.All others by Igby

CARRY NATION IS:
BIG FRANK-BASS
GAVIN-GUITAR
DAN-VOCALS
STEVE-DRUMS

G&P:How and why did Carry Nation form?
Dan:We formed in '85 as a bunch of friends who felt the need to make some intelligent noise.When Insted really took off,Gavin's school intensified,and Frank's workload increased,the Nation just faded.The next thing we know,Gavin and I were doing No For An Answer.Two years later after the fall of NFAA and with the availability of the other two members-reformation,at least to document the whole thing,was only natural.
G&P:What is the meaning of the term Carry Nation?
Dan:The name is a tongue in cheek reference to the prohibitionist of the same name.
G&P:I've seen flyers of CN so you have played shows.What is the response as opposed to the NFAA era?
Dan:With each passing show Carry Nation seems to emerge as a more aggressive outfit with a more dynamic stage presence.The crowd has reacted accordingly.
G&P:Steve,what is on the agenda for Insted?I've heard you were gonna tour Europe.
Steve:Insted is not on hold.We took a long break.We have plans to go to Europe.We just signed to Epitaph records and part of the deal was to go to Europe.Insted is stronger than ever.A new record out at the end of Summer.
G&P:I heard CN played a show with HR.Can you elaborate on that?
Dan:You are incorrect.Voicebox (One of my side projects with Chuck Treece) played with HR.It was an experiment in communicating with people that were not necessarily in our peer group.
G&P:Steve,with Insted,the Ep is definitely much heavier than the Lp.Since you are now involved in an even heavier outfit,can we expect this to be a continuing pattern?

Steve:Insted will be Insted.My drumming gets heavier as I get better and more proficient.It is not a conscious effort on my part,it is just natural.
G&P:Dan,I see you are doing some work in Flipside Fanzine.Do you have any plans on other fanzine stuff?
Dan:I do a scene report in Flipside mainly because I feel that is a large and influential local mag that might otherwise let the most productive part of the Southern part of California go un-noticed.I've also begun a semi-monthly collumn in MRR.
G&P:Is Carry Nation a full time band?
Frank:It depends on your definition of full-time.Dan and I both run a small record label.Gavin goes to school full-time and Steve works full-time and plays with Insted.I usually hold down 2 jobs.Somewhere in all that Carry Nation exists.I sometimes wish we could spend more time on the band,but so far everything has gone really well.
G&P:The Ep has gotten some good reviews from major HC zines.Why do you think that has been the case.Usually anything that is in any way positive is put down.
Dan:I feel MRR and Flipside are more capable of accepting CN because we are closer to their age group and share a common history and perspective on the underground.Furthermore,I feel they appreciate our concern with issues and ideals other than terms like straight edge and positive which are basically crutches to describe something which requires significantly greater thought.
Frank:Not to sound pompous,but I think people respect the fact that we've paid our dues in one way or another.We also don't label ourselves into any particular clique. We just play HC and try to write intelligent lyrics.
G&P:Does Carry Nation want to be known as a SE band?
Dan:It really,really depends on your definition of the term.Our attitudes are our and not the flagship of some movement.
Frank:Personally,I like to be thought of as a hardcore band.If someone wants to know politics,they can ask me.
G&P:If you saw a person wearing a"Fuck Straight Edge"shirt,what would you do?
Dan:I'd be hard pressed to give a damn either way.It seems like the petty action of someone consumed with in fighting.
Frank:If a clown doesn't have an audience paying attention,then he doesn't have a show and is easily ignored.
G&P:Frank,I haven't heard of you on the bass until the CN Ep.Were you in other bands?
Frank:I have had short stints with bands,but nothing aver really gelled.The Vandals, No For An Answer,and Skrewball are the only ones worth mentioning and/or the ones that I can remember.Carry Nation is the perfect band for me.It is everything I want in a hardcore band.If I wasn't in CN,I would be into them.
G&P:2-part question.1-what is new with Nemisis Records.2-How would a band come to be on Nemisis Records?
Frank:A new Visual Discrimination record,Walk Proud Lp,a couple of Hunger Farm 7", Pitchfork Lp,and a Chorus of Disapproval Lp. Basically,if I like your band and I think it can sell a few and if the band is down to Earth in expectations,(they'll be signed) I like working with local bands because we have close contact and we can deal in person with each other.I will work with bands from anywhere though.Most of the bands I work with,I also consider them friends.When it comes to business and not friends, then I cease to be interested.

it is discredited by their methods that I have seen first hand,ie.focused recruiting of the young and the lonely.Vulture time.
Frank:I am agnostic and believe that most organized religion is run by evil and corrupt people feeding on weak minds.

G&P:State your ages. When you are 30,do you plan on being into HC?
Dan:Dan-38,Gavin-64, Steve-32,Frank-9.Thirty seems like just a dusant memory.
Frank:Yeah,I hope to.
G&P:You have touched on the subject of religion on the 7".Can you elaborate on your opinion of religion today?
Dan:I don't absolutely denounce the possibility of there being a higher power,but it seems illogical.As far as the Krisna movement goes,I see some visdom in a little of their literature but I feel

The following pages are the result of many peoples help that responded to my request for photographs.G&P #5 was supposed to be a photo zine.Actually,it is. Anyway,thanks to everyone who helped make this section.You may notice quite a few shots of Gorilla Biscuits and Judge.Well I like GB a lot and as for Judge,these may very well be shots taken from their last few shows.One onea set was taken from the video show,another was from one of the shows in California with Lars.

RANDY-AGAINST THE WALL

INTEGRITY

BILLINGSGATE

BILLINGSGATE

GORILLA BISCUITS

GB-IN EUROPE

MURPHY'S LAW

INTEGRITY

JUDGE IN CA.

SOMETHING TO SAY

RESOLUTION

24-7 SPIES

ALEX

GORILLA BISCUITS-CHICAGO

INTEGRITY

WALTER

REFUSE TO FALL

DOWNCAST

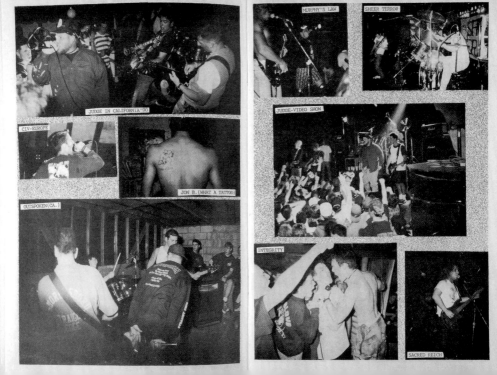

JUDGE IN CALIFORNIA '90

CIV-EUROPE

JON B. (WHAT A TATTOO)

OUTSPOKEN (CA.)

MURPHY'S LAW

SHEER TERROR

JUDGE-VIDEO SHOW

INTEGRITY

SACRED REICH

SICK OF IT ALL

END TO END

STEVE YOUTH

SICK OF IT ALL

FISTFIGHT

FISTFIGHT

SHEER TERROR

SUPERTOUCH

SHADES APART

DOWN FOR THE COUNT

MAXIMUM PENALTY

VERBAL ASSAULT

FALSE HOPE

BAD TRIP-SAFARI CLUB

INTEGRITY

Y.O.T.

FREEWILL

EXCEL

AGNOSTIC FRONT

DOUGH BOYS

D.R.I.

OUTSPOKEN

INSIDE OUT

EVEN SCORE

WRECKING CREW

EXCEL

EVEN SCORE-CLUB BLITZ

VERBAL ASSAULT-THE LIVING ROOM

MASADA

DIE HARD

OUTSPOKEN

A CLUB BLITZ SINGALONG

INTEGRITY

SOULSIDE

IMPLEMENT

INSIDE OUT

INTEGRITY

FUGAZI-THE ANTHRAX

VERBAL ASSAULT

VIC-INSIDE OUT

ROB-RELEASE

INNER STRENGTH

INNER X STRENG
TIME FOR REAL

SUPERTOUCH

BILLINGSGATE-CLUB BLITZ

INSTED-GILMAN ST.

JUDGE-VIDEO SHOW

SLAPSHOT

Y.O.T.

RITCHIE-UNDERDOG

Y.O.T.

JUDGE-FROM VIDEO SHOW

WEEDEATER

REFUSE TO FALL

YOUTH OF TODAY AND CO.

PHIL-THAT IS SUICIDE

UPPERCUT

SCREAM

Y.O.T.

SAY NO MORE
HARD CORE

Would you be surprised if I were to tell you that Nebraska had a cool HC scene? How about a cool HC band? Yes I said Nebraska. Well,Say No More is that band that has been putting Omaha on the map in the HC scene. They were in town for a weekend and I had the chance to interview them this time. They played 2 shows;one in In.. and one in Milwaukee.(See Show Reviews) And,oh by the way,they do have a 7" out on my friend Mike's label-Good & Plenty Prod. Anyway, read on and find out that there is more to Nebraska than corn.

KELLY-BASS
JEFF-DRUMS
BOB-GUITAR
TODD-VOCALS

G&P:This is your second time near the windy city,what do you think of it now?

Bob:No one goes to shows.

Todd:It has been around so long,it seems it has been divided up.Each group has their own set of shows that they'll go to.Milwaukee has a younger crowd.They all go.

Kelley:I thought more people would be at Medusa's the last time we were here... Especially since we played with Even Score.

Bob:I thought Omaha had a lame scene,but we get 300 people at those shows.

Todd:Omaha mixes well though.People who don't really like it go anyway.

Kelley:And still have fun.There is never any fights there.

Bob:I don't remember a fight there since Verbal Assault '86.

Kelley:There were a few,but nothing like the "riot" last night in Indiana. EVERYONE:**DON'T PLAY THE RINK IN SHEERVILLE INDIANA!!**

G&P:What is your second impression of the Wisconsin scene?

Bob:I think it is pretty hip.It is small.

Todd:It reminds me of Lincoln Nebraska.

Kelly:Milwaukee is all right,a good town.They saved our asses this trip.

Todd:Yeah,we sold a lot of stuff there.We love those guys.Now we may not owe too much on the van.

G&P:At the Indiana show,there was some turbulance in the air and you guys didn't really get involved.
Todd:First,I couldn't tell what was going on.I didn't want to get involved with something where I had to chose sides.
Bob:It also seemed kind of trivial.
Kelley:It was all over playing a fuckin' Motley Crue song.
G&P:Would you have taken part if it came down to it?
Bob:It didn't look like we needed to,because there was about 4 of them and 20 of us that were willing to go after it.
Todd:If it came to where they were cleaning house,we would have(stepped in). Probably earlier.But we're not going to provoke anything.
G&P:Are you happy with the EP?
Bob:We're happy with it.But I think the equalization of the 7" to the master is not as good.The bass was a little more,and the guitars were crunchier.
Todd:It was because we had to wait,and we only had the original to listen to, we had grown accustom to the original.
Kelley:We are happy with it,especially the drums.
Todd:And it really helped us a lot when you and Mike went to Rhode Island.(We sold 7"s out there)
G&P:Do you think it was to your benefit to be on G&P Productions?
Todd:Yes.Especially if you are talking about what we were going to be on.
Kelley:Flack Productions.(a burst of laughter fills the van)Fly By Night Prod.
Bob:Don't worry,next week everybody—
Brad the roadie gets in his 2¢.
Brad:Oh,by the way.We are stopping in Moline
G&P:What is on the agenda for you guys.
Brad:What for,Brad?
Brad:I'm gonna kick Mike Flack's ass.
Kelley:A tour this summer.
Bob:We are going to record some more.Just for the heck of it.
Todd:Even if it is just a demo or something because we have so much new stuff.
Bob:We came up with 9 new songs in a month.It is hard for us because we all work and it is hard to get the songs down.
G&P:What was the best show you ever played?
Bob:Blind Approach's second to the last show in Minneapolis.And our equipment got stolen.We played a really good show and our stuff was stolen.That is why me and Brad are sleeping in the van tonight.
Kelley:All of our records got stolen-even worse than our equipment.We had all of those bootlegs from Minneapolis.
Bob:That record store in Minneapolis bootlegs a whole lot.
G&P:What do you think of record collectors?
Kelley:I hate record collectors man.(sarcastically)
Bob:Kelly got a Sick Of It All t-shirt just for thinking about trading.
Todd:He also bought 2 Carry Nation 7"s,just so noone else would have them.

G&P:Do you think it is ok for people to make a profit from collecting records?
Todd:No.That record store from Milwaukee sold our 7" for $6. One kid paid $10.Half the time they don't even know because they aren't involved with HC.
Bob:They had one record for $10 and it said right on the record "Do not pay more than $3.
Todd:They had the NYC Together for $50,and I treat mine like shit.
Bob:And that Fugazi 7"on Sub-pop.They said it was going for $100-$150.I got mine for $3.
Kelley:Fugazi sucks.

G&P:Do you guys like emocore?
Kelley:The Forced Down record has the coolest cover.
Todd:That isn't even Emocore though.
Kelley:The Best Emocore isn't even from D.C.,and that is Verbal Assault.
Bob:They are on the edge of Emocore and Hardcore.The new Lp. rocks.
G&P:What is your opinion of Straight Edge?
Kelley:I love it.I have no problem.I was for 3 years.Most of that was when I did not know any other SE people.I didn't meet any others til these guys.
Todd:The SE pride strangled itself in Omaha.Now,the people who are SE are that way for themselves,and most of the people who were,are no longer.
Bob:I smoke,but besides that I drank one beer in my whole life,and I don't really have any urge to.
Kelley:Straight Edge is cool.I have lots of SE friends,most of the bands I like are SE.And Straight Edge Hardcore rocks.
G&P:Do you think it is taking it too far to put down people who aren't SE.
Bob:Yes,but it is like that with everything.People who aren't put down those who are.
Todd:You need both sides,that way you make your side stronger.
Kelley:At least now kids know that they don't have to drink.But there is still pressure the other way.
Bob:By the way,,this is the first semi-serious interview we have ever done.I mean we aren't talking about naval lint.We haven't said that Jeff will quit the band.
Todd:By the way,Becky,we are sorry for that interview.We got a little out of hand on the other one int.
A few people get in the inter.
Phil:You should get Mike G.in this interview and ask you about pornos and stuff.

Todd & Kelley:No,lets not.
G&P:What is your favorite co-ver song to play.
SNM:Sign Of The Times,Your-Mistake,Warzone-As One(laughter)
Todd:What is funny is that Bob plays the strings and I play whatever and it sounds just as good. My favorite cover was the song Underdog.
Kelley:Say it to my face is good.It gets the crowd going.
Bob:Another real fun one that a lot of people don't know is Reagan Youth's Regen-erator.Reagan Youth rocks.
Kelley:What is even sadder is-

people think that Warriors is done by Judge and they don't even know it is done by the Blitz.That kills me.I have that Blitz 7" and I will trade it.I'm not a record collector,but I will trade it.You set me up with a good deal,we'll trade.(irony)
Phil:Lets talk about Chicago.
Kelley:We allready did.I thought it was weak though.When we played at Medusa's with Even Score, no one was there.
Bob:How many people go to local shows here?
Phil:It depends on the band.For Naked Reagun you got 5000 people.But for Even-Score,sometimes they pack it,but lately you'll get about 50.
Bob:Any show in Omaha,we get 300.
Phil:That is great.Chicago sucks.
Phil:Do you do Motley Crue covers?
Bob:We are.We're gonna do Live Wire.That or a Kiss song...Ok,next question.Just don't ask us what our songs are about,cause you'll get a 3 page answer.
G&P:Do you ever plan to make any money with this band?
This was the funniest question,the whole van was hysterical.
Todd:I think this whole weekend was proof of that answer.Our goal is not to lose too much money.
Bob:To break even would be a dream.
Kelley:But we do have a good time.Chicago last time brought us down.we had the Waukesha show that had to pull through for us.Dude...A Waukesha Basement?
G&P:Did you know about the Miss America Pageant?They were giving away furs to the winner.I know people that protested that.
Bob:It is also kind of sexist.but we won't go into that.
G&P:No,that is interesting you say that.Let's get into it.
Bob:The Miss America Pageant is sexist as shit.It is putting women on a pedastol to find out which one is the most profound and prestige.If it is not to see who is the most beautiful,then why don't they have men & women up there to see who is the most perfect.
G&P:Who is your favorite wrestler?
Bob:Andre the Giant-for wanting to go out with Kelley's old roommate.
Kelley"This girl I used to live with.She worked at the most prestige hotel in Omaha.When the wrestlers came through,they would stay there.She met Andre,and he had a Giant crush on her.He used to call my place all the time and leave messages. One time he called from France to talk to her and she wasn't home...Phil,(who is from the Chicago area)what did you think of Milwaukee?
Phil:Me?I thought it was a lot cooler than most Chicago shows.Now that it is turn-ing into an interview of Phil,What I don't like is the prehistoric "punk" towns. When I was on tour,we played in Muskegan in a club where GG Alin lived.It was the worst.They had guns and they wanted to kill us because we were SE.This was when I was in Tuckmouth.(not the Ca.Tuckmouth).Any more Q's for me?
Bob:The Todd/Say No More interview.Oh,we do have a song named after him.What a guy.
Todd:Phil,you don't have it.It is only 10 bucks at Earwax.(Jokingly)Earwax?
Bob:Ask us about pornography?
Todd:Milwaukee is the porno capital of the world.It was a Sunday night there and the place was packed and doing business......I had to cut the interview here bec-ause I t went longer than expected.Thanks for SNM for a cool int.write SNM c/o Todd 3604 s.121 st. Omaha Ne.68164. The 7"s available for 3.50ppd to the label.

GOOD & PLENTY PRODUCTIONS

GOOD AND PLENTY PRODUCTIONS
P.O. BOX 339
WINTHROP HARBOR
IL. 60096

This is an old interview that was meant to be in G&P #4,but because of a delay,did not make it.Some of the stuff may be outdated,but I feel Turning - Point is a band that deserves the exposure.If you haven't heard them yet,get out of your shell and tape it from someone.Now on New Age Records,this NJ band is expecting an lp out soon.From what I hear,this could prove to be a great one.Thanks to Ken for taking time to do this through the mail. 1-22-90.I don't remember exactly what all the Q's were,so I'm rewriting them by ear.

JAY-GUITAR 18
KEN-DRUMS 20
SKIP-VOCALS 17
NICK-BASS 16

G&P:What is new with Turning Point?I haven't heard much lately.
Ken:Since the EP we have recorded a song entitled"Insecurity" which will be on the Foundation Records compilation EP.We also just fin-ished recording our Lp on New Age Records due this Spring.We are also planning to tour this Summer.
G&P:Was there any problem with Hi-Impact Records?
Ken:No.New Age really looked good so we got on that label.We were glad to be on Hi-Impact Records.Darren is a nice guy.
G&P:Were there any other offers?
Ken:We have had offers from a couple of different labels.but New Age was the best offer.
G&P:Lyrically,you write a lot about Straight Edge topics.Does the whole band agree on that?
Ken:Yes we do.Skip wrote most of the lyrics,but we all agree on them.Straight Edge is very much a part of our lives.
G&P:Why do you feel that so many people are"falling off the Straight Edge"so to speak.

Ken:I think a lot of bands that get out of SE because they weren't really into it to begin with.It's a trend for them.I know when people get older their ideals change.It doesn't mean as much as it used to.
G&P:Give me the lowdown on some NJ bands.
Ken:AS far as NJ goes,there are a lot of great bands.Vision.Release, American Standard.The main problem here is the club scene.A lot of people work to put on shows,but it doesn't last long,thanks to White-power morons who get places closed.The Anthrax in Ct.rules.We really enjoy D.C.also.
G&P:What is the situation with the EP?I think it is a great record and you did it in a short period of time.What is your opinion.
Ken:The first and second press are sold out.Third pressings are on the way.We are happy with the EP but the recording was a little weak.

There are a lot of thongs that we would like to do different.
G&P:On the EP,the sound sorta resembles Youth Of Today.I actually think it is better.Do you think that future Turning Point releases will stay on that same line.musically and lyrically?
Ken:A lot of people have said the same thing.I think we have gone through a little change since the recording of the 7".I think our new stuff is better lyrically and instrumentally.As far as our own beliefs... They remain the same.Straight Edge is still very much a part of our lives.
G&P:Thanks for the interview.Do you want to wrap it up?
Ken:Thanks to Gabe for this interview.Thanks and hello to Release guys,Edgewise,and Slow Joe.Keep an eye out for the Lp out on New Age Records in early Summer.A tour also this Summer.The 7"is available still on Hi-Impact.Check it out.

VISION

This is definitely an opinion-filled introduction to this interview, but everyone is entitled.If someone was to ask me which lp. was the best of 1989, I would have to say, Vision-In The Blink Of An Eye. You can set the needle on any song and I can guarantee greatness. This interview was going to be in #4 but didn't make it back to me on time.I think the fact that I caught up with Dave at the Anthrax helped speed it along.This was done over the mail with Dave,the singer.Thanks to Dave for sending a perfect promo pack.The result...Read on.   All Vision photos:Ken Salerno

VISION IS:
CHRIS-BASS
MATT-DRUMS
DAVE-VOCALS
PETE-GUITAR

G&P:Give me a little history of the band.
Dave:We have been together since January 2,1988. Matt was the last to join. All of our previous bands didn't do more than put out demo tapes.
G&P:Now that you have the album behind you, are you happy with it?
Dave:We are happy with it, but we feel personally that the musicianship could have been a little better. That's because we know our potential and we know when we made the slightest goof that someone else might not be able to hear.
G&P:On the Undiscovered 7",the song"The Only One"has a little more at the and. Sort of like the Dragnet mosh. Why did you cut it on the lp.?
Dave:The reason for that little Dragnet bit, was because we used to go into another older song called"Steps" (off of the first 7").Now we rarely don't really play that song, so we don't play the Dragnet either.
G&P:How did you hook up with Nemisis Records? What happened with Positive Force?
Dave:We got on Nemisis through Insted.After a short 9 day tour with them, they brought back 50 copies of the Undiscovered ep.to California. Thanx: About the Positive Force deal,they were gonna put us on record, but they stopped all together.
G&P:What is with the lines over the picture on the album cover?
Dave:It was shutter blink. We really rushed the album to come out. We wanted a photo on the cover. We put the lines over it to make it hard to make out.
G&P:From the looks of that picture, I see you have played big shows.What were some good ones Vision has played?
Dave:The biggest show we played was at City Gardens (NJ) with the Ramones. We also opened up a New Year's Eve show for Agnostic Front and 10 other bands.

That was at CBGB'S in New York,the place was packed.That was the one where A.F. did their video. We've also played with bands such as: The Exploited, 24-7 Spies, Verbal Assault, Dag Nasty, SNFU, and more.
G&P:When I hear Vision, I think of a blend of music.Does the band have any Metal influences?
Dave:We all have our Metal & Hardcore influences. We don't just listen to one particular type of music, because there is so much good shit in this world, so many talented musicians. How could we shut them out,or off?
G&P:In Vision, who writes the music and lyrics?
Dave:As far as music goes: Chris, Pete, & Matt come up with ideas, play them out, and Dave puts his ideas in wether he likes it or not. Lyrics are mostly written by Pete & Chris. Matt more or less fits the words with the song. Dave looks over the words,decides what makes sense, changes and rearranges.
G&P:I have to ask, are any of you vegetarians? How about straight edge?
Dave:None of us are vegetarians, although Dave does not eat red meat. Straight Edge? Well, Dave is straight totally. Pete and Chris, once in a blue moon have a drink. Matt does his own thing, nothing serious.
G&P:Do you have any tour plans?
Dave:Good question. Right now we are one for three on tours. That is right. So far two tours fell through for one reason or another. But hopefully someday we will get to play your city.
G&P:How much longer does Vision plan on being around? It seems a lot of bands aren't in it for the long run anymore. They put out a 7",

then maybe an lp.But they give it up.Why?
Dave:I think a lot of bands are formed be peo-ple who are kids, and just want to play for a while. But we are a bit different. Everybody in the band is very much into what we are doing.

cont.next page.

VISION

UNDISCOVERED

VISION AT CBGB'S

VISION

Hell some of us go to school. Now,Chris our bass player is going to be 25 in a month. But who cares. We love what we are doing.
G&P:Any closing comments? Dave:Thanks,Gabe for having the patience to wait for our late response.

Vision has some limited edition purple marble swirl albums.So any of you colectors, get it while you can.
Write:VISION
701 MEADOW RD.
BRIDGEWATER NJ. 08807

RELAPSE

SHOW REVIEWS

KILLING TIME

KILLING TIME

KILLING TIME

KILLING TIME

MAXIMUM PENALTY

Feb. 17 The Anthrax-At All Cost,Maximum Penalty,Killing Time. $8
After being at the Anthrax a few times I had no intention on seeing a cheap show. At All Cost was up first,and they were OK, for starters.Catchy,but that was just an opening band.Maximum Penalty hit it next, and after a new singer and a few new members,they still put a little pep in the crowds step.They did quite a few new tunes so expect something out by MP,but under a new name.Killing Time was up last and it was raining people.Someone even brought in a cushion and dove with it.(What a great idea).They did all the Lp tracks with tremendous crowd participation.This is hardly a band that can be described in a review, you really have to see them yourself.My only regret was bruising my knee the night before.But I did get some killer shots.

April 19 The Exit,Fl.-Sharon Tates Baby, Wrath,and Excel $10
Let me start by saying I missed the first band,sorry.Wrath was up when I get there. Actually these guys are very tight and have a clean sound.The only problem is,that gets old quick.Not so much response from the crowd except when they covered Ace Of Spades by Motorhead.The next band I had waited to see for three years.Excel.They opened with the Sanford and Son theme song on the pa.Then I finally got to see them live.Anyone who has ever heard this LA 4-piece will say these guys are the best band for this type of music.It is hard to describe,but blend Suicidal,and the best blend of time changes from fast to slow you could ever imagine.I have played their tape to all of my friends from all aspects of the scene,girls,SE,punk,and metal and they all agree these guys rock.They did many old favorites as well as the songs off the most recent Lp.The Joke's on You.Plenty of bass action from this band,and that is all I needed to hear.Check 'em out.That's Right.

Feb.9 The Anthrax-Courage,Intensity,Release,and Judge. $8
I was definitely ready for anything this night.After a 21 hour drive to Rhode Island you can imagine the intensity building.We had just got there and Courage had already begun.This band has ex Upfront singer,Roger.They delivered a heavy set that was very tight.I'm looking forward to a future release from them.Release was next,now with a new bass player.They were ok I guess.I'm not a real big fan.The best song was Drug Free Youth.Intensity was next,from Princeton.They were tight,but it wasn't anything I hadn't heard before.For some reason,few people got into them.Judge kicked in last. With an additional guitarist that night, (Ryan Hoffman COS)you better believe it was now twice as heavy.They did all the usual songs,but with slower dance parts.I dove with the camera in my hand and busted it so sorry no outstanding shot.Another dive-fest at the Anthrax.

EXCEL

JUDGE AT THE ANTHRAX

COURAGE AT THE ANTHRAX

COURAGE

March 17 The Rink,In.Gear,Billingsgate,
and Say No More. $5
  This show was interesting to say the least.
Picture a 6 foot stage in the corner of a
roller rink.That's right.Gear was first.If
you are into Dag Nasty type stuff,which I
am,then you should check out this band.They
now have a 7" on Your Future Records and is
worth getting.Billingsgate was next.This is
definitely the band to check out in the 90's.
I can't say enough about this 5 piece from
the Chicago area.They did all the 7" songs
as well as a new one called outlet that will
blow anyone away.Get the 7" from Victory
Records.Say No More was last.This was only
my third time seeing them play and I can
definitely say they are getting much better
with age.They have many new songs which they
did as well as some covers (as usual).Then
all of a sudden these metallers from the
back of the place request a Motley Crue song.
That didn't go over too well with Mike G.who
put out the Say No More 7" so a few words
were exchanged and the next thing you know
I dove on top of the metallers head (and yes
there was music playing).Now they were mad.
One of the guys told me,"If you want to ride
a horse,go back to your reservation".That
was a blatant racist statement.Needless to
say the show was stopped and we went home.
I'd like to say that there were several SE
people from Chicago who did not start any-
thing.Anyway check out SNM on tour soon.
And **never play the rink in Indiana.**

PHIL,AIRBORN AT
THE RINK

Feb.16 The Living Room,R.I.-Courage To Be,
Nasty Savage,and D.R.I. $10
  This is a show like no other.A whole new
concept was brought to my attention that
night.Courage To Be hit it and I see people walking on people.This was great.It did-
not take long before some "wicked" pit
action started.Sick of it all was supposed
to play,but I can truly say that these
guys were an adequate replacement.Nasty
Savage was up next.I had seen them in Milwaukee earlier on the tour,and nothing was
going on during them.Providence was a different story.The metallers there went off
for them.The best part was when the singer
body-slammed someone onto the crowd.D.R.I.
was last.Let me first say that if you have
50 metallers upfront,no bouncers,and a
waist high stage,you can expect air all day.
They played a long set including old and
new ones.For those of you who won't go see
them because they are too metal,I can only
say it is your loss.If you like to dive,
then this is the ultimate band to see.

D.R.I.-THE LIVING ROOM

Feb.10 The Anthrax-Heads Up,The Toasters.
This is not my particular type of show,
but I went anyway.Pack a couple hundred
people from all walks of the scene and un-
ite them in song.Imagine,the funkiest beats
of your life...That is Heads Up.They were
nothing short of one of the best live bands
I'd ever seen.With their ever popular style
of Punk,HC,metal you can be sure there was
plenty of diving in the house.After a long
break,including a nap,the Toasters were up.
There is not much to say about ska-Either
you like it or you don't.They did an extra
long set and there was a lot of mileage on
peoples shoes that night.

GOOD & PLENTY
May '89 FREE Issue #2
Special expanded version

Only The Strong Interview,Lyric Trivia,
Brotherhood Centerfold,Concert and
Record Reviews, and much more

  Since so many people were asking
about the past issues,and I no longer
have any to distribute,I decided to put
this piece in.It is a collage of photos
from the first 3 issues.In order for #5
to be out at this time,I had to scrap
my plan to reprint 1-3.

KEVIN SECONDS-THE EARLY YEARS

GOOD & PLENTY ZINE
GABE RODRIGUEZ
2116 SALEM BLVD.
ZION IL. 60099

JUDGE IN CA.'90

GOOD & PLENTY

$1.75 THE Zine No.6

QUICKSAND INTEGRITY SACRED REICH CHAIN GANG

As the musical landscape of hardcore continued to evolve and transform, so did the zines that covered the music. Issue 6 reflects this shifting territory.

    Quicksand had just formed in 1990, a few months before their *Good and Plenty* interview. Members had played in acclaimed hardcore bands (Gorilla Biscuits, Youth of Today, Bold, Beyond, and Burn)—all groups who appeared on the pages of *G&P.* Rodriguez notes, "On June 22, 1990, I had the privilege [of] doing a real interview with a band that had evolved from the ashes of many bands. They asked me kindly not to dwell on those bands, and I did. But you can be sure there [were] lots of other things on their minds, and this is the result."

    Quicksand is a post-hardcore band. The label "post-hardcore" itself denotes the sound coming after hardcore. What's the logical progression for something that already went as fast and hard as it could go? A hardcore zine like *G&P* naturally evolved to cover experiments and new musical endeavors. Rodriguez observed, "From what I heard tonight, it isn't a basic hardcore sound." And Tom Capone, guitarist for Quicksand, bluntly agrees: "We are not a hardcore band." Rodriguez continues to press, adding, "I was looking around at the crowd while you were playing and there were a lot of people who weren't into it. Do you think you are taking a risk by playing this type of music...?"

    Even a scene that positioned itself as being open-minded could struggle to accept change. Frequent *G&P* collaborator Kim Nolan (herself the editor of Chicago's *Bark & Grass* fanzine) contributed a letter in issue 6 that explicitly addressed sexism and gender relations within the scene. "Women are gradually getting a foot in the door, so to speak, but the greatest threat to us is not men, but actually, other women," she wrote, before presenting a plea against monolithic thinking.

    And so—in response to Rodriguez's earlier straightforward question about how audiences were responding to their sound—Sergio Vega, Quicksand's bassist, replied, "We are doing what our hearts feel now."

Issue 6
Winter 1990-1991
56 pages
7.5 × 10.6 inches
2,500 copies
$1.75

Opposite: Cover for *Good and Plenty,* issue 6, 1990-1991.

Fans could have a hard time accepting that musicians and bands could change and evolve, that they might be changing as well. In the *G&P* interview, Quicksand's singer Walter Schreifels was frank about the band's direction: "We are not trying to trick people into thinking we are hardcore mosh stuff."

It's astonishing to see how labels, which can help categorize and describe, were being used to limit and circumscribe. As Vega points out, "Once alternative music becomes a set pattern that everyone follows, then it is no longer alternative. No one is taking risks."

Rodriguez, Nolan, and Quicksand all felt the pressure of being limited by labels. Maybe that was the discovery: reaching for one's own goals could be more satisfying than fulfilling the expectations of others; rigidity invites stasis. So to continue to thrive, there needs to be movement, experimentation, and full-throated engagement with modern ideas.

"I did fulfill the promise of getting [metal] bands in this issue," Rodriguez stated. At least there was that. —C.S/K.S.

Good And Plenty Back Issues

#1-Sudden Stop,Word Search, show reviews. $.25

#2-Only The Strong,show reviews, Brotherhood centerfold,lyric trivia. $.25

#3-Gorilla Biscuits,Brotherhood, Insted,Bold,Judge,show reviews, lyric trivia. $.75

#4-Refuse,Even Score,Upfront, Inner Strength,7 Seconds,show reviews,tons of photos.$1.25

#5-Carry Nation,Say No More, Vision,Billingsgate,Turning Point, 19 page photos section.$1.25

Anyone who would like to dis- tribute G&P zines,please get in touch with me.I need all the help I can get.As an incentive,I will give a Youth Of Today Break Down The Walls lp on Wishing Well re- cords (blue vinyl) to the person who distributes the most zines. The winner will be announced after the zine is sold out.

GOOD & PLENTY ZINE
GABE RODRIGUEZ
2116 SALEM BLVD.
ZION IL. 60099

Good And Plenty #6 Winter 1990-1991

Thank you for buying this zine that was put together from all other G&P zines.I hope you understand that I had to raise the price $.50,or else I would have lost too much money.I feel that even this price is reasonable.I also gave all the photo credits that I could directly on the photos.Here is the offi- cial thanks list.These people I'd like to say thanks to...Jobs Printing,Tom Turner,Nathan (Chump),Chad A.,Good and Plenty (the band),Tim Brick,Greg Brown, Phil (Poison Free),Billingsgate,Say No More,everyone at Club Blitz,Tony B., Sacred Reich,Quicksand,Integrity,the Milwaukee scene,Kerry,Jill,the Unicorn, 911,Masada,Lori Hiple,Jules Ann,Zeds, American Outfitters,Pat Costello,Tony Peelman,Mario,everyone from North Tono- wanda NY who bought a zine,Audrey,Justin, Alejandrina,Kim Nolan,John Hughes,Molly, Megan Luther,Ms. Luther,John Handwerk, and anyone I forgot.I would especially like to thank the person who did most of the work on this zine Matt Garcia.

Cover photo:Billingsgate
p.John Handwerk
Back cover:Inside Out
bottom:Gorilla Biscuits
p.Dave Sine

It was not my intent for this zine to coincide with the war in the Per- sian Gulf.It really makes this whole thing seem trivial.But I wasn't the one who declared war on Iraq.I would be a fool not to voice my opinion,so here goes...No matter how you slice, dice,or try to justify war,it just is not right.These wars are actually supposed to happen.But it does not mean that I have to support it. Be- sides all of that,soon there will be a war to end all wars,and I do hope that I come out on the right side. That pretty much sums that up.

As far as this zine goes,it is a combined effort of Matt Garcia and me. All things expressed by the bands are not necess- arily the opinions of ours.It was the intent to show the reader how the bands really are.Keep that in mind before you make any quick assumptions or whatever.I did manage to fulfill the promise of getting metal bands in this issue.(depending on your inter- pretation of metal)I even almost got DRI in here.But no such luck.

In past issues I have addressed how I have been ripped off in mail order. This will be no exception.Here is a list of people who combined have scammed over $200 from me.Ryan Huffman(Chain Of Strength),Jon White(Open Your Eyes Zine), Tim Owen(Action Packed/Jade Tree Records), Matt Dunmyre(Divide and Conquer Zine),and as of Jan 22,Jordan Cooper(Revelation Rec.) Please refrain from fattening these people's wallets.

Also,you will not see any reviews on my part due to my inability to criticize any sincere effort by a person.I had lots of ads,but they slowly got old as the days went by and I was waiting for my arm to heal.

Over the 2 year span of this zine,there have been numerous people that have helped in the most ways possible.Here I would like to give recognition to all that have done their part either physically.or emotionally or in some cases both...John Handwerk

These people are the Bread and Butter behind what you are about to read.

If anyone has any comments about the opinions expressed in this zine,feel free to write.Or if you just want to say hello. Enjoy.

Jen Kulawas
Greg Brown
Tim Brick
Tony Brummell
Alejandrina Reyes
Say No More
Billingsgate
Kim Nolan
Ms.Luther
Megan Luther
Matt Garcia

PLAYLIST...

After almost 2 years of zineage,and the oncoming of cheesewhiz,it is no surprise that the playlist has been through a makeover.Notice,even top 40 has made it's way in.Check it out.

MATT	GABE
Only The Strong comp.	Deee-Light
Shove Bang Mecca	Julie Cruise
Julie Cruise	Celtic Frost
Megadeth	Misfits
Slayer	Samhain
Insight	Integrity
Integrity	Belinda Carlisle
Outface	7 Seconds
Iron Maiden	Reason To Believe
7 Seconds	Sacred Reich
Shelter	No Mercy
Quicksand	Suicidal
Tad	Excel
Soul Side	Billingsgate
Social Distortion	Wilson Phillips

Lately,there have been many charges of sexism in the straight edge scene. These claims are not unfounded,as our scene is still largely run by males, with females playing a small but vocal role.Women are gradually getting a foot in the door so to speak,but the great- est threat to us is not men,but actua- lly,other women.

Have you ever been to a show and wit- nessed a squealing group of girls who are pointing out guys to each other? These girls will go to a show to find a new boyfriend and/or hit on the band members.Most of these females don't know anything about the bands they have come to see,much less care.Some of them have no clue as to what hardcore is all about.They come to the shows to be so- cial and fashionable.These women are the biggest threat to our struggle for equality because they are complacent and unquestioning.Their sexist (yes,- sexist)behavior disqualifies every inch of ground we have fought hard to gain.

Not all women are like this,of course. There are so many women out there who really care about what this thing called hardcore really means.These wo- men are the ones who care and are try- ing to contribute and accomplish things.

Please do not lump all women you see at a show in one single group.We are as diff- erent as black and white.

A friend once told me that women are just as sexist as men.I hadn't really thought about it.I was still trying to change my- self inside,and wasn't too concerned with what I was presenting myself as to the out- side world.In a way,my friend was right. Yes,the men hold the cards in this thing, but most of them are now more than willing to support the women coming in,or that al- ready were.Nobody wants to be labeled a sexist.Today,that is almost as bad as being called a racist.I,like other women, have unconsciously taken this to my advantage, and realize now that I have said and done some pretty sexist things.I am not for sup- eriority,I am not about men bashing,I do believe in equality.It is time for women to rethink their ideas and hear that they are really saying to each other.Are you really striving for equality, or are you becoming what you are fighting against?

Kim Nolan

On the night of June 22,1990,I had the privilege in doing a real interview with a band that had evolved from the ashes of many bands. They asked me kindly not to dwell on those bands,and I did.But you can be sure that there was a lot of other things on their minds,and this is the result.Who knows how long this will last,but Quicksand is definitely in my opinion a giant step away from the rest of the pack.Here is what they had to say only a few months after being together and ½ way through the tour...

Sergio-bass
Charlie-guitar
Tom-guitar
Alan-drums

G&P:How long has this band been a steady line-up?
Walter:We have Charlie for the tour for the effect of two guitars. The four of us have been together since April.
G&P:Do you think this is a good time to tour knowing that few people know Quicksand?
Walter:I think it is the best time.We have to learn how to do it,getting comfortable on stage and rockin' out.Like you said,noone has heard us.I think it is better to play and then put the record out.
Sergio:It is definitely good experience for me to play in front of people who have no concept of who we are.
Walter:We don't have the ease of people knowing our stuff.We get into it regardless of how much people are into us.Whether they get into it by rockin' out or just applauding or whatever.We have to put more into it than a band that is established.
G&P:From what I heard tonight,it isn't a basic hardcore sound.
Tom:We are not a hardcore band.
G&P:I was looking around at the crowd while you were playing and there were a lot of people who weren't into it.Do you think you are taking a risk by playing this type of music as opposed to the norm?
Walter:The bands that are playing now (Bad Religion,All)are like 9 years old.A lot of bands that were together when I first started playing about 3-4 years ago have all broken up.There has to be something more to drive them.We have all played in hardcore bands.We did that for a long time.
Sergio:Basically we are doing what our hearts feel now.
G&P:Do you like playing this more?
Walter:No,it is just that this is the time that we're at.We have played millions of shows,with the same songs,same styles.We go to the shows even when we aren't playing. We are going to play what we are into...now.It is not like..."Oh,that was then".We are just trying to start something fresh.People who want to see us will see us.We are

not trying to trick people into thinking we are hardcore mosh stuff.It does have power that people into hardcore can relate with.
G&P:Can you give me a little insight on your lyrics?
Walter:We are still trying to develop lyric-wise.A lot of it is just things that I think and am concerned about.
Sergio:We don't really know...Once alternative music becomes a set pattern that everyone follows,then it is no longer alternative.Noone is taking risks.
Tom:The lyrics are mostly personal.We don't know what our goals are.
Sergio:We do have individual goals,but we haven't been together long enough to get them to develop.
G&P:Since you are on tour with Shelter I have to ask your views on the whole Krishna movement.
Walter:It is not something that I want to become involved with.They do have some points that I can relate with.
Sergio:We are not supporting Krishna consiousness (by playing with Shelter),we are just good friends.We are doing our own thing.It just so happens that we hooked up with them.
Walter:They have been very helpful.We have had lots of troubles and they have been supportive.But,as a movement or a philosophy,it is not something that we focus on in any way.
G&P:All of you are from New York except for Charlie,right?
Charlie:I play in a band from Cleveland called Outface.They wanted to have the effect of two guitars on tour.On the record,Tom and Walter play guitar.
G&P:There are a lot of negative things going around about New York.Is it like it is dead.
Walter:There is definitely stuff going on,but it is not as commercial.
Alan:It seems that it comes and goes in waves.
Walter:The new scene is not something that we mix in with.And it is not because..."Oh they suck".That is not it.It is just not our thing.
G&P:I don't want this interview to result in someone becoming dork of the month.
Walter:Obviously you know a little about it.That is what is going on.You can't say it is dead.It is not something we are a part of.People outside of New York may think it is dead because they don't hear about it in a big way like some of the bands before.
G&P:On the flyer tonight,it said,"Former members of so and so".Wouldn't you think that people would get the impression that you are a straight edge band?
Alan:I don't think we have much control over that right now.That is up to the promoters who book us however they feel.I think we have to establish ourselves and get the record out and it will change.

Tom:The more we play shows,the more people will see.We are not a straight edge band.
Walter:I don't people to think that is what they are going to get because that is like a violation and false advertising.
Sergio:We are all individuals and accept each others lifestyles.We work together as friends.
Charlie:All played tonight.The flyer said ex Black Flag and Descendents.For someone who hasn't heard All,they are in for a surprise.Is is all up to the promoter.We do have to attract people to the show though so we can go on and play.
Walter:To be honest,we specifically said lets avoid that.But in a lot of cases we cannot.I know a case in Europe where Fugazi went and everywhere they played they were promoted as "Ian of Minor Threat".That is the way they were promoted.You are forced into that position.I am sure after the record comes out we can stand on our own identity.Although it is nice to have people who are into the stuff we've done in the past.It has a lot of the same spirit.
G&P:Would you like to say anything about the record?
Sergio:We hope you enjoy it.
Walter:It is going to be very available.It is also on CD and cassette single.I think it is a great record.Even for the people who are expecting the mosh thing.I really can't see how they would be disappointed.It has a lot of power to it.You can get power musically in a lot of different ways.It is not the same type of thing that we have been doing.I am not sure what you can interpret from the live set?
G&P:It is heavy and slower.Actually,I like the slower crunchy stuff.
Tom:We are trying to reach a broader audience.
G&P:I heard the Moondog tape and I came here expecting that type of thing.I would say that I like this just as well.
Walter:I am into the whole hardcore thing and have been for many years.If you keep doing the same thing in everything not just music,it becomes stale.What is the point of going through the ritual of going to a show and moshing to the music when you've done it a thousand times.It becomes a ritual.
Sergio:It becomes mindless.Saying "ritual" gives it too much meaning.
G&P:You have been in other bands,past and present.Is this band going to interfere with any of those?
Walter:I really don't think so at all...We do have lots of plans.When you talk about the focus of the band,we do have a lot of goals.A lot of bands wait to do things.
We want to be aggressive.
G&P:Do you plan on staying on Revelation Records?
Walter:We are looking for the best label we can get.
Tom:Revelation is basically a demo label,to attract labels that produce bands.
Walter:At this point,nobody wants us on their label.I think that Revelation is putting out a lot

p.Justin Subn.Zine

p.Justin Subn.Zine

Chicago...July '90

---

of neat new stuff,that isn't typical to what they've done in the past.They've sold a lot of records to the same people.I think a lot of the new stuff will hopefully get across to different people who would not have ordinaral appreciate the past releases.
Sergio:Revelation wanted us,and I'm very thankful that they've given us a lot of support.If we grow to something bigger,that's nice,but if we stay on Rev. that is fine too.It is not a stepping stone at all.It is where we are now.
Walter:Our van broke down (while on tour).2 seconds later we got on the phone and wired us $2000 to get it fixed.They are awesome.If we can stick with them,it's great.If we can do better,and Jordan is totally supportive of that too,that's cool.
Alan:There are good and bad things about getting on a larger label.There's positive things about it,and it has its drawbacks.You have to weigh them out.
Walter:I'm not holding my breath for anything.I just consider ourselves lucky that Jordan did the record.
G&P:Anything that you would like to add as we call it a rap?
Walter:Just that I want people to pick up the Ep. I'm not gonna brace people and say "Wait til you hear this guys,I hope you can handle it." It is not like that.
Sergio:Listen to it with an open mind.
Tom:It is definitely a step up to what Revelation has put out in the past.
Walter:(Jokingly)Since Tom's work on the Bold EP.
Tom:Revelation is broadening it's sound.Since the Slipknot record.It is pretty different.
G&P:I haven't heard it yet,but a lot of people say that it is not the best.
Walter:I think that they don't like it because it isn't what they expected.I listen to it.From my perspective,I don't think that it is my favorite record in the world,but it is definitelt one of mine.A lot of it has to do with the people of New York.The whole network of people aren't doing that kind of stuff anymore.It's just not the thing to do.
Sergio:It is a natural progression.It is not about saying that this isn't worth playing anymore.We are just evolving and we hope people are open to it.
Walter:I appreciate all the stuff that I listened to 4 years ago,but I also find a lot of new stuff that I like.I think that people who were into the Revelation stuff can hopefully get into this.
G&P:What was Moondog?You did get one song on a that NY compilation.
Walter:That band came and died.That song is called expression.The compilation is called."Look at the Children Now."It has a lot of the stuff from the ABC No RIO scene.Those hardcore bands that are coming out of New York now,they are really grass roots.
Alan:It seems like it is back to the underground.
Walter:The bands won't sell their stuff to stores and stuff like that.Really idealistic people.If you get that compilation,it is a good document of what is happening.
Sergio:It is sort of hard to get access to what is going on on that level.
G&P:What sorta stuff are your lyrics based on these days?
Walter:For me,it is just when I hear something or someone will point something out to me.I do not see myself writing a free South Africa song.One of our songs has political applications is called Clean Slate.It is politically inspired,But not very literal......(End of the tape)

Quicksand-The Anthrax p.Tim Brick

"... They made me stand on a chair, put blankets across my arms, and tied me to a cross with ropes. When they took away the chair, I was hanging by my arms."

Through The Weeds Part 1

I'm in eighth grade and thinking about what classes I will take in high school. Following the daily routine of walking to school through the weeds everyday in the bitter cold of a Midwest winter.Jim has got some home grown that he says will kill. Why not?We have a little time to spare before first period.All we had was an Old Style can that was in the bushes and it was all that we needed.Don't ask who was the one who thought of using an beer can as a bowl,but whoever it was must have really wanted it badly.I was hesitant to be first because I wanted to see how it was done.No one knew it was my first time.They fired it up.Steve was first.He gags as if he was swallowing fire.I'm next.Ok,here goes.Just inhale and hold it in,but I couldn't because my lungs were on fire.One more time.This time I had done it.It wasn't long before we were late for school,so we walked to school...or should I say we floated.Finally I got a chance to sit down and feel the warmth of a math class.Paranoid as I could ever be,it was my turn to talk to the school councelor.I did it.It was easy.The day went on and it was business as usual.

Next day.Should I go for it again?Why not?I got away with it the first time.This time we had more time...and more pot!So obviously we got more wasted.Don't even remember how cold it was outside,but it sure got warm inside.The heat triggered my high as soon as we walked in the school.I remembered that I ate Cheerios that morning. Not smart!Made it through first period with no problems.Went to Science lab and they were disecting a chicken that day.You can imagine the smell.It wasn't long before the cereal wanted to be back in the bowl that it came from.I couldn't stop it.Everyone was staring at it.There I was with puke that was still in the shape of O's all over me.I ran out to the bathroom and hid for about an hour.Cleaning myself off as best I could.

That is all that it took for me to decide that pot wasn't for me. I guess the only reason I tried it the first time was because everyone else was.The second time was because I got away with it the first time.Now it is five years later and I had only had the urge to try it one more time and I thank my friend Matt for not giving me any.It may not have been a conscious thought on his part,but he didn't. My body has a way of telling me what I can and cannot do.And I think that more people should listen to their bodies when they speak.I do not know too many people who can say that they never threw up while high or drunk.So what is the problem?

Into LaLa Land Part 2

How many of you can remember the first tape you ever bought? For me,it was back in 1982,and that was Business as Usual,by Men at Work.For the next two years,I was satisfied with radio music and all my brother's albums,like Rush,Foghat,Boston,REO Speedwagon,and Journey.It wasn't until Halloween of 1984 that I first got a metal album,Stay Hungry,by Twisted Sister.That winter I gave my brother Tom $10 to get me Powerslave,by Iron Maiden.That became the biggest turning point in my life...

(part 2 cont.)That started a spur of record buying that to this day,I still very much adhere to.I always said to myself,"All I need now is this album and I will be satisfied."You know what,I was never satisfied.Records were not enough.Posters,buttons,magazines,hats,I had it all.But I had never seen Iron Maiden live.Meanwhile,my brother Tom was getting into the much harder stuff like Slayer,Venom,and Exodus.Not me,that crap was evil.

My family moves to Zion right before I was to start high school,and that was not the easiest adjustment for me.I kept to myself,passing the time by drawing on my folder in classes,not talking to anyone.One of my brothers friend wrote Venom on my folder and that is how I met my friend Matt Garcia who is now the biggest contributer to this zine.He came up to me in Social Studies class and asked if I drew the Venom piece.He was wearing an Iron Maiden Purgatory shirt,and that was all it took for me.To this day,he is the only one from High School or before that I still know.Meanwhile,my father who thought that my music was very wrong and evil for me,took all of my Maiden stuff,about $500 worth and threw it all away.That was a big blow to me.So, what next.You guessed it-now comes thrash.I started borrowing Tom's tapes,and Matt had several gems of his own such as Celtic Frost,Possessed,Megadeth,and Metallica.Being the Freshmen that I was,I ate all that stuff up and more.But it wasn't a while later that I got into hardcore.Matt always tried to get me to like weird stuff like Septic Death,the DK's,and Minor Threat.But it wasn't until he gave me D.R.I.Suicidal,and the clincher...The Misfits.

The next few years,after I got my driver's license,I find myself taking my dad's car 50 miles to record stores all over the place.Going to every show that I could get to.My first show was Ozzie and Metallica.I spent many a day with whiplash after shows,(you metallers know what I mean).

It wasn't until the summer of '88 that I saw my first real hardcore show.M.D.C in Milwaukee.I was friends with Mike Good then,and another guy named Mike B.I was pushed in the pit at the show,and I came out with a bloody lip.That must have been my body telling me again what was good for me,but like a fool,I didn't listen.

After numerous trips to the record stores,I finally picked up the one album that made a difference in my lifestyle.New York City Hardcore...The Way It Is.From that,I ordered all those Rev. singles,blowing check after check on mailorder.Mike and me decide to pass the time by with a little zine.And after a few issues,I find myself interviewing all the bands that got me into straight edge in the first place.The Chicago straight edge scene was going strong and a few more zines passed by and I was on top of the world.I was so caught up in everything,that I graduated from high shool and I realised that I didn't really know anyone of my classmates.All of a sudden,the scene flopped like a pancake and shows were really scarce. I ended up tweedling my thumbs because there was nothing ever to do.Depression set in very quick and it didn't take long before I realized that I had dug my own grave.Luckily,I wasn't covered fully with dirt and that, was when I had to make a change.

The whole point of this life story is to point out something that bothers me very much these days.Back in eighth grade when I decided not to ever do pot again,I engulfed myself in music and everything accompanied with it.I find myself with a fractured wrist from what I now see as the stupidest thing I ever did in my life...stagediving.I am 19 years old and have to come up with $2,000 to cover my doctor bills. I was living in a world where all that mattered was shows and that is not how it is.I can truly say now I know what 7 Seconds meant by "Farewell to Seven Years."I feel that is why I am making this the final issue of the zine so I can start a new chapter in my life.I don't regret my days that I spent at shows and all,but I only wish I could have had the brains to know how to separate reality from fantasy.Thanks.Matt for all the memories.

I am a slave to nothing...Not even music.

Integrity

I may get a lot of slack for doing this interview on account of the band and their views,but let me get this out up front.I do not agree in any way to most of these guys ideas,but I do however like their music.Before you call me a hypocrite,think about all the bands that you listen to and tell me that you agree with everything they say.Now,you may not agree with Integrity,but you can be sure that I got every word from their mouth.It is true that there are many rumours abourt them,but this interview will lay it on the line.The interview was done after their show in Milwaukee on Nov.4 1990. Integrity is:
Aaron-Guitar
Len-Bass
Dwid-Vocals
Bill-Guitar
Chubby Fresh-Drums

G&P:How long has this line-up been together? Chub:A month ago we added our second guitarist. G&P:What happened to the long-haired guy? Dwid:He is in a band called Outface on Crisis Rec. G&P:I saw you throwing out a lot of skate stickers. What's with the whole skate trip? Dwid:We are sponsored by Vans,NHS,Jimmy Z,Zorlac, Santa Cruz,and Thrasher skate boards. G&P:How did that COME ABOUT? Dwid:We all skate,except Bill and he is gonna skate. We are not good,but it's just fun.Getting free stuff is also very cool. Len:We just sent out letters to the skateboard companies. Dwid:We are also on the new Skate Rock Compilation. G&P:The new record is supposed to be on Progression Records,and then I hear it may not.Tell me about that. Dwid:We don't know. Chub:When it does come out,it will be a 12" most likely record in February or March. Dwid:Brian is just kinda lazy about it...He never calls us so we don't know if we are on his label or not.

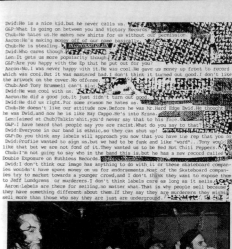

Dwid:He is a nice kid,but he never calls us. G&P:What is going on between you and Victory Records? Chub:He hates us.He makes new shirts for us without our permission. Aaron:He's making money off of our name basically. Chub:He is stealing. Dwid:Who cares though. Len:It gets us more popularity though. G&P:Are you happy with the Ep that he put out for you? Aaron:No,I was never happy with it.He was cool.He gave us money up front to record which was cool.But it was mastered bad.I don't think it turned out good.I don't like the artwork on the cover.No offense. Chub:And Tony Brummell can't sing. Dwid:He was cool with us. Aaron:He did a good job,it just didn't turn out good. Dwid:He did us right.For some reason he hates us. G&P:We doesn't like our attitude now.Before he was my Mr.Hard Edge Dwid.He thought he was Dwid,and now he is like Ray Cappo.He's into Krsna. Len:(aimed at Chub)Talkin'shit,you'd never say that to his face. G&P:I have heard that people say you are racist.What do you say to that? Dwid:Everyone in our band is ethnic,so they can shut up! G&P:Do you think any labels will approach you now that you have the rep that you do? Dwid:Profile wanted to sign us,but we had to be funk and like "word"...Tony would like that but we are not fond of it.They wanted us to be Red Hot Chili Peppers. Chub:I'm not going to say who in the band this is,but he has a new record called Double Exposure on Ruthless Records. Dwid:I don't think our image has anything to do with it or these skateboard companies wouldn't have spent money on us for endorsements.Most of the Skateboard companies try to market towards a younger crowd,and I don't think they want to expose them to Jeff Lundgrens or murderers.I don't think labels care as long as it sells. Aaron:Labels are there for selling,no matter what.That is why people sell because they have something different about them.If they say they are murderers they might sell more than those who say they are just are underground.

Club Blitz 6/16 90 p:John Handwerk

Milwaukee 11/4/90 p.Matt G.

Club Blitz p.John Handwerk

HARDCORE

Dwid:I have a label and I am putting out Confront because I've liked them since I was fifteen years old.I'm also putting out this band Committed and they are total skaters and shit.But I don't want to make money,I don't care about money.
G&P:So how much did you make tonight?
Dwid:Nothin',like 20 bucks or something.
Chub:30 bucks.We were promised gas money,but now the kid says we get paid after the sound guy.There was no sound system there what so ever.
Dwid:Yeah,he made more than us,and he sucked.I could have done a better job.
Chub:The sound guy wasn't even there so some kid worked it.He got 75 bucks.We only got 30 and it cost us more than that to drive up here.
G&P:There is a big change lyrically from the Ep and the cassette single.What is the meaning behind the song Darkness?
Dwid:What it is,is that I can't keep on one subject for too long.It is about a lot of things. A while back,me and a friend got our asses beat because we were white kids.It had something to do with that and with him being messed in the head.It has to do with life,racism,it's about a lot of stuff.Most of my songs,you can't find something set about it.Maybe Live It Down and Dead Wrong you can.Other than that it kind of floats around.It is overall pretty much a view of shit I hate.It is everything that I thought at the moment.
G&P:What are your views on the Hare Krsna movement?It is getting to be a lot bigger than people expected.
Chub:It is just whatever Ray Cappo does.When Youth of Today first came out,they were vegetarians.Now Ray is a Krsna,and a lot of kids wear Krsna beads around their necks,and they are Krsna's and all of this is good.
Len:Mindless followers.
Chub:I think it is good that the kids got influenced because Youth Of Today had a good name.I know that the Krsna's approached Ray and they helped him "see the light",so to say.They had a lot to do with him being a Krsna.They did it on a marketing basis,not for curing or religious reasons.They just wanted him as a figurehead to sell stuff.

(cont.)They have got a kickass van,and all the shit.They ride in luxury,that's materialism. This is non-materialism,this shit-ass van that breaks down all the time.We get no money.They always get their guarantees and all the shit. It's hypocracy.It's good that they are vegetarians,but it's hypocracy.If you question the song In Contrast Of Sin,where we say "The Age Of Kali",which is the age of quarrel,hypocracy, that is exactly what they are.They are all lying sacks of shit,that is what I think.Ray Cappo is a nice kid,but he got used by those people.
G&P:Someone told me that people who have long hair have no place in straight edge. What do you say to that?
Aaron:That is funny.What a nerd.
Len:You should do what you want wether you are straight edge or not.
Chub:I think long hair is excellent.I want my hair to be like the singer of Skid Row.
Dwid:Just because we have long hair doesn't mean that we are gonna sell crack or do anything or do drugs.I don't wear Champions,but I am straight edge.
Len:Personally,I'd have long hair,but it would be an afro if I did.
G&P:Have any of you had any bad experiences with mail-order?
Chub:I do get a little bit of money for integrity shirts,so anyone who sent money, I'll send your shirts as soon as they come in.I swear to God you'll get your stuff.
Dwid:With the Blood Books,we try to do it through the label.Victory Records does the first one.Progression does the second one.I don't want the responsibility of having it delayed,because the labels are always slow.W try not to screw people over.
Aaron:It sucks!
Dwid:Violent as always.Confront are back.Everything is the same except Erba's on top now.Erba is the king in Cleveland now.He used to be the prince,but now he is the king.He was a straight Edge kid with long hair.He had long-ass hair,bells,blue x's, a Project X shirt and bi-focials.
G&P:I have heard strange things about you from reliable people.One guy said that someone from Integrity threatened his Mother on the phone.
Chub:First of all,I didn't threaten his mom.He wrote a letter to Frank who plays guitar in Confront,and he said he loathes us,we're the worst band ever and this and that.So I called him up and...
Dwid:You are a geek.
Chub:I don't like his Mom if that helps any.If I did say something to his mother I'm sorry.

Dwid:Who cares is he loathes us.Everyone does but they still come to our shows.
G&P:When I was on the East coast,I heard a lot of rumors about Integrity.One was that Dwid wanted to fight someone who said that he couldn't sing.
Dwid:I can't sing...I scream.Yeah!Raid are mean to me,and I'm not fond of them.I like Sean.I just think some of their stuff is like dreaming...I don't think it is going to happen like that.But,people living on that kind of diet is great.
Aaron:That is cool,but if you want to eat a juicy hamburger with mayo,that's ok
Bill:They shouldn't try and force it on anyone.
Dwid:I know you guys are Jewish and you understand what the Holocaust means...Hell, that is what they are going through.
Chub:Vegetarianism is cool,but as long as I don't kill the animal I will throw it on a piece of bread and eat it.
Bill:All that stuff is cool.You can believe whatever you want to believe in,but don't push it on me.If you do then you're messin'with me and that's not cool.
G&P:I have read a lot of interviews with you guys,and this seems to be a different Integrity that I know.
Aaron:Dwid calmed down.
Dwid:It is all a front dude.Some people just make them up.
G&P:What do you think will cause the fall of Straight Edge?
Chub:I think it has died.
Hardcore is dying.
Dwid:You know why it is dying.Because you think you're a rockstar.We're not a rock band,we're punk!
Aaron:I think it is dying because a lot of people gave their allegiance to it like that,and it didn't mean anything to them.
G&P:What is the song March of the Damned about?
Dwid:It is about people living in a set way of life.
G&P:Do you regret any of your lyrics?
Dwid:NO!

ONE LIFE DRUG FREE

G&P:So when you talk about fighting being a sport,you mean it?
Dwid:Yeah,it is fun.The last fight I was in I got my head bashed in.It comes with the territory.I just got cocky and I almost died!
G&P:Don't you think there is something wrong there?
Dwid:No.
G&P:Do you go picking fights?
Dwid:Most of the time I don't.Last fight I was in was a couple of weeks ago.We played with this metal band and there were these Nazis and they don't like them. (the band)So I took offense to it and because they are my friends,and I'll beat anyone's ass if they mess with my friends.I understand that by writing the songs, that I do people want to challenge me.But it is not like a Tyson thing.
G&P:I don't agree with any of that.
Dwid:That's cool.I don't want you conform to be like me.
G&P:Would you fight girls if they picked on you?
Dwid:We fought girls,yeah. We played in Philadelphia and there were these girls that were as big as They were bigger than us and they kicked our van.They were huge and we were like "Come on!" I was scared for my life,I beat the shit out of them.
G&P:Any last comments?
Chub:Thanks to Cloonfor helping us out with the show.Hello and thanks to Kim for not coming up this weekend.
Dwid:I want to thank my dietition and I'm glad I'm back.That's all!

A CHAIN IS ONLY AS STRONG AS ITS WEAKEST LINK

Club Blitz 6/16/90 p.John Handwerk

Milwaukee 11/4/90 p.Matt G.

Total Shrine...
Shove Bang Mecca...
Burn Baby Burn...

maher-bass
zends-guitars
Brent Spain-drums / Vocals

The following pages are a comp.
of photos accumulated over the past
several months. I have about 5 times
the amount of these at my home, so
anyone needing any, just ask. Also,
to explain the literature on rape...
I was recently on a delivery at my
work and stopped at a place that
handled problems related to rape and
abuse. I thought these were very infor-
mative, so I used them. They are in no
way intended to be pointed at any of
the bands. Please read.

Ice-T p.Cam

Dirty Rotten Imbeciles

Recognize and share your feelings

All men and women experience a wide range of feelings—pride and compassion, sensitivity and competitiveness, fear and acceptance, vulnerability and hate, just to name a few. These emotions are natural reactions to events in our lives. However, we have learned to divide feelings into those slow and feminine, with very little overlap. The range of feelings acceptable to men is very narrow. We are told that men are only to be aggressive and strong, logical and unemotional. In fact, we are also at times confused, nurturing, sensitive, and sad. Our adherence to traditional gender roles distorts our sense of ourselves and prevents us from seeing others as they really are. Because we have learned that our own reactions are unacceptable, we deny having them. We project them onto women—and onto other men—to hold ourselves up at their expense. We avoid making emotional contact with men and depend entirely on women for our emotional connections. Our discomfort with our own feelings makes it harder for us to be ourselves with others, and our intolerance makes it harder for others to feel comfortable with us. On the other hand, exploring how we feel helps us decide whether we are comfortable with our own behavior and with the behavior of others. Letting others know how we feel helps us understand and sort out conflicts when they do wear, instead of running from conflict and pretending that everything is fine. If we are willing to risk changing the ways we relate to men and women, we can begin to develop trust in our ability to relate to people as people. As we learn to be aware of our feelings and to express them honestly, we develop more confidence in ourselves and find it easier to form and maintain deeper, more rewarding relationships.

Encourage women's efforts to empower themselves

Men who have never experienced what it is like to be singled out as the victim of a crime based on their gender often have difficulty understanding women's fear, and they may discount it as paranoia or man-hating. Supporting Chimera and other self-defense training for the women in your life—relatives, classmates, friends, and mates—is not promoting division between the sexes, but rather a more powerful, intimate relationship based on equality and mutual respect.

Gorilla Biscuits p.Dave Sine

Confront woman-hating attitudes in ourselves and others

Misogyny is the often disguised yet widespread fear or hatred of women, including the attribution in ourselves which are traditionally labelled feminine. Think of the power we give to the accusation "sissy" or "fag" when our fear of not fitting in drives us to act out the most extreme macho behaviors, including rape. We all have the potential to listen, accept, and nurture. Realize that developing emotional strengths and skills is something all men need to do.

p.Gabe R.

PRETENSE: THAT SUBMISSION IS CONSENT
RAPE AND SEXUAL ASSAULT
EMOTIONAL WITHDRAWAL
THREATS AND VIOLENCE
PORNOGRAPHY

RAPE SPECTRUM

SEXIST JOKES
RAPE FANTASIES
SEXUAL HARASSMENT
SEXUAL OBJECTIFICATION

GB-the Ritz Amnesty show 8/10

Ask women
what makes them feel unsafe

GB-the Ritz Amnesty show 8/10/90

p.Gabe R.

Ask women
what makes them feel unsafe

Over 80 % of rapes are committed by someone the victim knows. Women have cause to fear not only the stranger in the bushes, but also their classmate, their co-worker, their friend, or a member of their family. What makes you feel unsafe may be very different from what frightens the women you know. At times which seem harmless but may increase a woman's fear include standing too close or touching any part of her body without asking. Don't try to bully a woman into not trusting her own sense for when she is safe or in danger. There is no reason why a woman should know that you are "one of the good ones" without evidence. Find out how your behavior affects the women in your life. Once you know, it will be easier to act in ways that help them feel more secure and to avoid doing things that they find threatening.

GB-somewhere in Europa

GB-Gilman p.Dave Sine

Encourage women's efforts to empower themselves

Men who have never experienced what it is like to be singled out as the victim of a crime based on their gender often have difficulty understanding women's fear, and they may discount it as paranoia or man-hating. Supporting Chimera and other self-defense training for the women in your life—relatives, classmates, friends, and mates—is not promoting division between the sexes, but rather a more powerful, intimate relationship based on equality and mutual respect.

Uniform Choice

Carry Nation p.Chris Amouroux

Rape hurts all women

Whether a woman has been assaulted or not, she lives in a rape culture, one which limits her freedom. Women cannot walk where they want, or when they want. They are restricted in how they can jog on demonstrate physically. This includes limitations on the type and amount of make up, style of dress, and even how they can walk. The clearly send a message that women are invisibly merely by being female. We measure our role as victims from a woman as a sexual intimation. The must remain silent, and feel good for access to be "safe." Women are not allowed to relate in even strong assaults, or in the risk of assault, is endless. This state not invisible for making and stops of rape are sometimes. Women are not permitted to exploit continuity of their own choice. Fear of rape is used to control women who dare to commit their own rules of behavior. Rape is the punishment for those who enjoy a spontaneous, violent sexuality which does not fit into accepted definitions.

Statistics estimate that 25% to 90% of rapes are committed by male acquaintances family members, co-workers, classmates, dates, boyfriends, and husbands. A woman is told that she needs a good man to protect her from the bad men. Accepting this message tells a woman up to be the servant by my acquaintance male no defense. A good man is what makes acquaintance rape so devastating. When a woman feels forced to depend on men for safety, her relationships are not freely chosen. Seeking a protector can lead her to accept a man looking after important qualities, and she might still be raped—by her protector.

People who a woman are targeted for rape as women, rape plays a part in maintaining women's subordination and inequality. Nowhere is this as clear as in the justice time of marriage. A woman gives up her ability to bind for herself by being protected and supported. The worst assumptions concern in this unbalanced relationship are the justify the attempt for all the women sexual being paid every term for every dollar paid to men. This system is very profitable, and as long as rape is used to enforce women's second-class status, the threat of rape will continue to be a part of every woman's life.

Uniform Choice
Uniform Choice

Upfront-Fenders p.Dave Sine

Respect other's feelings

Have you ever tried to express yourself to someone who refused to listen to you or said you had no right to feel the way you did? Frustration and hurt are understandable responses to such emotional abuse. Being discounted like this also makes it harder than it already is to share feelings. In the extreme, our disregard for others' feelings is at the heart of rape. On the other hand, if we treat others the way we would like to be treated, they will be more likely to communicate with us honestly and directly. It is not necessary to agree with or even fully understand what someone says in order to respect their feelings as real and true.

Uniform Choice

Uniform Choice

Say No More p.Justin Subn Zine

Discuss your expectations

Expectations are hopes crystallized by silence. Acting on our expectations without sufficient information can cause serious misunderstandings and lead to rape. There is nothing wrong with feeling sexual desire, but, all too often, we do not communicate our desires, find out our partner's feelings, or establish consent. Instead, we project our interest in sex onto our partner, or assume she or he feels as we do, and we misinterpret any friendliness as invitation. Establishing consent for sexual or playful intercourse is morestep we used to justify each indignity as woman's work being paid sixty times for every dollar paid to men. This system is very profitable, and as long as rape is used to enforce women's second-class status, the threat of rape will continue to be a part of every woman's life.

A person's consent to come to your apartment, to kiss you, or to touch you is not the same as consent to any other sexual acts. Neither do so-called nonverbal cues such as someone's winking at you, drinking with you, or alerting to undress imply consent for sexual intercourse. Even if we think our partner is sending us "mixed messages," it is up to us to get clarification. Acting on our assumptions may seem more spontaneous but often leads us to be dishonest, manipulative, or to use physical force to get what we want.

Most of us have grown up with the bias that talking about sex is "just not done." But without romance about gender stereotypes are our only guide to behavior; men are encouraged to push for as much sex as possible. Women are forced to take all responsibility for deciding where to stop. This double standard is unfair and destructive to all of us. Discussing sexual expectations, especially in new relationships, is the best way of confirming mutual agreement, and the only way that we as men can take responsibility for the consequences of our sexual behavior. Share your hopes, feelings, fears, and fantasies with friends, dates, and lovers. Such sharing creates possibilities for freer, more honest, more mutually satisfying relationships.

Uniform Choice

Stop being violent

No disagreement requires a violent response. There are many alternatives. Talk it over. Think again. Develop and accept a compromise. Take "time out." Talk to someone else. Turn it over to a third party. Making threats and hitting people are power plays that freeze our differences at the most dangerous level. Violence makes communication and fair resolution of conflict impossible.

Insight

Supertouch p.Dave Sine

THERE CAN BE NO FREE MEN UNTIL THERE ARE FREE WOMEN!

NO=NO!

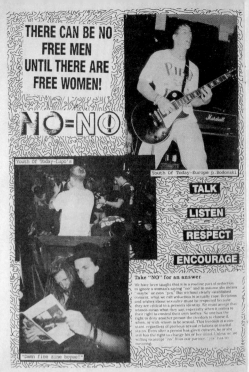

Youth Of Today-Lupo's

"Damn fine zine boys!"

Slayer-Gabe's Basement '85

Youth Of Today-Europe p.Bodonski

TALK

LISTEN

RESPECT

ENCOURAGE

Take "NO" for an answer

We have been taught that it is a routine part of seduction to ignore a woman's saying "no" and to assume she means "maybe" or even "yes." But without clearly established consent, what we call seduction is actually rape. Decisions and wishes about sexuality must be respected because they are critical to a person's identity. We must accept that women mean what they say, especially when it comes to their right to control their own bodies. No one has the right to deny another person the freedom to choose if, when, or with whom to be sexual. This freedom is a constant, regardless of previous sexual relations or marital status. Even after a person has given consent, he or she still has the right to change his or her mind. Unless we are willing to accept "no" from our partner, "yes" has no meaning.

Big Drill Car p.No Thanks

Big Drill Car p.No Thanks

Billingsgate 10/7 McGregor's p.John Handwerk

Billingsgate 10/21 p.John Handwerk

Go-Go's singalong, p.John Handwerk

Billingsgate 9/8 Kitson's p.John Handwerk

DEVELOP FULL RELATIONSHIPS WITH MEN AND WOMEN
RECOGNIZE AND INTERRUPT SEXUAL ASSAULT
CONFRONT WOMAN-HATING ATTITUDES
DISCUSS YOUR EXPECTATIONS
RESPECT OTHERS' FEELINGS
TALK ABOUT SEX

SUPPORT
SPECTRUM

JOIN MSR
GIVE WOMEN SPACE
TAKE "NO" FOR AN ANSWER
SUPPORT ANTI-RAPE ORGANIZATIONS
ASK WOMEN WHAT MAKES THEM FEEL UNSAFE
ENCOURAGE WOMEN'S EFFORTS TO EMPOWER THEMSELVES

Trademark-Milwaukee p.John Handwerk

MEN
Be All That You Can Be:
Join Men Stopping Rape

Insted

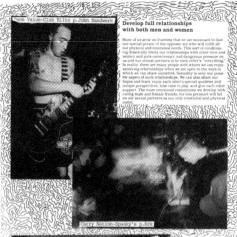

Face Value-Club Blitz p.John Handwerk

Develop full relationships with both men and women

Many of us grow up learning that we are supposed to find one special person of the opposite sex who will fulfill all our physical and emotional needs. This sort of conditioning drastically limits our relationships with other men and women and puts unnecessary and dangerous pressure on us and our sexual partners to be each other's "everything." In reality, there are many people with whom we can enjoy satisfying relationships when we are open to the ways in which we can share ourselves. Sexuality is only one possible aspect of such relationships. We can also share our hopes and fears, enjoy each other's special qualities and unique perspectives, take time to play, and give each other support. The more emotional connections we develop with caring male and female friends, the less pressure will fall on our sexual partners as our only emotional and physical outlet.

Carry Nation-Spanky's p.Krk

Murphy's Law p.Chris Anda
Metalfest #2 Milwaukee

Give women space

Sexual assault is an ever-present threat for women. On the street, in lines, and in crowded situations, leave space between yourself and the women around you. Consider that many women aren't comfortable with a male stranger that near. If you are approaching a woman walking alone at night, try crossing to the other side of the street. The difference it makes in your life may be only a few seconds, but for her, it may be the difference between walking in comfort and walking in fear.

Stop using pornography

Pornography and advertising use images of violence and subjugation to turn us on. They portray women (and children) in subordinate roles, as objects available to us and at our disposal, enjoying rape and abuse. When we buy pornography, we buy a limited perception of women as nothing more than bodies. The damage done by this male institution vastly outweighs any damage done by the handful of women's sex magazines. Consider how images of rape and domination have shaped our attitudes about women and sexuality.

Men Stopping Rape is not against the egalitarian depiction of nudity or sexual activity; we are against mainstream and hardcore material that presents only one gender, in unrealistic and dehumanizing ways. The assumptions pornography creates are degrading to all of us and destructive in maintaining equal relationships.

Give women space

Sexual assault is an ever-present threat for women. On the street, in lines, and in crowded situations, leave space between yourself and the women around you. Consider that many women aren't comfortable with a male stranger that near. If you are approaching a woman walking alone at night, try crossing to the other side of the street. The difference it makes in your life may be only a few seconds, but for her, it may be the difference between walking in comfort and walking in fear.

**Men Stopping Rape, Inc.
Box 316
306 N. Brooks St.
Madison, WI 53715
(608) 257-4444**

Statement p.Dave Sine

Stop telling sexist jokes

Many sexist jokes trivialize the hurt and pain women and some men suffer from male violence. Others perpetuate myths about rape and what women and men are really like, or reduce us to the functions of our genitals. Men who tell sexist jokes are usually trying to build themselves up at the expense of women, or with heterosexist jokes, at the expense of gay people. These jokes divide us into factions and stifle communication. When we laugh at these jokes, we laugh nervously, trying to fit in with "the boys." Such male bonding at the expense of women promotes rape. We don't need a laugh at that cost.

Reason To Believe p.Dave Sine

Stop withdrawing emotionally

As men, we are taught to fear exposure of our feelings. We learn to deny them to ourselves and others. Our fear of vulnerability often leads us to take a position of dominance and control. In order to remain "strong," we deal with frustration and hurt by withdrawing emotionally and refusing to communicate, sometimes without realizing what we are doing. In the end we never learn how to work out our feelings with others, and our attempts to maintain a position of "strength" only isolate us. We may try to force others to guess what's wrong or to give in to what we want. If this doesn't work, we sulk, bluster, or even threaten violence. However, if we can trust that there is a reason for our feelings the way we do, we can learn to express our feelings directly and find non-causative ways of communicating.

Inside Out-the Anthrax p.Jen Kulawas

Confront woman-hating attitudes in ourselves and others

Misogyny is the often disguised yet widespread fear or hatred of women, sustained by the attitudes in ourselves which are traditionally labeled masculine. Most of our society teaches us to act "strong," "cool," or "big" when our emotions of fear or tenderness threaten to burst forth. Because we equate emotions with weakness, we learn to despise the "weaker sex" who express emotions we fear. We seek to control women instead of ourselves, and to control ourselves we smother the gentler, "weaker" parts of ourselves. We all have the potential to learn compassion and unlearn violence. We need to accept and express the full range of our feelings, understand our emotional strengths and skills is something all men need.

Recognize and interrupt sexual assault

Assault can occur anywhere: on the street, at a party, a football game, or the workplace—any time, day or night. It ranges from forced sexual intercourse to any unwanted touching, and also includes verbal abuse. Many actions learned as normal, such as a "friendly" pat on the behind, are in fact assaultive if they don't involve the consent of all parties. Be aware of women being assaulted physically or verbally. Notice what is happening and who is involved. Intervene with comments, questions, disruptive noises, or physically if necessary. Asking if a woman wants help is important. Responding to a call for help is essential. Getting involved makes the violence visible and may stop a rape. Acknowledging a responsibility to interrupt assaults does not imply that women need male protection. The belief that women need men as protectors from other men only reinforces the myth that women are powerless, and puts us unhealthy burden on us. Do not expect a woman you assist to trust you any more than her assailant.

Develop full relationships with both men and women

Many of us grow up learning that we are supposed to find one special person of the opposite sex who will fulfill all our physical and emotional needs. This sort of conditioning drastically limits our relationships with other men and women and puts unnecessary and dangerous pressure on us and our sexual partners to be each other's "everything." In reality, there are many people with whom we can enjoy satisfying relationships when we are open to the ways in which we can share ourselves. Sexuality is only one possible aspect of such relationships. We can also share our hopes and fears, enjoy each other's special qualities and unique perspectives, take time to play, and give each other support. The more emotional connections we develop with caring male and female friends, the less pressure will fall on our sexual partners as our only emotional and physical outlet.

Respect other's feelings

Have you ever tried to express yourself to someone who was too afraid to listen? How did it feel when someone gave you advice, changed the subject or interrupted when you only wanted them to pay attention? Because men are conditioned to believe that we are supposed to know everything and always be in control, it is harder than it already is to admit when we don't understand or need support. Respecting other's feelings means to listen openly and carefully, to encourage others to share their feelings, to resist the urge to give advice or "fix" things before really listening, to respect the limits others set on what they want to share, and to let the other know, by our words and acts, that we empathize. We need to really listen to others, and understand what someone is saying before we respond with our own feelings and opinions.

Bad Religion...Chicago

Billingsgate-Milwaukee p.John Handwerk

Slapshot McGregor's p.John Handwerk

Slapshot McGregor's p.John Handwerk

Straight From the Heart 9/25/90
last Club Blitz show p.John Handwerk

V11-Milwaukee p.Mike G.

Excel p.Dave Sine

Men *can stop* rape.

Excel p.Dave Sine

Excel-somewhere in Europe

● **SEXISM**

● **VIOLENCE**

● **WITHDRAWING**

Cro-mags-Cubby Bear p.Chris Anda

Stop fantasizing about rape

Sexual fantasies can provide us with a rich outlet for feelings and desires that we cannot always gratify in life. However, rape fantasy is rape in your head. When we construct rape fantasies, we write detailed scripts for every step of a sexual assault, although we often pretend it is a seduction. In fact, most actual rapes consist of the acting out of pre-planned rape fantasies. Such fantasies are dangerous, because they eroticize violence and encourage us to become excited by a woman's struggling against us. They blur the distinction between sex and sexual assault and numb us to the reality of rape.

Henry R. p.Shannon

Henry R. p.Shannon

Henry R. p.Shannon

Stop pretending submission is consent

Men often assume that if a woman doesn't say "no" she means "yes." There are many situations in which women have submitted to men's demands when they did not truly consent. Women may feel pressure to submit because of the legitimate fear of physical violence, abandonment, withdrawal of monetary support, damage to reputation through malicious gossip, and social rejection. These fears can make submission seem like the only alternative. On the other hand, communication opens new possibilities for satisfying each person and is the only way mutual consent is ever confirmed. Consent requires understanding, respect and agreement between equal partners.

Crivits

Swiz-Gilman p.Dave Sine

Rape hurts all men

1 in 6 boys are victims of some other sexual assault before their eighteenth birthday. Many of these boys grow up to commit rape...

Talk about sex

Many of us grow up with unrealistic beliefs about sex: that we should instinctively know what to do; that we should be ready to achieve an erection instantly and maintain it for hours; and that it is uncommunicative to have to talk about what gives us (or our partner) pleasure. These beliefs and others keep us from knowing our own sexuality and from enjoying our sexual relationships. Sex without discussion does not allow consent, or even minimal expectations, to be communicated. Without mutual agreement, sex becomes rape. Sex is healthy when it reflects the free and mutual sharing of one another. When we discuss what makes us comfortable and uncomfortable and try one way to express ourselves, we also greatly reduce the risk of sexual assault.

Billinsgate 11/90 p.Gabe

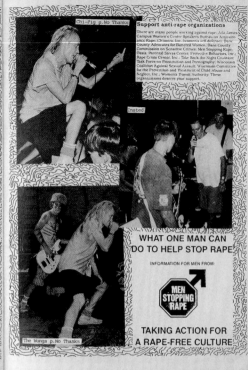

Chi-Pig p.No Thanks

Insted

**WHAT ONE MAN CAN
DO TO HELP STOP RAPE**

INFORMATION FOR MEN FROM:

MEN STOPPING RAPE

**TAKING ACTION FOR
A RAPE-FREE CULTURE**

The Wongs p.No Thanks

7 SECONDS

In 10 years, you would think that after over hundreds of shows and recording 10 releases, it would take a toll on a band. Meanwhile, they would obviously accomplished a lot if they were really into their work. Well, this was the case for 7 Seconds. These next four pages are our way of saying thank you to 7 Seconds and family.

Milwaukee 6/2/90 p.Matt G.

Chicago 6/1/90 p.Matt G.

Milwaukee 6/2/90 p.Matt G.

Cactus Club-San Jose p.Bob Conrad

Milwaukee p.Dan D.

Milwaukee 11/89 p.Mike B.

Waukegan Il. 11/89 p.Dave J.

ESCAPE AND RUN

Milwaukee 6/2/90 p.Matt G.

Kalamazoo 11/89 p.Matt G.

Reno 12/88 p.Bob Conrad

Reno 12/88 p.Bob Conrad

Reno 12/88 p.Bob Conrad

Milwaukee p.Dan D

Milwaukee p.Dan D

Tribute Freedom Landscape

Milwaukee p.Dan D.

WHEN ONE FALLS.

Chapel Hill N.C. p.Josh Lance

MOLLY RINGWALD

You may be wondering about this page. Well you may have heard rumours about me giving away a NY City Hardcore 12" comp TEST PRESSING.This may seem to be an off the wall contest,but I guarantee it will be well worth it for the winner.The person who answers correctly the most of these trivia questions about Molly Ringwald will win the Test.This is no joke!So all you Ringlets get off your duff and enter today. I will announce the winner after the sale of the 300th issue of this zine.Please include full names when possible as you answer the q's.In case of a tie,I will have a drawing to determine the winner.Send all responses to me along with a SASE. These are not easy.Good luck!

1.At what age did Molly make the cover of Time Magazine?
2.Who sings the song "Pretty In Pink"?
3.Which actors have been in more than one movie with Molly?
4.At the age of nine,what popular Disney children's show did she appear on?
5.Give both her parents names.
6.Madonna beat Molly for a role in this David Mamet play.
7.Which Designing Women co-starred in Pretty In Pink?
8.Out of all of her films,which one grossed the most at the box office.
9.What T.V.movie did Molly star in as a suicidal teen and is often shown in High Schools across America?
10.In 2 movies Molly speaks a language other than English,what language is it? Name the character that Molly portrays in the following movies.Full name when possible
-The Facts Of Life
-Tempest
-P.K. and the Kid
-16 Candles
-Surviving
-The Breakfast Club
-Pretty In Pink
-For Keeps
-The Pickup Artist
-Fresh Horses
-King Lear
-Strike It Rich
-Betsy's Wedding
-Women & Men...Stories of Seduction

NEW YORK CITY HARDCORE

▲ TWIN PEAKS ▲

As you can see,I have been watching a lot of t.v. lately. Not much else to do in a dead city with a fractured wrist.One of the shows that really caught my attention was Twin Peaks. I figured that since I did a Molly trivia page,I will do the same for all you Peak Freaks.This time I am giving to the person who can correctly answer these questions a NYC Hardcore "Together"ep.After the sale of the 300th zine,if noone has all of them correct,I will give it to the person with the most correct. Good luck!

1.Who killed Laura Palmer?
2.Name the High School dropout waitress at the RR Diner.
3.How did Cooper know that the video of Laura and Donna was filmed by a biker?
4.Give the one-armed-man's full name.
5.The character of Donna Hayward is played by _____.
6.Actress Sherilyn Fenn (Audrey)has been in this pornographic publication recently.
7.What girl did Cooper find in his hotel room bed naked?
8.Give the full name of Laura Palmer's cousin.
9.Ben Horne owns a Casino/Brothel by the name of _____.
10.What is the letter that is on the back of Bobby Briggs jacket?
11.Who was Ben Horne with the night Laura was killed?
12.Ben Horne's original lawyer was _____.
13.What was found inside Laura's safety deposit box?
14.Who played Gordon, the loudmouth-hard of hearing FBI agent?
15.What is the population of Twin Peaks?
16.Did Laura Palmer ever have sex with another woman?
17.Where in Laura's room did Laura hide her cocaine?
18.What was written in blood at the scene of Laura's murder?

THE BAND IS:
GREG-DRUMS
WILEY-LEAD GUITAR
JASON-RHYTHM GUITAR
PHIL-BASS,VOCALS

When I saw Sacred Reich in concert,there was no doubt in my mind that these guys really back up their lyrics with authority.Imagine being in a jam-packed club with about 200 metallers and half of them smoking whatever was avalable to them.Then off go the lights,and over the P.A. there is the Martin Luther King Jr. speech,"I had a Dream.Well,this was the setting for the show and all hell broke loose during the show.But for a few minutes,the whole club was united in listening to MLK.I warned everyone that I would soon do an interview with a metal band,and I jumped on the chance to get Sacred Reich. Phil was interviewed before the show in Providence on August 16 1990.

Milwaukee 1/89 p.Gabe

G&P:so how old are you now?
Phil:I will be 21,everyone else is 22,23,24.
G&P:How long have you guys been playing as Sacred Reich?
Phil:Since 1986.
G&P:I take it that you were in High School. Did that become a problem,for shows?
Phil:I was only 16.But,no.We didn't have a record out until 1987.We didn't do much touring anyway.We'd play like Phoenix,Los Angeles,Detroit, Toronto,Cincinnati,and Cleveland.Then we went back and did Surf Nicaragua.Then we did a tour with Atrophy.

That was about 9 weeks in the U.S.,then we did 5 weeks with Forbidden.Before that, like about 2 Christmas's ago,we went over to Europe and did 4 shows with Motorhead. Destruction,Coronor,and Candlemsass.That was our first time in Europe and we got to hang out with Motorhead and shit.It was a killer.
G&P:So how has this tour been so far?The album was released not too long ago.
Phil:Yeah,about 5 weeks ago.It has been pretty cool man.We have our own bus.We had to share buses before.We have new equipment,new songs.Things are going pretty good.
G&P:Most people would consider Sacred Reich a metal band,but your lyrics wouldn't identify you as such.What influences you to write?
Phil:At first it was old MDC,DRI,COC, and the Subhumans.Those bands showed me that you can say something.I went as far as to rip off MDC lyrics and shit.In the song "No Believers",it goes,"Get off your knees there's no God in heaven."And MDC goes, "And there's no God in heaven so get off your knees".There was another one by COC. Actually we used to cover "Holier" a long time ago.We just played not too long ago in England and they opened for us.I was telling them how it was cool to meet them. It was weird.I said that we used to play one of their songs.They asked if we were gonna do it that night.I said no because we haven't played it in a couple of years. I was with them as they were writing there set list and they were going to write "Holier" and one guy goes "No, these guys are gonna do it.(meaning us).We went to the side of the stage before the encore,and they asked if we were gonna do it. So we said "What the Hell", and we did it.Our drummer almost killed me,cause we hadn't played it in so long.We just totally screwed it up.Carl came out and sang. It was really fun.
G&P:I was looking at the new album,"The American Way",and it includes this little speech by you that was direct and to the point about a lot of things.Do you think you went out on a limb to stress your opinion?
Phil:Fuck it man.That's what I believe.I don't think I went out on a limb.If people can't accept that as the truth then obviously they are not down to what the truth is.
G&P:I think that would have startled some people just by the fact that a metal band said that.
Phil:I hope that it would open some eyes. I mean,I do it because I think it's right. Regardless of what other people do with it.The point is that it's out there for them.Whether they want to believe it,not, change the way they think about things, question things,or think it out for themselves.I don't want anyone to think what I say is the truth just because I'm saying it,unless they already think that. Maybe it will smack them in the face and go,"Hey maybe he is right?"Everyone has to figure what the truth is for themselves.Nobody can tell you something that is that important and have to accept it as such.We say what we say in our songs cause we want to and it gives it more validity in our music.It's coming from our hearts.We have no say if people believe it or not.We do it because we know it is right.
G&P:Do you ever regret anything that you ever wrote in a song?
Phil:Not regret.Regret is a bad word. I don't ever regret anything because it was done at a certain time,and that is how it was when it was done.

(cont.)Things like "No Believers" from the first album,"What is this lie,there is no truth.There's no God,there's no proof."I don't agree with that stuff anymore and we don't play it.It's not right and we're not gonna play it.I don't regret,because at a certain point in time,that is where my head was at.But we have moved on.I was sixteen,what the hell did I know about anything.Everyone goes through that somewhat satanic "screw religion" stage,and that's where I was.
G&P:Would you mind telling me what your religious beliefs are now?
Phil:I was raised Jewish,so I have a lot of that.I also get into some Eastern Religions.Hindu,Bhuddism.It's more of a frame of mind.God is such an abstract suject. Morally I know what's right and wrong.Everyone has to figure it out for themself. That is the thing about religion.All religions are searching for the same things and that's no reason to hate each other.That's the thing I like about Hinduism.It says that there are many paths to the Summit.There are different religions for different cultures.
G&P:The song on the new album 31 Flavors is a change for you guys.Would you like to elaborate.
Phil:People always ask us "What makes you different?"Well this song isn't going to make us different than everyone else.But it is different, and it's kind of like a challenge to our fans to see where they are coming from.You know?A lot metallers have blinders on. Sort of like tunnie vision. All metal,maybe a little hardcore.It's just a smack in the face.I like it.It comes across as to open up to different music,cultures,and everything.There's so much out there.I have always wanted to use horns.It is just like a challenge...Something you wouldn't expect.
G&P:Do you play it live?
Phil:Yeah.Either people like it or they don't.A lot of people boo,but that's fine. We don't expect everyone to like it.We didn't think everyone would,but who cares. It's our record.We can do what we want.If they don't like us because of it,fine.
G&P:Have you ever had any problems with the PMRC?
Phil:No.We are too small for them.And what can they say?What have we done that is so...It is not satanic,and it is not about sex.There's a thing called freedom of speech and they can't touch that.Our lyrics are about politics and life.

Milwaukee 1/89 p.Gabe

G&P:That 2 Live Crew controversy was a big issue.
Phil:You know what it is the 2 Live Crew and the Jello thing...It is about sex.They are so uptight,man.Those people don't know their dicks from their assholes.The sex issue really scares them.They don't know how to act.They are afraid that their 16 year old will go out with black guys. Sex freaks them out more than anything,even more than the satanic thing,because satan is abstract.It is not some band member screwing their daughter.Luther says it is all about racism,and you know everything is in a way.He said that why don't they go after the Dice Clay's and all of those guys?It is because Luther has his own money and he is his own entity.They can go after Luther and get him a lot easier than someone who has a corporate backing.Luther is a black man making a lot of money and that pisses lots of people off.
G&P:This is your third album,do you feel that you will get better offers from bigger labels?
Phil:Enigma put out The American Way which was a step higher from Metal Blade.They gave us a lot more money to record,and do videoes and stuff like that.
G&P:I haven't seen the video.Is it being played?
Phil:Yeah,on Headbangers Ball.It's for the song The American Way.It's pretty cool.
G&P:I read in some magazine the story behind the song Administrative Decisions.You were supposed to play on the school football field or something?
Phil:Yeah,it was like a fund raiser with all the school clubs and those booths. Bands were going to play and people would come and spend money so the clubs would make money.If they would let us play,then they would make money.Isn't that the object? So I brought them our demo.I don't think they dug the No Believers thing.I said that they should let us play,because there were a lot of people who wanted to hear us. They said no.I said "All right.I'll come back".I went and got like 2/3 of the school to sign this petition to let us play.The school rejected it because they said the thing had to be OK'd by us first.The fact was that they were saying we couldn't have a petition.Then they said that the kids would sign anything because it was against the school.Come on,you got to give them more credit than that.I told the principal that without those kids he wouldn't have a job.Censorship is a big thing now,so I

called all these newspapers and stuff.Some radio station called and I talked on some radio talk show.After all of that they still wouldn't let us play.I even went up to the district superintendent and asked him,but he had to back up the principal. Not because he was right,but because of all the bureocracy and that just pissed me off.I said to the principal,"Man you are fucked!"I just winked out.I went back the next year to get some school records for college or something and one of the assistant principals asked me how the band was.I said,"Oh,we have been to Europe a few times yov dick.How many times have you been there?"I hate them.It's not a good feeling either.I dropped out of high school.I was 1½ credits short of graduating and I had it.I knew I could have done it.It was the principle of the matter. In the whole grand scheme of things,I know it was right for me.It is not about learning,it is about doing what you're told and I'm not gonna play your game.See ya.
G&P:Yeah,that isn't too hard to see.But what would you say to the everyday person who is struggling in school these days?

Phil:It really sucks,but if you're not going to be in a band,you got to play that little game man.You have to go to school so you can get a job so you don't end up pumping gas.It sucks and I feel really bad because you have to get out in that world and play that little game.They teach you in school to raise your hand and to be on time so your boss doesn't get mad.It encourages good habits while you are in school. Such as paying attention so you are prepared when you get out in the work world. But there are good teachers out there also,and you just have to find them.I had some really nice teachers in school that helped me out.You need to find them because education is where it is at.Knowledge so you can move up and distance yourself from all of the B.S.The further away the better,and the more sane you will be.
G&P:Are you familiar with the hardcore scene today?

Phil:A lot of the straight edge kids are trapped by all metallers because they drink and get high.I know that drinking and getting high isn't the right thing to do,but I do it anyway.I'm trying to get away from it,but I still do it.It is not for anyone else to tell me I can't and it doesn't make you any better than me cause you don't do drugs.And that is the problem- this "Holier than thou attitude."I don't need drugs or booze".Why don't you bring yourself off your mountain and mingle with the little people.
G&P:There are obviously different people at your shows. How is it?

Phil:It is mostly metal kids.But some hardcore kids. And there is no reason why people can't get along just because they are different.
G&P:Are there many fights?

Phil:Not really.If they do break out,we just stop playing and say that this wasn't why we came.Say we were playing then "One Nation"and a fight breaks out.Come on! Isn't anyone listening?
G&P:The last time I saw you you came out with the Martin Luther King Jr. speech,and at the end all these people applauded.Then you played "One Nation".It was cool.

Phil:That was a killer.I want to do that some more.We haven't been doing it on this tour.We are not one of these precision tuned clockwork bands that do the set,stop,

and then there is the taped intro with the stage black,songs into songs.We're just not like that.When we try to pull stuff like that off we humble because it's not what we're about.I'd like to do the King speech thing again.It would give me chills.
G&P:You seem to tour a lot.What is next for Sacred Reich?

Phil:Another tour.We never really tour that much.We went to Europe,we did the Rock Hard Fest in Germany with thousands of people.We played Holland,London,and Paris to kick off the album over there.Then we came back here to do this tour for 5 weeks.We're gonna get ready to go to Europe for 7 more weeks,then come home for a bit.Then we go to Japan.Then we'll play the U.S some more.There are other things in the works but I won't mention them until they pan out.
G&P:So how is the European response compared to that of the U.S.?

Phil:We have sold as many records there as we have here.To go gold in Europe,you have to sell 60,000 albums.Over here it is 500,000. So that shows you how much smaller the record buying public is over there.To sell equal amounts is really good.It takes longer in America because you're not getting played on the radio.Circus and Hit Parader aren't as cool as Kerrang and Raw,as far as letting bands happen.
G&P:I saw a review for a live album from Sacred Reich.What was that?

Phil:There is this thing called Live At The Dynamo that was only released over in Europe.It wasn't the greatest thing in the world.It wasn't our idea and we told them not to release it here.Some kid wrote me and said he paid 25 bucks for it and it sucked.Well I didn't tell him to buy it.Why do you think it wasn't released here? I don't want a bunch of letters.We didn't want to do it.
G&P:Those 2 extra songs on Surf Nicaragua that were done live,are they really live?

Phil:they are live in the studio.It was like we set up our stuff and our friends came and we recorded.It's another stupid thing we did.But we live and learn.That is how Slayer did their Live Undead thing.But it is definitely us playing live with all the messups.
G&P:Do you want to wrap it up?

Phil:Just to get the record and to and to read that little paragraph.It seems so simple.There are a lot of different types of people.But we have more similarities than differences.Let's just get over it and live together and the world will ne a better place.Don't you feel better about yourself if you are nice to someone,then being an asshole. It seems so simple.

Milwaukee 1/89 p.Gabe

CHAIN × OF STRENTH

Kurtis-Vocals Rine-Guitar
Cris-Drums   Rosty-Guitar
Allicks-bass

When I found out that the Chain Gang was doing a show nearby, I had to jump on the chance.This band has a reputation that is misunderstood by most people and I thought that I'd set the record straight.Here goes.

G&P:I hear things about you guys and since there are so many people that say them,I do wonder.Just curious,what is the most you ever got drunk?

Rine:That was at the Soundgarden show a while back.I think it was when they shot the video.Yeah,I was real messed up that night.
G&P:What were you drinkin'?

Rine:Anything I could get my hands on.It was at the Whiskey,(fitting name.)That is a good place to get drunk at...Loud music,booze,girls,the works.
G&P:What happened that night now that you got me curious?

Rine:I don't know.I only remember Soundgarden coming on.That's it.
G&P:Come on Rine,I've seen the video of you and someone else in the band,(Rosty), a sheepdog and a jar of mayo.Tell me about it.

Rine:That was a girl,not a sheepdog.
G&P:Come on ,I want to give you a chance to clear yourself, what really happened that night?

Rine:I have nothing to say.I don't remember any of it anyway.
GP:Is Chain Of Strenth a straight edge band?

Rine:Yes,we are.We believe in moderation.Then,it's ok.
G&P:Does that include masturbation?

Rine:You have to ask Kurtis about that.
G&P:A lot of people say that you guys are dicks.

Rine:Yeah,well most people are dicks.
G&P:Who said that?

Rine:Ludicrist.Bands like them are what holds us true.
G&P:There seems to a connection to straight edge and pornography.Can you explain that?

Rine:That's another thing that holds us true.Some of my favorite movies are,Backdoor Romance,Hottest Show In Town, Take it from Behind,I could go on.
G&P:What do you think of the SE scene today?

Rine:Well back in my day,when I was green in the scene,it wasn't such a big deal if you were SE or not.That's where I get my ideals about the Old School.All you have to do is call yourself SE, and you were.Today,the best thing about it is the money.I put this ad in this zine and you read this thing,I have all this cash in front of me.I did what any other person would have done.I kept the loot.Everyone has to make a buck. It came in handy,I got a lot of pizza in a short time.I made like a bandit.
G&P:You are saying it is ok to hide behind the SE mask and rip off all of the green"Johnny-Come-Lately"kids?

Rine:It's the American way.Capatalism at its finest.Look at all those Misfits boots, someone made a pretty penny off those.This is my way of spreading the wealth.

G&P:It sounds to me like a poor justification for your greed for wealth.
Rine:Well,a man's gotta do what a man's gotta do.Whether you are selling dope on the street corner or whatever.Everyone has to make a buck.
G&P:Were you guys ever supposed to play at Club Blitz in Illinois?

Rine:Oh yeah,I remember.We were on tour a while ago,right before the Foundatiom Records Ep was released.The night before the show,we were stuck in Montana and our van broke down.We knew we weren't going to make it so we stayed in some city named Missoula Montana.
G&P:So what did you end up doing there?

Rine:We just hung out,looking for things to do.It was a woody city with lots of trees.It didn't look like we would meet much people there so we went up to the border of Canada and found this little casino type place called One Eyed Jacks.We did gamble a little,but after a while when we were all tipsy,we had fun with friends in the back rooms.We spent a lot of cash that night.
G&P:I thought you had a flat tire?

Rine:That's what we told the guys at the club.There were rumoursgoing around that the kids at the club would have skinned us alive if we showed up.
G&P:Why would anyone want to do that?

Rine:I don't know.People have this idea that we are bad guys but we're not.We are doing our own thing the way we want.It's all how you see things.It's ok,we had tons of fun in Canada instead.From what we heard,Chicago isn't too fond of us. I don't know why.I don't want to start trouble with anyone.So we didn't show.
G&P:Have you ever seen a zine called Fists Fight?They have a page in it with a picture of Kurtis hanging from a noose.I thought it was pretty funny.

Rine:Oh yeah,we've seen it.We live it.The other day,we were all over Kurtis' house and ended up spending the night.The next day when we woke up and went outside,someone had set up a booby trap with a noose over the front door.I was almost lynched. It comes with the territory.When you're on top,everyone wants to bring you down. We try to ignore those idle threats.It is hard though.One time in Connecticut we played a show and about fifty kids jumped on our singer for a singalong.I don't think they even knew the words.It looked like they had it all planned out.
G&P:What can we expect to see in the future of this band?

Rine:Well,I am going to try my luck as an actor.I have been working on one film with some friends.It is kind of a low budget type thing.I was talking about it earlier.It is called Backdoor Romance. Check it out.Later.
G&P:One last thing.What ever happened to you and Judge?

Rine:Well,I wasn't actually in the band.I was just filling in for a double guitar sound.It worked out cool.I stole a few riffs from them,and I learned some more.Listen to the new Ep, you can hear it easily.

> *The greatness of a nation and its moral progress can be judged by the way its animals are treated.*
> — Mahatma Gandhi

WHATs HOT? WHATs NOT?

WHATs HOT?

HEADBANDS
JUDGE BOOTLEGS
JULIE CRUISE

ALMONDAYSE
TACO BELL
HOSTESS LIGHTS
SHERILYN FENN
LARA FLYNN BOYLE
DEP-LIGHT
MOLLY RINGWALD
SLAYER
IRON MAIDEN
THE GO-GO'S
TWIN PEAKS
INTEGRITY

SHOVE BANG MECCA
WILSON PHILLIPS
TRIXTER
NELSON
SUSAN VEGA

CANVAS SHOES
X COUNTRY TRIPS
BLUE VELVET
TATTOOS
GABE'S TOSTADA'S

MADONNA
VICTORY RECORDS
LIVING COLOUR
P.B. CRACKERS
SCHISM LONGSLEEVES

WHATs NOT?

CORDUROY PANTS
SPIKED HAIR
JERSEYS
WIDE-LEGGED PANTS
MALFA INDIA
GYM SHORTS
CHEESE WHIZ
SLIPKNOT
OVERKILL
CHICAGO
THE BOTTLE
LUNCHBOX ROCK
ATOMIC RECORDS
MISFITS BOOTLEGS
THE NAVY
JON P. ON BASS
REVELATION REC.
G&P PRODUCTIONS
ICE-T

NEW YORK HARDCORE
TC3 ON BOOZE
SUB-POP
FUNK
MRR
MASTURBATION
WAX TRAX
ROB RELEASE
SATAN
BOB

After a four hour conversation at 3:30 am we came to the conclusion to do a "What's hot/ What's not" segment. I am sick of reading these things in Vogue and Esquire that only appeal to a much older and richer audience. These are strictly the opinions of Gabe and Matt and are subject to a little humor.

GOOD & PLENTY ZINE
GABE RODRIGUEZ
2116 SALEM BLVD.
ZION IL. 60099

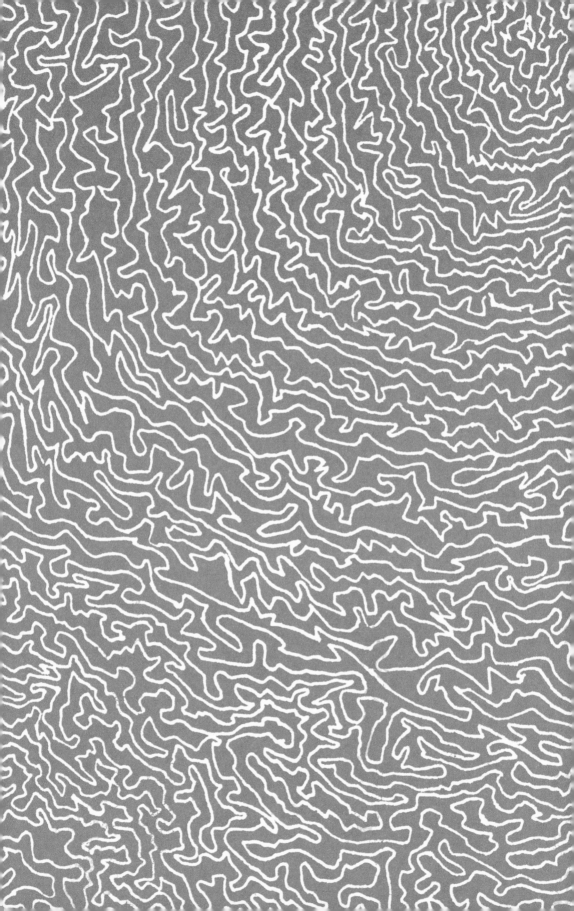

Backwards from Boston

Anthony Pappalardo

How do you get the photos to not look like ghosts?

Ah, shit. It's going to take a few tries to figure out which way to feed the paper back in to get the pages to line up—is there a name for that?

OK, we have a stinky, inky ream laying here, waiting to be collated but a "regular stapler" won't stretch to the gutter...

No ad money. No backing. Maybe free copies from shop class, so why not sell it for a single dollar for an optimal profit?

In the late-1980s/early-1990s, making a fanzine was a learning curve, especially if you had no mentor [you probably didn't]. That was the charm. If you were a fan of zines, well, I'd liken the obsession to ice fishing. When I was eleven, my father drove us from Massachusetts to somewhere in Maine to sit in a wooden box and eat unshelled peanuts while we stared at a hole in the ice, waiting for the bait to catch. It was so mundane that it was almost psychedelic.

At one of the last hardcore—not punk—matinees at the mob-associated Channel Club in Boston, Mass., someone handed me a free fanzine with a terse Judge interview and some record reviews. I owned a few copies of *MRR* and some scattered zines, but this half-sizer was particularly epic because it had advertisements for other mags that were precisely relevant to my interests. Most notable was an ad for a zine from Illinois, edited by a Latino that featured a flip on the Gorilla Biscuits logo and a penny candy theme. I didn't know much about Mr. Rodriguez's home state other than sports, and there were few people of color in the Boston scene at the time, so this was a must-order, along with a few others displayed in the small zine. I mean, I knew Chicago had bands but what the fuck was Zion?

aybe the next time we get together,my hair won't turn
s someone trying to tell me something?

know I don't pay you for your services,but I is wort
ery penny.Thank you.

PHOTO BY ALYSSA CHUNX:GABE A[
OUTSIDE OF FENWAY PARK.

Boston

I recently spent the new year in Boston and had a fabulous time. Me AND my friend Tom drove 1,000 miles to get away from the norm. That we did... We used a lot of film on the trip, and I thought of using a few shots...

I couldn't resist this one →
Alyssa, Tom, + Shawn on the run.

JAN. '92 P.GABE

JAN. '92 P.GABE

At 4:00 AM, on a weekni Tom, and Shawn decide to by lip syncing to classic S It was broken up by the po Try explaining that one t

Here we were introduced to a famous past-time amongst the locals... Hedgediving. If you have never tried it, Do try this at home. It beats stagediving.
Pictured: Gabe, Jon Reed, Tom T., Alyssa, + Rich on top.

These 10 days were definitely unforgettable, to say the least. Thanks to all who helped to

P.Justine De M

Months later, folded up photocopied communications packed with intel started showing up in my mailbox. I would approach my cul de sac, hoping to see my mailbox with a red flag boner standing straight up—psychically willing there would be. I was hoping a 7" or zine was inside and not those shitty things called "bills" that I didn't yet understand.

One such delivery of note was a blustery weekday in November, where I received a shattered Powerhouse single and a copy of *Good and Plenty*—the last issue but more importantly, the "Boston" issue. OK, it wasn't all Boston bands, but Eye For An Eye, Kingpin, Seven League Boots, Alyssa Chunx, and Doc Hopper (who counted) and that was cool. These were regular-ass people I saw every weekend: peers, friends, creatives who had different POVs, and enough to digest over-and-over for weeks.

G&P was funny, poignant, relevant, and relatable. Even though I worked backward through the few issues that existed, it was especially cool to see a changing scene being broadcast—both the local bands I experienced every weekend and larger acts of a like mind—challenging the conventions of hardcore. Essays and interviews were discussing more than the standard topics of the day, specifically sexism and gender roles in hardcore, reproductive rights, race relations, the corporatization of hardcore, environmentalism, and animal rights.

Maybe some of these points aren't as salient and informed as a well-composed tweet, but they're honest and indicative of something germane to hardcore punk and much larger than it: the work is never done. Hardcore being smaller and less specialized in the 1980s and 1990s led to me being exposed to more than my immediate surroundings, background, and world. It put personalities to logos and photo credits and challenged me to listen and learn.

Folded pieces of paper penned by teens may not be subculture tomes, but they chronicle the human condition and connect the past to the present.

The issue ends with a "What's Hot and What's Not List." Included in the NOT are Andrew Dice Clay, Roseanne, David Duke, hardline, hate core, gas, and the Chicago Bears.

Spot on, Gabe. Spot on.

Opposite: Detail from paste-up for *Good and Plenty*, issue 7, p. 58, 1992. "Exploring Boston" feature.

GOOD AND PLENTY

#7

7 LEAGUE BOOTS

EYE FOR AN EYE

ALYSSA CHUNX

INTO ANOTHER

DOCHOPPER

ICEBURN

KINGPIN

$2.00

411

Three years passed, and the final issue of *Good and Plenty* arrived as a fully realized, mature publication. It's respectably printed, with better paper than many other scene publications. Your hands won't get dirty with ink when you read it.

Issue 7
Winter 1991-1992
60 pages
7.75 × 10.7 inches
3,000 copies
$2.00

Opposite: Cover for *Good and Plenty*, issue 7, 1991-1992.

Issue 7 wasn't intended to be the last issue. Rodriguez shares his intentions in the introduction: "I hope to continue [*Good and Plenty Zine*] for a long time, but I'm taking each issue one at a time." He's recognized and grappling with the idea of transition, declaring, "I welcome change. Change is what attracted me to the hardcore scene to begin with." Alyssa Chunx, a frequent collaborator to *G&P* and zine-maker herself (*Blowin' Chunx* 1-5), writes, "hardcore is what you make it. It is whatever you want it to be. It is always changing."

The cover design of *Good and Plenty* 7 has reached a level of sophistication and refinement that exceeds previous issues. A crisp black-and-white texture covers the background; band names are in all capital letters, set in a typewriter font. The *Good and Plenty* masthead is blurrily distorted, likely the result of experimentation with a photocopier. In an unusual move, Rodriguez included a printer test pattern in the actual design. Initially a full color or grayscale image, the pattern has been converted to black and white during the printing and production process. The resulting graphic has shifted to flat black and white, with no areas of gray. It's an apt visual metaphor for youthful naïveté, where ideas can be overly simplified and nuance lost. As a disgruntled reader writes in this issue: "Since you sold all those zines, does that make you more straight edge? We sold zines too."

G&P 7 features eight interviews, twice as many as the previous issue, and includes conversations with Into Another and Iceburn, two bands that defined change and evolution. The pair pushed boundaries and made people rethink preconceptions. In the Iceburn interview, Rodriguez notes, "It's not every day that you see a band that plays 10 minutes songs." Gentry Densley, the guitarist, replies, "Do you think they get boring though?" Later, he continues,

"It seems that kids today are looking for an image... not looking for a message." Chad Popple, Iceburn's drummer, adds, "It seems with music, lots of people are closed-minded about it..."

Rodriguez reveals in the issue that he's always wanted to interview individuals who aren't band members. "Many of the most interesting people in hardcore I have met aren't in bands," he explains. He chooses to talk with Alyssa Chunx, a punk rocker from Boston who Rodriguez met when she was attending the University of Michigan. Asked what it would mean for her to quit making *Blowin' Chunx*, she replied, "I thought I could quit doing a zine, and it would be over, and I could put it behind me. But I realized, and I know a lot of people who stop doing zines, that you feel unfulfilled when you're not doing it. Whenever you are doing a zine, you are always working on another issue, or it is always kind of hanging above you."

If that's true, maybe there's another issue of *Good and Plenty* in the works, just waiting for a few more photos, a few more interviews... —C.S/K.S.

GOOD AND PLENTY

Good & Plenty #7 Winter 91-92

I'd like to thank you for buying this zine. I have put lots of hours and trips to the xerox machine to come up with this baby.Way back in September of 1991.I decided to start work on this zine and five months later,here is what came of it. I take all the credit for the typographical errors you may come across.I'm kinda lazy when it comes to proof-ing my work.I'd like to explain the raise in price also. Last year when the postal service decided to raise the price of postage,I got burned.This issue is also a bit thicker,more pages,hence the raise in price.I still feel it is fair.I have yet to meet a zine person who has made money on their zine.I am no exception.I don't keep track of my zines money.All I know is that after making trips to the post office,I am broke.They know me well there. Now I'd like to take the time to thank the people who have helped,inspired,and contributed to this zine(or all of the above)I have to give credit to these people,for without them,you wouldn't be reading this...Scott Larsen, Nathan Rodriguez(CRUMP),Tom Turner,Tom Rodriguez,Greg Brown,Dan Werle,Phil Jean,Doug Justine D.,Carl Riple, Meagan Montrose,Into Another,Iceburn,Seven League Boots, Ringpin,Lloyd and Eye For An Eye,Chris and Doc Hopper, Sean Coleman,Max and Lean To Go,Kelley and Say No More, Billingsgate,Good and Plenty the band,Slap of Reality, Megan Luther,Special thanks to the one person who has been there the longest,Matt Garcia.Even though it may not seem I am always grateful.I do appreciate all of your efforts.

I'd also like to especially thank Kim Nolan and Alyssa Chunk for their tremendous effort and support throughout this issue. Maybe the next time we get together,my hair won't turn pink... Is someone trying to tell me something?

GOOD & PLENTY BACK ISSUES

#4-Refuse,Even Score,Up Front, Inner Strength.7 Seconds,show reviews,tons of photos.$1.25

#6-Quicksand,Integrity,Chain-Gang,Sacred Reich,tons of photos. $1.75

all others sold out

DISTRIBUTION

I HAVE HAD GOOD AND BAD LUCK WITH DISTRIBUTION IN THE PAST.FOR THIS ISSUE,IF ANYONE IS INTERESTED IN SELLING G&P,PLEASE CONTACT ME.I DON'T REALLY HAVE A SET POICY.SO SPECIFICS ARE NEGOTIABLE.I NEED ALL THE HELP I CAN GET.

CONTEST WINNERS

IF ANYONE REMEMBERS,IN THE LAST ISSUE I HAD 3 CONTESTS.HERE ARE THE NAMES OF THE WINNERS...
1.(DISTRIBUTION) GREG BROWN
2.(MOLLY RINGWOLD) DREW KATCHEN
3.(TWIN PEAKS) KIM NOLAN

GOOD & PLENTY T-SHIRTS????

I do have a new design again.One sided,colored tees. These will be available as I make them.Please write first.

GOOD AND PLENTY ZINE
GABE RODRIGUEZ
2116 SALEM BLVD.
ZION IL. 60099

PHOTO BY ALYSSA CHUNK: GABE AND TOM OUTSIDE OF FENWAY PARK.

Hello again,and welcome to Good and Plenty Zine.Some of you may remember in my last issue,I said that it would be my final issue.I would be lying if I said that I never thought it to be true.So,I guess you could say that I lied.It has been a year since I last put out an issue,and a lot has happened since then.I met some new friends, and I lost some old ones.I've bought lots of records,and seen lots of shows,and done lots of mail.I never actually "stopped" doing the zine.I guess what happened was I had gotten bored with things at the time of my last zine.Actually,not much has changed as far as being bored,that has been constant.So why am I doing another issue?Basically,the same reason I started this baby three years ago.I am sick of sitting around and complaining and whining that nothing is going on.If I am not active myself in some way,I don't feel I have the right to complain.I hope to continue this zine for a long time,but I'm taking each issue one at a time.

This issue has been the hardest one to do for me,because of the fact that I had to start from scratch,and had to come up with most of it myself.I thank all those that have offered to help,but I know if I don't work day and night,it will never come out.Some may say that G&P has a new look.I have to agree.I welcome change.Change is what attracted me to the hardcore scene to begin with.A few people even suggested that I change the name of this zine.I wouldn't think of it.G&P is known for being a certain kind of zine,and maybe that is my fault,but I have no problem with that.One thing that has been constant throughout this zine,is me.I am still the same person now than I was 3 years ago,or 20 years ago when my parents named me.I don't think the same way as I did when I was one year old. so should I change my name?Fuck no!As long as this zine stands,it will remain G&P. I welcome all replies that anyone may have.I also welcome everyone to write the people interviewed in here.I gave addresses for that reason in particular.To anyone who sent stuff for review,I am sorry,but I don't review things.I am very picky with a lot of things,and I don't think I could ever be fair.You may notice a few ads,if anyone has problems with them,please let me know.

I hope you enjoy this baby as much as I did making it.I can't take all the credit.I was inspired by a lot of things,and I did have lots of help.Til next time-Enjoy. G&

I am confused. It's a good and a bad thing. It's good because it means I am thinking,it's bad because it drives me into states of insanity. Is hardcore more than music? Is it a mindless, teenage angst which ends when the participant turns twenty? Is it nothing more than a religion itself? Is it restrictive ? With the downside and sometimes mindlessness at a majority of shows, this may seem true at coming from the outside.

But hardcore is what you make it. It is whatever you want it to be. It is always changing.

Hardcore is hard to define because there are no limitations; the only walls placed up are knocked down by a group in opposition to them. That is one reason I don't see much unity within the "scene" and never have. This cycle of building up and knocking down keeps punk from ever becoming stagnant and sort of keeps it within the concept of an anti-establishment. But there is the argument that in being an anti-establishment it is itself an establishment. Punk though depends upon the individual, as not needs change so do the desires, concepts, struggles, and further to the direction of the bands, zines, clubs.

Perhaps I am struggling in my attempts to define or not to define it. I don't want to set up "standards" for anyone. Standards suck. I know what punk is to me. I don't know what it is to everyone else, but I do know that some of my closest friends are punks.

Knowing what punk is to me does keep me from feeling trapped within the scene at times . There are certain fucked up things that are happening within the scene, like in life that I just can't understand or accept. But it is the individuals interpretation of what punk/hardcore is. It may not be mine but it is someone's and I will disagree and voice it as well as set up an alternative to their definition(s). To me punk/hardcore is not about making money, is not about consuming, it runs more true than that. The fight to keep punk off their level is another battleground within our lives. It is another level to take action on for ourselves, and our expression, and thus our lives. It's the relationship and dichotomy that gives our lives control.

For some it is only punk, it is only money, it is only fashion. For some it is only an idea, only alternative, only a way of life. For some it remains on one level of life, for some it extends to various levels.

I hope this essay hasn't destroyed itself in existing. It's just these things are always on my mind and they continue to confuse and enlighten me. - Alyssa

---

SECOND:GUESS

Good & Plenty
FUGAZI
Reno Punk Fest

Second Guess, an offshoot of 7 Seconds' Second Thoughts, containing an interview with Fugazi's Brendan Canty, Good & Plenty's Gabe Rodriguez, an article on the Reno Punk Fest and much more. Please send $.75 and 2 stamps to Bob Conrad, PO Box 9382, Reno, NV 89507. New issue out in Spring.

INTO ANOTHER

When I heard that Ritchie from Underdog had another band,I was more than enthusiastic to hear it.I got all these descriptions from friends about them,like Ozzy,Judas Priest,and Bad Brains mixed.When I heard that the closest they were playing Chicago was Green Bay Wi.,I just had to go,and get the long awaited interview with Ritchie.(The Summer of '89 I was unable to get the Underdog interview.)Well,all I can say is listen to these guys with an open ear,and you may like it.Into Another are powerful live,and worth driving out of state to check out.

Tony-Bass
Drew-Drums
Peter-Guitar
Ritchie-Vocals

G&P:Who is all in the band?
Ritchie:Drew plays drums,(Bold Crippled Youth),Tony from Whiplash,a speed metal band plays bass.Peter Moses plays guitar.He's a guitar genius that we found.I sing.
G&P:How long have you been together?
Ritchie:We got together back in the summer of 1990.
G&P:What were you doing between that time,and the Underdog breakup?
Ritchie:Actually,Underdog was finished in the Fall of '89.That was when we played our last show.Drew and I have been talking about this since midway through Underdog.Even during my brief stint in Youth Of Today,we talked about doing something that wasn't really too hardcore.As soon as I stopped playing with Underdog,I got together with Drew and hung out and wrote songs.
G&P:Why did Underdog break up?

PLAYLIST

GABE
GREEN DAY
SAMIAM
BELINDA CARLISLE
EYE FOR AN EYE
KINGPIN
QUIT
JONES VERY
FUEL
PEARL JAM
SLAP OF REALITY
SEVEN LEAGUE BOOTS
RORSCHACH

DOWNCAST
FARSIDE
BAD RELIGION
SOULSIDE
CELTIC FROST
ICEBURN
BILLINGSGATE

TOMMY T.
SLAYER
EMBRACE
FARSIDE
SUPERTOUCH
KINGPIN
EYE FOR AN EYE
LEEWAY
INTO ANOTHER

MATT
HELMET
COFFIN BREAK
SOUNDGARDEN
SEVEN SECONDS
DROP ACID
L7
BABES IN TOYLAND
LUNACHICKS
HOLE
LOVE BATTERY
AFGHAN WHIGS
MUDHONEY
SKIN YARD
PEARL JAM
MOTHER LOVE BONE

ALYSSA CHUNK
GIVE ME BACK CONF.
X-RAY SPEX
EMBRACE
RORSCHACH
ARTICLES OF FAITH
ECONOCHRIST
JIMMY SWAGGART
HELMET
FURY
BLONDIE
FUEL
PISSED HAPPY CHILDREN

Ritchie: broke up the band by quitting.I wasn't really happy anymore.I wanted to play with-I hope nobody gets mad at me for this-better musicians.I love the guys in Underdog, but I wanted people who were more into writing and rehearsing and doing a full time thing.

G&P:Is there any chance that some Into Another songs or riffs are maybe "later" stuff that was really Underdog?

Ritchie:At first,Drew and I started writing songs and I was like using later Underdog riffs that I was coming up with.But eventually it just turned into an entirely different thing.There isn't one recycled Underdog riff.

G&P:How did you hook up with Revelation Records?

Ritchie:Isn't it weird that we are on Revelation?(Laughter)We were getting our money together to make a demo.We figured with the stuff we wanted to record,we were going to need a sizeable chunk of money.I don't know.I ran into Porcell one day at-Oh,he was working the juice bar at a health food store in New York.He just said to me,"Why don't you guys do your record on Revelation,and we'll pay for everything and it will be like an elaborately packaged demo,no strings attached?"And we were like,"Well,why not?"As it turns out,they have been very cool so far.A lot cooler than Caroline was with Underdog. Of course they don't have the money that Caroline has,but so what.They are 100 times more honest...I was less than happy with the way Underdog was handled by Caroline.

G&P:I have seen some pretty impressive ads for the Into Another lp. in Metal Forces and magazines like that.

Ritchie:Yeah,actually we weren't trying to hit everywhere.We also have ads in Option, Seconds and Maximum RockNroll.It is just,I guess those bigger mags have more circulation and colored ads.People see those and freak out on them.I don't know,Jordan was willing to spend a lot of money on advertising.I guess we're not really a metal band per say.

G&P:How has the turnout been at shows?

Ritchie:The shows we have played in New York have been well attended,with the exception of the New Music Seminar.On the tour,there have been moderately sized crowds,except Cleveland,but we've only played 3 shows so far.Pittsburg,and Columbus were farely small halls,and crowds.In Cleveland it was farely packed,probably because Shelter played.

G&P:Is the Album out?

Ritchie:Good Question.I hope so.(It is out now)It was actually supposed to come out on june 1st,but we ran into delays.It will be out in a few days.We do have cassettes on tour.All the formats are manufactured and packaged and ready for distribution.

G&P:I remember in Underdog,the lyrics hit a lot of subjects,how are they this time?

Ritchie:The songs are much less topical,and less heavy-handed.With the lyrics I am writing now,there is a lot more subtlety,analogy,and imagery.There aren't any political anthems.The songs range from masochism,to sexism...That is one topical song.

G&P:How would you describe Into Another musically?

Ritchie:We were joking about this yesterday.Our music is very involved.That's what we've decided.People have said (comparisons are so corny),they hear everything from old Sabbath,to Queen,Bad Brains,Judas Priest,Rush. I don't know.

GREEN BAY WI.PHOTO:GABE

G&P:Has it mainly been hardcore kids whoa have attended your shows?

Ritchie:Yeah,that's because of the bands we get booked with.I don't mind it at all. I just hope we play lots of other types of bills too.I want to play with all manner of bands.I don't want to play just HC shows,the way a lot of other bands composed with former HC band members do.

Ritchie.I'll never stop.I love getting tortured for 8 hours at a time. I am just completely addicted to them.I will be a Circus Freak someday...

G&P:I see you've gotten a lot of tattoos since we last saw you.

Ritchie:Outside of the music/hardcore scene, who or what influences you positively in your day to day life?

G.B WI.PHOTO:GABE

Ritchie:Do you know who John Robbins is? He wrote a book called, A Diet For A New America.He was the sole heir to the Baskin Robbins fortune,and he turned it all down because he is vegan,and completely against the exploitation of animals.He is totally against dairy farming.He went and lived in a log cabin for years,that he built.He wrote this book about vegan nutrition,and just world vegatarianism.He is one person who inspires me.

G&P:What is it like in New York city,for bands these days?

Ritchie:New York is a really awful place for bands to play.There is literally no place to play,except for CBGB'S.The whole musical world in New York is in bad shape.It's sad. Most bands pay to play in New York.The only bands that are making money or that are successful are the older bands that were successful years ago,and are just going through the motions...

G&P:Milking it?

Ritchie:Precisely.

G&P:What are some cool places to play?

Ritchie:Just from past experiences with Underdog,Minneapolis,San Francisco,Berkely, Seattle,Spokane,Green Bay...We played a boxing ring in Green Bay once.Lawrence Ks.

G&P:How does the future for Into Another look?

Ritchie:All we do is write songs.We have about three albums worth of songs written. Hopefully someone will want to put them out.We just want to tour.Basically stay out of New York.We didn't even book a tour this time in New York.

GET A LOAD OF THIS!

GET IT STRAIGHT!

BAD RELIGION · NEW ALBUM AVAILABLE NOW

ALL PHOTOS BY G-FORCE PHOTOGRAPHY
KEN RICHARDSON + CHRISTIAN KING
(except where noted)

3-17-91:THE CHANNEL

In the Spring of 1991,a friend of mine made me a video compliation of bands,all taped in the Boston area.He took it upon himself to throw on a few locals,one of which is a band called Eye For An Eye.(Thanks,Ed.)Since that time,I have tried my best at getting a hold of anything I could by them.They have quickly become one of my favorite bands.I just can't say enough about them.They have a 7" out now on Blackout Records,but that doesn't do them justice.Only seeing them live,can you get the full impact of Eye For An Eye,for which I have not had the pleasure,yet.While in Boston,I knew I had to get an interview with them.I was not disappointed.

EYE FOR AN EYE IS:
THOS-DRUMS
KEVIN-BASS
LLOYD-VOCALS
JAY-GUITAR

This is a very in depth,personal interview,that touches on some very important topics that I feel need to be addressed.Several time in this interview,when the Boston scene is referred to,any scene could be inserted,to apply in a more general sense.Present at the interview,was the whole band,Alyssa Chunx,and myself.At times,it does get kind of heated up,I only hope I didn't distort any of the feeling behind it by transcribing it on paper.I wish you all could have been there,but that is impossible.I encourage everyone to read on.Special thanks goes to Alyssa for coming through with the hot q's at the right time.And obviously,thanks to Eye For An Eye for being so honest in this interview.You may or may not agree with everything,but at least read it for yourself, write the band,talk about it.If this interview sparks conversation,I think it has served an added bonus.

G&P:How long has this line-up been together?

Kevin:About,since the spring of 1989.

G&P:Obviously,you have had other members when you first started out,but did you honestly think that you'd last this long?

Thos:Honestly,I really didn't think about it.I was in this band,and just having a good time.Originally,I thought,wow,maybe someday we could play a show.That was about how far I was thinking at the time.And after that I thought,maybe we could play the Channel,(a big club in Boston)or maybe even the Rat.Some place with more than one or two hundred people.

Kevin:There are different levels of a band.When you first start out,it's like,"Wow,maybe we'll get paid."Then maybe play another city,then maybe do a little tour.Now we are like,maybe if we could get on Warner Bros.and make millions of dollars.(jokingly)It's the next logical step.

Lloyd:Obviously.

G&P:You have a 7" on Blackout Records that has been out for a while now,(March '91)how did that come about?

Jay:We me Bill (Blackout) in NYCity a while ago.We used to go down with Wrecking Crew,to New York a lot when they'd play.We had met lots of people and Bill was one of them.It came down down to the fact that he was interested in a Boston band,and at the time we were the most favorable Boston band unsigned.-But we never did sign anything.You can quote us on that.

Kevin:That is why we are gonna get snapped up by Warner Bros.

G&P:I saw your 7" in the store the other day,and it was $4.99.What is the deal with that?

Jay:That is a hard issue.I found out about the price when I saw it in a record store.

Lloyd.Distributors get it for $2.50.What happened was,when we were sitting down talking about the possibilities on how to do the format etc.,Bill asked us about having it be a full color poster.We were all like ,"Great." Brilliant idea.Once the reality actually hit that it was going to cost money,and it was going to cost him a little bit more money,and when it hit the stores,the stores will see it and think that it is kind of thick.It isn't just folded cardboard with a record in the middle,they thought then they could put an extra dollar on it easily.We never thought that people would think about that.The record company didn't put any restrictions on it saying that it couldn't be sold for more than $3.50.Record stores do their own thing. →

Alyssa:Does it bother you that it is that much?

Lloyd:Yeah,endlessly.

Thos:I would never spend that much on a 7".

Kevin:It is kind of embarrassing.

Jay:It puts us in a vice practically.It is not our fault that the record is that much.If we had it our way, it wouldn't be.Our image gets pinned because of it.I have gotten letters asking why it is so much.So,(it seems) the reason being it so much falls in our hands.Besides designing the record,and playing the music,that's all we had to do with it.The rest was in the hands of somebody else.You are kind of powerless in terms of how much it will be.

G&P:With a name like Eye For An Eye,do you ever get like a bad reputation by that alone where people would misinterpret what you are about?

Jay:The zine No Answers,well I have never met the guy,and I respect the zine a lot though.He thought,that before he even read the record,or heard of us,and was about to play the record for review,he thought we were going to be some hard,up your ass,paddle thrash,macho,harder than nails band,because of our name.Then he heard it and thought differently about it.We even had an incident with Sam McPheeters about that too.

Lloyd:Yeah,that was really funny because he even knew us personally-or at least he knew me personally.We played a show with them in Boston and he didn't even step inside to see the band.We just heard that Sam thought we were some sort of Slapshot wannabee band,because of our name.And then,come to find out,he knew us. I was like,"Sam,that is my band."And he was just like,"Oh."It was really funny.

Kevin:I think we got booked in DC,at that recent Fall Brawl because of that type of thing.They were all the "tough guy"type bands.I'm not dissin' them or anything,but that was my perception.We got booked at that show, and kids were like,"What the fuck?"

Thos:This is a place where kids are getting hit with chairs and bottles outside.

Jay:Talk about first impression of the DC scene...We get there and everyone was like smoking some sort of drug,taking some sort of drug,or drinking some sort of drug.

Thos:Yeah,the show ends where everyone gets maced.There was a smoke machine running,and I think it got caught in there or something.It was everywhere.

G&P:I have several live tapes of you guys where you talk about a song that you recorded for a compilation that I never heard or saw anywhere.What happened to that?

Thos:Well,John was supposed to come tonight,and he would have been the man to ask.How many people have never finished a product that they started.I think it's safe to say everybody has.

Lloyd:Yeah,that's exactly what happened.But,unfortunately,it was hyped quite a bit.Because it was one of the first compilations of the "new" Boston bands.It was about 2 years ago.We recorded,"What It Means" for it. Actually,it has gotten some radio airplay.(the song)

Jay:The comp. was supposed to be called,Boston Hardcore 1990.

G&P:I have noticed that a lot of your newer songs are quite different from your older style of songs.A lot bands get slack for "progressing",or whatever.Have you experienced any of that?

Lloyd:Yes,over this year especially.If you look at our single,the songs are old.When we were recording it the songs were old.And now it's even older.Actually we didn't write songs for a while because the single was coming out.Since then we've written quite a few new songs.And 4 or 5 songs definitely will change a set quite a bit.This year we have been getting feedback saying we've slowed down,some people say the power isn't there anymore.We've gotten the whole array of opinions,the good and the bad. →

3-17-91:THE CHANNEL

EYE FOR AN EYE
SOUL IN MIND

Kevin:We are just trying to stay contemporary.I don't want to play songs that go 100 miles an hour,cause I don't like really listening to that shit.

Jay:We were just listening to Gang Green today.

Kevin:Yeah,but it was cool when they did it because it was like 10 years ago.Some bands can do retro music well,but I'm better doing stuff that is new.

Jay:That is definitely a strong point of our writing,is that our ideas of what we want to produce are so completely different.We conflict when we write,but as a whole,that is what makes us unique in our songs.

G&P:Yes,I do think you do have a unique sound,and there isn't a whole lot that you could be compared to.

Thos:Thank you very much.

G&P:You did do a short tour over the summer,correct?

Kevin:Short,yeah.Brief.If you can call it a tour.But I thought on tours,people went to see you.

G&P:So it really didn't work out well for you?

Lloyd:That's the thing.We were working pretty hard,and we got a chance to jump on a tour that wasn't really ours originally.It was done by a promoter that has done pretty well in Boston up to that point.We knew him personally,so it was like,"You need us to tour,fine we'll do it." But come to find out,the tour was pretty...Well,a lot of corners were cut on that tour.(laughs)

Thos:Yeah,kind of a round tour.

Kevin:We got stiffed like every single night.

Lloyd:We lost amazing amounts of money.We played to disgustingly small crowds.

Thos:But it was an invaluable experience that I wouldn't trade for anything,If I had to do it again,I'd definitely do it differently.We learned more in 17 days than we did in the past two years.

Jay:We learned about ourselves,about our limitations,or how to deal with certain things like diet...It was like,I had just gotten back from California,and the day I got back,they were like, "We are leaving for tour in 3 days."I was all excited.But it was kind of miserable.

Thos:But it was a good kind of miserable.

Jay:No.If it wasn't for like eating nachos, bread,and water everyday for 2 weeks.

Kevin:If it wasn't for losing money,it would have been good.

Thos:If I wasn't with you guys,I would have snapped.

Lloyd:Tours are definitely a hands on-do it yourself thing.

Alyssa:What is this about Eye For An Eye having a lawyer?I am just curious as to what made you decide to get one.

Jay:Specifically,because we have a merchandising contract.

PHOTO:JUSTINE De METRICK

Alyssa:Ok,can you start from there?

Kevin:When you get to a certain point in a band,where you get contracts thrown at you,like record contracts,t-shirt contracts,or even shows.When we play out we give a contract.

Alyssa:Like a guarantee?What is yours?

Kevin:It varies.When we played ABC NO RIO,we got paid 30 bucks.

Lloyd:We book everything ourselves. I have booked every single show we've played this year except the tour.John Regan helped us out a little bit.

Kevin:But you need a lawyer.Because when you deal with business people... Contracts are set up to screw you,and I don't know exactly what is standard for the industry.

Alyssa:Is it like,where your lawyer is your advisor?

Thos:Yes.But you have to realize,we have a punk rock lawyer.She just graduated from college,she's pretty punk rock.We know her. →

ALYSSA,EYE FOR AN EYE,+ TOMMY T.

Kevin:We payed her fifty bucks.It's not like any of us are rich.She said if we play her party,she'll do it and we'd pay her 50 bucks to look at our contracts.It's is not like we are this hube conglomeration,cause we haven't fucking made anything since we started

Jay:It is also good to have a lawyer, in the sense that,if you ever get into trouble,legally you may need help. Whether you want to avoid it,deal with it,or glorify it.We don't know anything about the music business.We know about music.If we need a reference point,or if we need to say,"Don't talk to us,talk to this person." That's why a lawyer helps out.

Thos:This person is an entertainment lawyer also.This is not somebody who goes to murder trials,or sues big corporations,or does headhunting.This is an entertainment lawyer,whose business is music.

Alyssa:Let's talk about your merchandising contract.Do you have a 2 year contract?

Thos:yes.

Lloyd:I actually work at this place too...People have got to realize.It's like,punk rock has been around for about twenty years now.

Thos:According to the guy in MRR,it has only existed for 5 years.In the "What's the Scoop" section,the question was,how do you see punk rock in 10 years.This guy answered that it only existed for 5,so he didn't think it will exist in 10 years.

Kevin:It is about playing music.Our band is at the point,where we can't just shake someones hand and say it's cool.People aren't nice on a whole.

Lloyd:They never were.Think of the Sex Pistols,EMI.The earliest scandal in the world.It is like, since there has been money in it,since day 1-Iggy Pop,Velvet Underground,whoever you want to talk about.Since day 1,since punk rock bands have been commercially applicable...

Alyssa:See,that's not what it's about.

Lloyd,That's not what it is about,but...

Alyssa:That's what it has turned into.

Lloyd:NO,NO,NO.That's what it was from the beginning.That's what it was when I was sperm.Ok.

Jay:It only has become a big issue now because there is money in it.

Alyssa:There seems to be a bigger dichotomy now.You are either a band like Born Against,that doesn't even make t-shirts,or a band that makes their own shirts and sells them for 5 dollars,very do it yourself.Or you are a band like Bad Religion.

Jay:Bad Religion have a huge merchandising contract.

Thos:We tried to do our own shirts,they suck.They looked really bad.

Alyssa:It seems to be,that there is one movement that is about being very DIY,and they want to bring that back. They say,Fuck the lawyer,we want to do things ourselves. They are only concerned about getting to a certain level, and then staying there.Like Fugazi for instance.They are the epitome of the DIY thing.

Thos:If I had the biggest independent record label for the past 10 years,we'd be on it,and we'd be doing it ourselves.If there was a Dischord Records we could be on, we'd be as pure in our ideals as Fugazi.

Kevin:I am sorry,I don't have any fuckin' money.I can't start my own record label.I can't make my own t-shirts. It's the fuckin'90's,you just can't.Maybe these kids can because of their parents.I have no fuckin' money.

Lloyd:You just started to say it,the big issue that these people just don't understand.See,Ian MacKaye is not a poor kid.He never was a poor kid.It's like,Sam McPheeters is not a poor kid,he has an inheritance.They have capitol.We don't have capitol.

Kevin:We don't got no money. →

7-91;the EDGE

Alyssa:There are ways of going about it,I think...
Kevin:You got to understand,I play bass.I'm not a fuckin' t-shirt manufacturer.I have to work.
Jay:What you (Alyssa) are trying to establish here,in the big picture,is you are trying to say what is right and what is wrong.
Alyssa:Right.But I don't it isn't as black and white,I know.I am just trying to give a perspective that I know a lot of people would say about hearing you have a lawyer.I don't think things are as black and white. A lot of people do.
Thos:We do have a lawyer,yes.And we do have a merchandising contract,but if people took the time to talk to us about it,they'd realize that it really is DYI.-(laughter)DIY...whatever.It's really DYS.
Jay:DOA.
Lloyd:It's DYS.They are behind it all.They always have been in Boston.'
Thos:It is very DIY,because our lawyer is our friend.
Lloyd:We knew her a year before we knew she was even going to be a lawyer.
Thos:We are doing her a favor.We are her first paying client.And she is doing us a favor because she is using knowledge she has to help us out.Just like the guy who started our merchandising thing,he used to work for Zec Records-a very punk rock place,which is very PC...meaning punk correct.(laughter)Zed records is a cool place.It's very hip.
Lloyd:But they bootleg like crazy.
Jay:The whole thing about bands selling out,or trying to stay pure or keep the values of what we have defined as hardcore music, but when I was a kid,hardcore was always about doing what you wanted to do.And whether you wanted to be pure.or trade in all of your artistic freedom for contracts,that is what you wanted to do.
Lloyd:That is not what we want to do.
Jay:The funny thing about hardcore in the '90's,is that when I was younger,and more of an observer than a part of the controlling aspect of it,I always saw it as something that was entertainment,but as well as an educational thing at the same time. Something that spoke out against all the hypocrisies,or something that spoke out about something positive.These days,it seems at least in my eyes.to have split.There was a happy medium when I was a kid.
Alyssa:Now it seems like a bigger dichotomy.It is incredible. It's like there are two different races.In Boston,you have Cringe Productions,(which is the big promoter of national acts.)There is also a smaller,more grass roots group of people trying to do shows in Boston,called Tools of the Revolution.There is a big dichotomy there.I see it getting bigger and bigger.You were talking to me earlier how when you played the show that Tools Of The Revolution,(TOR),put on,it was a bad experience.
Lloyd:We have had bad experiences at Cringe shows also.
Jay:The thing about that TOR show,was people put preconceptions on us,that we were rockstars.I am sorry,but that's bullshit.I went into that show with an open mind.I was like,"These kids are what I'm about.I'm vegetarian,I'm straight edge,I'm so rebellious up your ass,you couldn't believe it.I can really relate to these people."I got it thrown back in my face.That's bullshit.
Kevin:This is Kevin speaking now,not Eye For An Eye,this is me. These kids who have been into hardcore for 2 years,who have all these preconceptions about us...We've been doing this more than most bands do,and we make no fuckin' money.Make no beefs about it,we make shit.So,we can have all these contracts and shit,and we'll still make no money.We do shows,and we lose fuckin' money. So all you kids who talk about us as money grubbin' whatever,can go suck my dick!We make no money,probably never will.I bust my ass in everything I do.I'm not a t-shirt manufacturer,I'm not a lawyer,I can't look at record contracts to see where I'm getting screwed.You need people to do that,at least we do.Maybe some people are gifted and can do their own record company,or have rich parents to help them out,I don't.We make no fuckin' money. You can kiss my ass.I'm just sick of kids coming up to me like I'm a fuckin' rock-star making millions of dollars.And the fact is,I'm getting my car repossessed,cause I'm not responsible,and work and shit.It fucks my job up.You can't lead a normal life and do the band thing,for the most part.I put my heart and soul into it,and to have these kids think I'm a money-grubbin'-bastard because I want to make 500 bucks at a show,when we draw 350 kids. Cause if we don't make that money,the club does.When we don't get paid,it goes to the club or the promoter.So,I feel like,we are bringing the kids there,we should get a little of the money to pay for our bills.We have rehearsal space,we have vans we have to rent,cause we never make enough money to buy a van.
Lloyd:We don't even hold on to enough money to make t-shirts regularly,and that's why we are doing the t-shirt contract.That's the specific reason we entered into it.We are gonna finally free up some money so we can do what we want with it.We're gonna do a newsletter,we're gonna have some mail-order stuff. →

SUN. DEC. 8 2PM
WELL WEED OUT THE SHIT
5$
FOR AN
1.6 BAND
MereL
Doc Hopper
V.F.W Hall
Tools of revolution

STATEMENT of PURPOSE

As a group of people who go to Shows, we are getting pissed off at only seeing huge bands with a lot of records out and local Boston bands. We hope to provide an alternative to the money sucking, big business venues of the Boston scene. There are a lot of bands that work totally hard and tour constantly, yet never show up in Boston. WHY? Because the bands can't guarantee thousands of dollars at the door. For example: Jawbreaker, Destroy, Fuel, Admiral, cringer, M.D.C, Subvert, 15, Citizen Fish, Monsula, Econochrist, Oi Polloi, Green Day, Filth, NOFX, Phleg Camp, Inflatable Children, Screeching Weasel, etc... All of these bands have toured within the past year and a half and have played nearby cities, but not here. Now we want to offer a place for all bands to play. We aren't interested in kissing ass of bands or people, so leave your attitude at the door! In order for this to last more than one show we need the cooperation and hopefully the involvement of everyone. We are responsible for this hall, and it cost a lot of money, so please don't wreck it, graffiti, etc. With the help of everyone, this could be a springboard for a new spark in a stagnant scene. See you at the show.

contact: Sean-[redacted] NICK & JUSTINE [redacted]
TOOLS o f REVOLUTION

P.GREG BROWN BALT.MD. 7-91

3-17-91:THE CHANNEL

Kevin:I see these kids with their $90 Stussy shirts,telling me how I'm screwing them.
-the conversation goes on...
Alyssa:I go to the big Cringe shows,and I fucking hated going to them half of the time.I'd just feel so alienated,and stupid.and I'd ask myself,why am I doing this?
Jay:(To Alyssa)How long have you been going to shows?
Alyssa:About 4½ years.
Jay:That's good.Because we've all been going to shows since about '85.I'm not bragging or anything.But I know I have felt that community feeling.(that you feel)
Thos:I felt more alienated at that TOR show,then at the biggest show we ever did at the Channell.
Kevin:Those kids don't like us.There's two different scenes.
Alyssa:Yes,there two totally different scenes.
Lloyd:But why?They are not.
Alyssa:I think a lot of people have been alienated,and pushed out so to speak,at the Cringe shows in Boston.
Jay:Why do you think they have been pushed out?
Alyssa:You go to a Cringe show,and it is sometimes the most alienating experience.
Lloyd:Why?
Alyssa:Maybe because when I go to those shows,I am sick of big men,standing up there yelling at me.
Lloyd:You mean the jock,skinhead type people?
Kevin:Hardcore has been that way since 1981.
Lloyd:I got chased out of one of the oldest clubs in Boston,at one of the first shows I went to in '84,being called "nigger" all the way out the door.And it's like,I didn't stop going to shows.That's a little bit of an alienation.I felt alienated at that show.But I went back,because I loved what I was feeling.I didn't care that three guys,bald shitheads,who were no better than the rednecks who beat me up all my life,were gonna sit there and call me nigger and chase me out of that show.That means,all right,I'm out of that show.I go back to the next one,and I go back.Who gives a shit.
Alyssa:I kept going back to shows also.
Kevin:This whole "PC" thing has been going on for how long now?
Lloyd:And it is an elitist movement.It is such an elitist movement.It's like,"Oh,we are sick of dealing with the moron scumbags who don't have the intelligence or the education to understand where this music trully come from,or what the bands are truly trying to say to you.So let's make our own shows and tell them."
Alyssa:It is more a thing like,"Fuck everything else,we'll make our own thing."
Lloyd:No.Because it has been around for too long,and includes too many different people,too many different attitudes,to subdivide.I just don't understand how can people narrow it down;the color of a person,the type of person,the way they dress,a mindset,and say,"Now,this is the right way to be punk!"You can't...But they are (saying that). "They" being a very general term used for people in HC that follow rules such as these we are speaking of.It is like,you can't be sexist,homophobic,racist,a meateater,or you can't condone violence. It is like,who do you think you are?It's like,you are trying to tell me that you are not a racist,sexist, homophobic,etc...You don't even know yourself yet.You are 18,19 20 years old.I don't even know myself.I'm discovering myself everyday.
Jay:(to Alyssa)This isn't a two-sided thing.We are on your side.Another thing,Cringe is not an ideal situation,because he is not from hardcore.He is trying to apply himself to something that he isn't about.I'm not putting him down.What he is doing is his interpretation of what he thinks audiences will like,it isn't always the correct thing.The other thing I wanted to say,about Lloyd's point,is about all of these rules;straight edge,racism,sexism,meat eating etc...It is a really tough thing to explain,but are these things really you, or are they consuming you,or are you consuming them?I'm not saying that what I'm about is bullshit,or that I have had second thoughts about this or that.This is really tough to explain,but a lot of times,you can't apply these rules to a general consensus,because everyone feels different ways.A lot of people become violent about being peaceful,and about being vegetarian. →

Kevin:It's like the whole youth crew thing.Jay has done it.But a lot of kids who were in all those youth crew bands,burned themselves out on it,because they had all these rules.
Jay:It is a surface thing,these rules,and it will pass with time,as we have seen a lot of rules pass.When it is a spiritual foundation,then it will stay.When it is really internalized,then it will remain a part of you.
Lloyd:Spirit meaning not body,not mind.
Kevin:A lot of these kids follow these trends so much that they completely go in the other direction.Look at me,I used to drink and do drugs.But a lot of kids do the opposite,and really fuck themselves up,just to rebel against the whole straight edge thing.
Jay:I am glad we are talking about this,we are actually getting a lot out,that I've been thinking about.
Kevin:I used to go to shows,and just watch bands,and I never really thought about the stuff that people ram down my throat now.It's almost like going to church.It is...It's a fun thing.(shows)The bands should kick some knowledge to the kids,But I don't want to see a sermon.If I did I'd go to church.
Lloyd:The church of your choice.
Kevin:And at least your priest would know what the fuck he was talking about.I'm about 95% on that "PC" shit, but I hate those kids preaching to me.They are like preaching to the converted.If they want to preach to people that are like the things they are against,then go to a fuckin' mall.
Jay:People who are that black and white,bands,individuals,they are practically doing exactly what the so called Christian church is doing.
-the conversation goes on...and on...and on...
Jay:A lot of times I feel that I can't escape hardcore,and sometimes I feel the need to.You can't tell me there isn't one person in this room ,who at one time or another has said to themselves,"I just want to forget the scene altogether!"
Thos:(to Gabe)I should be paying you for this.This is like therapy.
-I got into a conversation with Jay about Shelter for a while.I feel it is important to include some of it, but not to dwell on it since this really isn't the place for it,considering he is only 1/4 of the band.
G&P:Jay,what is the deal with you and Shelter?I have heard your name pop up with theirs a few times.
Jay:If we talk about this,this is not the bands opinions.These are my personal ideas.
Thos:Ray and Jay go way back.Check out the back cover of Break Down The Walls,over Ray's shoulder.He snuck out past his bed-time to see that show.
Kevin:Lloyd is on the Sick of it All lp.
Lloyd:If you want to see how hard I am,(sarcastically)see me in the pit at a SOIA show.
Kevin:Afterwards,he helped them carry their money back to the van.(laughter)
Jay,if you want to talk about me and Shelter,last summer I was going to play second guitar for them.Ray Cappo as a person,has been a very influential person in my life.Whether you think he is a complete loser,or whether you think he is god,I see him as a friend,not as someone who I want to be,if you can catch my drift.I learned a lot from him,but I don't want to be him,I want to be me.If you want to tag me or label me as a Hare Krishna, that is your business,but there is a lot more to it than that.
Thos:As far as tying that into the band,well that is Jay.And people can call him whatever they want,but he's still my friend Jay.He may be thinking what he's thinking,but I may be thinking whatever.I think we can all agree that there is more to this world than what you can see.
Kevin:Everybody has got their own thing going on,and we really are individuals,but we all work well together, and respect what everybody else is doing,even if we don't necessarily agree with it.
G&P:What is in the future for Eye for an Eye?
Thos:I think it's about time we put out some new recorded material.We've got a lot of new stuff,and lots of new things to say.
Jay:It's really hard to say,because a lot of the confusion that was sparked in this interview does effect how we feel,our motivation towards the band,towards hardcore.It's hard to predict the future.We'll definitely still be together.We are going strong.Criticisms will come and go,either negative or positive.Thats the way it always works.As cheesy as it sounds,we're gonna do what's in our hearts.A lot of thanks and love goes out to people who have supported us.It can be an ego soother,but it can also be a thing that keeps you going.
Kevin:We're also looking for a second guitar player.Send us a tape.Obviously you'd have to move to Boston.
Thos:Unless you have a really nice Wireless.

EYE FOR AN EYE

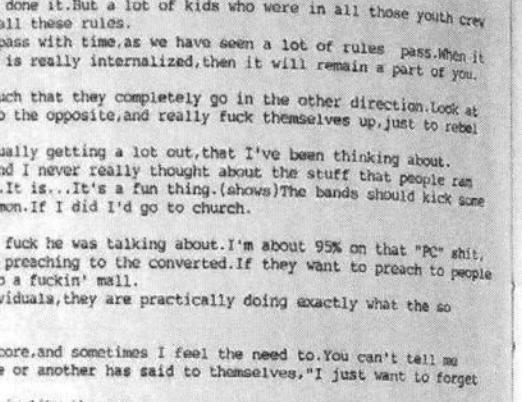

7-91:THE EDGE

EYE FOR AN AYE; C/O J.GROTIAN
24 FISKE PL.
CAMBRIDGE MA. 02139

7 LEAGUE BOOTS

Seven-League Boots

A league equals 4·828 kilometres, and seven-league boots enable their wearer to cover 33·696 kilometres at a single step. Little else is known about this footwear, except that it fits anyone who manages to steal the boots from a previous owner. For example, Hop o' My Thumb, the smallest boy of ten who ever wore shoes, stole seven-league boots from a giant and they fitted him perfectly. The boots played an essential part in his subsequent career as a king's messenger.

GREEN BAY WI. P.GABE

BOW THAYER-GUITAR
MICHAEL PRESS-DRUMS
RICHARD FEINS-BASS
BOBBY SULLIVAN-VOCALS

On March 12 1989,I had the chance to see Soulside in Chicago,and it was nothing short of spectacular.Good and Plenty zine was barely even a thought in my head back then,but I regret not up to them and interviewing them.Well,in September of 1991,i had the chance to see a band called Seven League Boots.I admit,I was inticed by the fact that Bobby Sullivan sang for them, but as you can hear from the music,this band is a lot more than just a singer from an old hardcore band.I had a chance to interview Bobby after the show.At the request of Seven League Boots,I am going to try my best to make this more than just a transcribed interview.He talked forever,so that is going to be kinda hard.Here goes:

Bobby:We are getting together a policy of not doing interviews, just because,like transcribed interviews,well I never read 'em. Also,like the problems in Soulside were when we did interviews, a lot of the shit was addressed to me,and we felt differently about things,that caused tension in the band.Especially with personal ideology...What you say really doesn't make a difference,it's what you do and how you live.It is easy for people to talk about things without really subscribing to what they say.That is why I don't have much faith in interviews when I'm reading them.I do like to read ones of new bands.
-the show was very small in Green Bay,because the location changed at the last minute.But a 2½ hour drive was well worth it to see this band.I had never heard them before,but it only took hearing one song of their soundcheck to hook me.I asked Bobby what it was like touring on a smaller level than he was familiar with in Soulside.
Bobby:You know,in Soulside,we never thought we were that big.I don't know,it's like I don't remember.In Boston we played to pretty big audiences.Since we are more accessable,we get booked on bigger bills,like EMF,Bob Harvey,lots of bad bands.In Boston,if we wanted to, 7LB could play with Jimmy Cliff,or we could play with Fugazi. Now,it's nice to play to different audiences,and try to open their minds,rather than play to people who supposedly have open minds.Actually,an audience is an audience...It also seems the bigger the audience gets,the less communication there actually is going on.So it was like......

...the bigger Soulside got,the less people were actually listening to what we were trying to do,which was make people dance in a different way than slam dancing.

-Seven League Boots have been playing for about 2 years,and have a 7" out on Constant Change.Which is a sub of Flux records out of RI.If you are having trouble finding the record, write:2028 W.Main Rd.Middletown RI. 02840 USA. I asked Bobby about the focus of the band.

Bobby:We don't have one message or idea that we all agree on.If there is anything that we are about,it's being individuals,and not being part of a large group or following,whether it be straight edge,Rasta,or whatever.I think aligning yourself with a group is like selling your individual self short. You may have a lot of things in common with people in the group,and unity is real important,especially when you are a minority.But alot of times you think you are a minority ,when you are really not.

-of all places 7 League Boots originates from Boston. with the reputation of that scene being the one of the harder than you attitude,I didn't see that as true with these guys.Here are some thoughts on Boston...

Bobby:It is almost like you can't even depend on a draw,because the kids are in and out.During the school year.it's packed with all these kids and they all just want to party.Come summer,it's an entirely different group of people.Or if you play one club,it is this type of crowd,and another club has that type of crowd.If possible,I'd like to play to a new audience every night.I enjoy that a lot better than playing to the same people,cause I don't expect people to like us that much,that they would see us that often.It's really demanding on an audience to expect them to keep coming back.In any sense,it is like,it gets started,and the same people got to the same shows and so on. As soon as people get sick of a band,it's like ,they shouldn't have to go to the show,if they don't like the band,just because they are part of the scene.It is hard to tell if there is a scene any-where ANYMORE.It seems the same people go to the same shows,but it's less of a cohesive thing... Before,in the hardcore scene,you had to be playing hardcore to be liked.But now,you could play about anything.

G&P:How did Seven League Boots hook up?
Bobby:I was the last to admit that Soulside was done,or at least the last one to realize it.I was finishing up school in Boston.Basically,Soulside was pretty much broken up,but I figured that I'd go home and at least practice and see if we wanted to keep doing it,but that just never happened.When I was up in Boston,I played with a bunch of people.I actually played with a bunch of guys in Slapshot.It was like when the Stars and Stripes thing came out.The other people in the band wanted to do an answer to that,basically...the opposite..It was Jaime from SSD...

...Stever Steve,and me.We just did a few practices,and it really didn't work.They wanted to do more of a rocknroll type of thing...Our bass player Richard and I were freinds up in Boston,and one day he was telling me he was going down to jam with these guys,and if I wanted to come with.I said,"What the fuck".We wrote 3 songs right off the bat.We had a set like after a month.We just really clicked together.None of the guys had ever heard of Soulside.Richard was into punk rock.The drummer andthe guitar player had been in a band since high school,and were doing Rolling Stones,Grateful Dead type stuff.So of course they never heard of Soulside.It is funny.My influence on the band is doing the reggae stuff,and they all want to play hard now,cause they have been laying back all their lives.

-It seems that 7 League Boots may draw a crowd a little older than the average teen may relate to.This creates the delima of over 21 shows.I asked him about that.
Bobby:Yeah,we'd play them.I don't think it's fair.The problem is, and this is something that the hardcore scene has done to themselves,it's that when you play at all ages show,you are going to be playing an underage show.It's not all ages.That's because the HC scene is so violent,that someone who is my age is not gonna want to go to the show.You know,I don't want to go to a show and have to watch my back.I want to watch the band.And the HC scene did that to themselves,they deserve it.From a band standpoint,you know,you get offered a show,and it's with a band that you want to play with and even though it is restricted...I can't justify it. But we would play one,because it is so hard to survive today as a band.

-Since I did have Bobby Sullivan in the car for an interview,I had to ask a few Soulside questions...
G&P:Did you ever play a show with the Cure?
Bobby:We had a show with the Cure in Budapest. but they bumped us.They said it was cancelled. Our bass player and Drummer like hitchhiked their way there anyway,cause we had a day off. The show was still going on.It would have sucked anyway.

-the conversation turns to a comparison of 7 League Boots and Soulside...
Bobby:A lot of people we see say they like us better than Soulside...Soulside was something we grew up on,and couldn't seperate ourselves from.It ended up hurting us,especially our relationships with each other.That kind of red the fuel for the band.Toward the end it was like me and Scott were going head to head.The only way I could justify it was to put it in the music.It was like,well if we do feel differently about these things,then we'll fight it out on stage,and that will be our music.That is why the last album is...I don't know,I think it is a kinda depressing record.A lot of the shit that I wanted to say,I had to say in a different way that wasn't so obvious.because the people in-

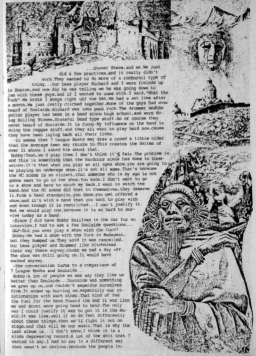

PHOTO:BRIAN SIMMONS

Bobby cont...:the band were reacting against my outspoken views.Meanwhile,I didn't want to impose my views on the rest of the band just because I feel that way and my instrument is words.It's not fair to impose them on everyone else,and have them have to answer to my words.It was a dilema, but it worked itself out.We really couldn't have gone any farther.

G&P:Would you consider maybe a solo effort so that you could express all your views?
Bobby:No,I don't like bands that have one person as the leader.Like the Henry Rollins band.Most-likely,he isn't the main leader.You know,they got such incredible musicians.. Part of the thing about music that brings people together,is the example of those 4,5,or 9 people on stage.It's what brings them together.Even though they're different,they coexist on the level of spirituality or whatever you want to call music.

-During the set,Bobby mentioned something about the pot fest happening in Madison soon.The conversation moved in that direction as I asked him about it.No sooner did a cop stop by the car to check on things.
Bobby:In boston,when we started,we did a lot of stuff about marijuana and decriminalisation and stuff like that...(To me)Is that the cops?
Johnny Law:There's been a lot of alcohol consumption and pot smoking here,and we're just checking it out making sure there's nothing illegal going on.
G&P:We are just doing an interview.
Bobby:We're doing an interview about this very thing.
Johnny Law:Do you guys have any I.D?
-after checking my I.D.,he left.
G&P:You mentioned PotFest in Madison during the set.Have you ever been to one?
Bobby:No.
G&P:I was at one.I got there late,but people were telling me about how helicopters dropped all this marijuana in the middle of the city,and all weekend,there was people smoking it everywhere.On the streets,on the capital building,everywhere.The cops did not bust anyone.

Bobby:I think the whole thing with pot is...Well,to thrive on it would be exploiting it as a symbol.We included an insert in our 7" about marijuana and it's history.I think it's important because.mainly just as an example of how the US gov't works.During colonization,there were certain things that people didn't understand.They classified things as European and Non-European,and pot was one of the things that they didn't understand.Basically,they don't have public health in mind at all when they make pot illegal.It's solely a business venture.That is how the US gov't works.Business is above everything.You can pick up lots of books on the subject.the Emperor Wears No Clothes,and more. George Bush is even personally tied in with it because a lot of his money comes from pharmaceuticalcorporations,which marijuana would eliminate some of their business,because of its therapuetic use.Even the leaves and fabric,the reason it was edged out as a resource and because Dupont was apt to lose a lot of business.I wouldn't want to thrive on it,especially since I smoke pot,and you know,people wouldn't really take me serious about it.But I think people should do as much research on it ,so they can.And the insert in our 7" comes from this book that is written pretty well,and an out-of-print book that you would never be able to find.So I sampled it and put it in.But as like,"This is our manifesto",just as some reading material!

Write in Seven League Boots coming
Constant Change,2028 West Main Rd.
Middletown RI.02840 USA

PHOTO:BRIAN SIMMONS

SEVEN LEAGUE BOOTS

Big Book

How can I be aware
  of where we are
When all our history
  does'nt seem to be
Taught to children rightously

We celebrate Columbus Day
When he found our land
he was looking for slaves
Sailed the sea by an evil wind
to kill the American Indian

Heard the news in Italy
  bought Bury My Heart at Wounded
  Knee
He sailed the sea by an evil wind
to kill the Arawak Indian

What kind of problem solvers
  are we going to be,
Without some truth in history

iceburn

After a long trip to Dekalb Il,and a long and powerful set by Iceburn,I decided to interview them,even though I had
quit the zine.Have you ever seen a band play a set,and just kicked
back and watch,but break out in a sweat anyway?Well,I did just that
after Iceburn's set.They are starting to develop their own style and
when they perfect it,and put it on vinyl,be sure to pick it up.
Any band that makes you sweat should be taken note of...

Doug-Bass 20
Chad-Drums-19
Gentry-Guitar-20

G&P:So you guys are on tour now right?
Gentry:We have been on tour for four days.The van broke down today.
G&P:Are any of the shows worth mentioning?
Chad:Denver was cool,but Lincoln was a dud.Denver was cool because we played with
a band called Lungfish.
G&P:What did you think of tonight's show.(Dekalb Il.)
Chad:I don't know.I slept about one hour last night,and ate very little.
Gentry:It is funny to see peoples reaction to us.
G&P:It is not every day that you see a band that plays 10 minute songs.
Gentry:Do you think they get boring though?
G&P:If the music is there and it packs a good punch,then I think it doesn't.And that
is how I perceived it tonight.I was way into it.
Gentry:Our songs develop with each part.It is just that we can't put everything into
three minutes.We probably could,but it would be weak.It is our style.We don't want to
be like everyone else.
G&P:How long has the band been playing as a three piece?
Chad:About 4 months,since April,'91.It was pretty tight as a five piece,but it actually
is tighter as a three piece.It will take a while to get the vocals down but it's coming.
G&P:Why are you playing with two less members?
Gentry:Those guys just have different interests.
Chad:They were just not as involved as all of us were.
Doug:They were at first.They were like way into it when we recorded the ep.
Chad:We recorded that ep after being together for about a month.It was recorded quickly.
G&P:Have you recorded anything since then?

7-19-91 DEKALB IL. P.MATT G.

Chad:Yeah,we have seventy minutes worth of music
recorded.We just have to mix it and add vocals.
Gentry:We started recording it around the first
of june.Tony (Victory) is supposed to put it out.
G&P:Supposed to?Is that definite?
Chad:Well,he gave us money to record.
G&P:Are you happy that Victory is interested in
Iceburn?It is kinda a step in a different direction compared to past Victory releases.
Gentry:If he wants to put us out,that's cool.
Chad:If he doesn't change his mind after seeing
us play tonight.
G&P:How serious is Iceburn?Do you plan on keeping
this band going?
Gentry:Yeah,as long as it works for us.You know,
it is our way of expressing ourselves thru
the music.We have to be challenged in our music,
not just by playing a few chords.It has to have
emotion in it.We just like music.
G&P:Do you feel that Iceburn is in any way a
continuation of where Insight was headed?
Chad:Actually,it is totally opposite.I don't feel
there is any continuation.That is why I think that
Insight broke up,because we were sick of it.In-
sight got to be such a dud.Some were into it,and
some weren't.Doug pretty much got kicked out or
whatever because he couldn't go on tour with us last year,and had a kid on the way.
Mark was being closed-minded about Doug having a kid on the way.So he kicked him out.
Then we got a new bass player a couple weeks before the tour.It was like everything
was pretty much fucked up.It wasn't even Insight anymore.On tour,everyone decided that
it wasn't what we wanted to do.Mark and Jeremy were still into it,but me and Jaimie
were not.So we wanted to get back into it.we started a band with Gentry,and we
picked up Doug.
Gentry:Originally,Jeremy was going to sing and play bass.I don't think that would've
worked.Jeremy sang on the cassette single thing.
He sang for Brainstorm,the band I was in.
G&P:Are you still using his lyrics?Did he write?
Gentry:I wrote the lyrics to Fall,and he and I
split on Burn.He'd let us use the words he wrote,
but with some of the songs,we didn't think his
words fit the feeling.It was like where he was
kind of getting out of it,and not putting much
into it.
G&P:I think the people who came tonight expected
to see something different than what you delivered...What do you think?
Chad:Definitely.I don't think any crowds are
open minded.Not from what I have seen.In Salt Lake
when we changed,everyone was so fucking closed-
minded about it.On the road,everyone has been
like,"WHAT?".But people who understand music and
have the first clue about it can understand it
and appreciate it.People who are into hardcore
just for the sake of being "punk rock" or whatever
don't get it.So it is like,"Well,they're different
so fuck them.They aren't the same as they were."
G&P:It seems to be that way with every band.
As soon as they change in any way,that's it.

7-19-91;P.MATT G.

PHOTO:GABE

Gentry:It is weird.It doesn't seem we've
changed our course.It is what we were always doing.It just develops.It's what is us.
Chad:A lot of it in Salt Lake was the
image thing too.Jeremy had a pretty popular image there.(Insight)Lots of kids
liked him.So when he left,that popular
role wasn't there anymore,and the people
were ;like out of it.
G&P:Insight had the big straight edge fol-
lowing also.Has it dwindled down because you haven't followed suit with it?
Chad:A lot of people hold that against us also.They go expecting something like what
Insight was.Or they think that we have the same thoughts as Insight,and we don't.Or
they expect Iceburn to sound the same as we do on the single,and we don't.
G&P:What do you want to get accomplished with this band?
Chad:A good feeling.Almost like a release type of feeling.
G&P:It is not like we are trying to get our sound to fit the masses to sell
records or whatever.
Chad:We are not popular,sp we must be doing something...
Gentry:(Interrupts)RIGHT!
G&P:How far are you going on this tour?
Chad:Boston,Florida,and back to Salt Lake.Then a few weeks later,we'll go all the way
up the west coast to Seattle.
G&P:What are Iceburn's lyrics about?
Gentry:We write about emotions.
The music is pretty heavy and we
try to portray what we are feeling in the music.The song Burn
is about you know the feeling you
have in your stomach burning,
when someone does something to
you,or what you see on tv.,or
just around burns you.
G&P:What kinds of music has
influenced your writing style?
Gentry:All sorts...Anything that
is good to us.I am studying a
lot of jazz,so I get into that.
Chad:A lot of jazz,some classical,a lot of DC stuff.
Gentry:You can probably hear
some classical stuff in Iceburn.

photo;gabe

Gentry:We are just trying to get
our own voice,thru our instruments
and through our music.Primus is good.They
are totally original.Naked City,The Melvins.
G&P:Well,I hope you guys stay together and move
forward after todays show.
Chad:It has just been a drag of a day.Our van broke
down and we wasted a lot of time doing nothing.
Gentry:I'd like to say something.It seems weird,It seems
that kids today are looking for an image,and they are not looking
for a message.We are all still I guess straight edge.None of us
drink,because we think it is stupid.None of us eat meat.It is just weird
how kids are turned off by the music.I think sometimes it is just too much.
I'm not trying to flatter myself.The kids want something where they can just...
Chad:Not have to think about.
Gentry:They want to grab onto some ideology.We are kinda against religion also.
I guess,organized religion in that right.
Chad:It seems with music,lots of people are closed minded about it.For example...
If someone is straight edge,and a beer band comes to town to play,they won't like
them just for that aspect of them.
Gentry:Maybe our hair is too long!
G&P:THAT CANNOT BE IT! (a burst of laughter)
G&P:What do you think of straight edge today in 1991?
Chad:I haven't heard anything that impressed me.But it is hard to impress me though.
Gentry:It was a big part of our lives and stuff.
Chad:Yeah,when we were young,we were into it and it was fun.And we weren't totally
lame about it either.Not me,but everyone in the band Insight used to do drugs,
and noone was down on anyone.The Salt Lake scene was cool,because it didn't
involve so much the SE scene.We were (SE),but we had freinds that weren't.
Gentry:It seems that the SE scene is really big now,and that is why we are
getting popular,because were are on Victory records.
Chad:And if we were on a different label,I'm sure noone would know
who the hell we were.I know freinds in Salt Lake who like us,and
they just go out and buy Billingsgate or Face Value stuff cause
they are affiliated with Victory.I 'm sure they never even
heard it either.I also think that a lot of people who
like Victory bands go out and buy our stuff cause we're
on Victory.Then they listen to us and say,"Fuck,I
hate these guys."That's what happened tonight.
G&P:Any last words?
Chad:Where is the nearest Denny's?Thanks to
all the people who helped set up this tour.

In past issues of G&P Zine,I have included tons of photographs.
This will be no exception.Again,some of the photos may be of bands
that I don't totally agree with on their views on things,but that
is the case with everyone in this world.There isn't one band,group
of people,or person in this world that I have found to be totally
in agreement with on everything.Whether you think this is a complete
waste of paper,or you think this is cool,that is your opinion. I am
really into capturing the visual aspects of what I see in hardcore,
and I will continue printing photos until I become bored with them.
The following photos are a collection that I have acquired from
generous friends who sent them.Thanks to all who sent shots.

BILLINGSGATE-PHOTO:JOHN HANDWERK

HEADFIRST-PHOTO:GREG BROWN

OUTSPOKEN-PHOTO:ERIC FORTNER

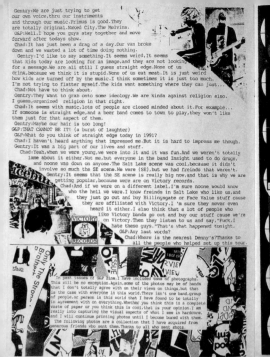

SLAP OF REALITY-P.AL QUINT
ALYSSA'S BASEMENT

SNAPCASE-11/15/91 P.JOE PARTYKA

CHORUS OF DISAPPROVAL
PHOTO:DAVE INDECISION

FARSIDE-PHOTO DANE MANDEL

SNFU-PHOTO MARGRET

BULLET LAVOLTA

7 SECONDS-P.BOB CONRAD

JAWBOX-4/91-PHOTO MARTY

UP FRONT-LAST SHOW
DAN LADD

INSIDE OUT-PHOTO DAVE INDECISION

L7

FAST FREAK DIET SLIDE SHIT LIST SCRAP LOST CAUSE SHOVE JUST LIKE ME

PHOTO:HEATHER P.

PHOTO:HEATHER P.

PHOTO:HEATHER P.

PHOTO:HEATHER P.

CHICAGO IL. 11-91 PHOTO:MATT G.

CHICAGO IL. 11-91 PHOTO:MATT G.

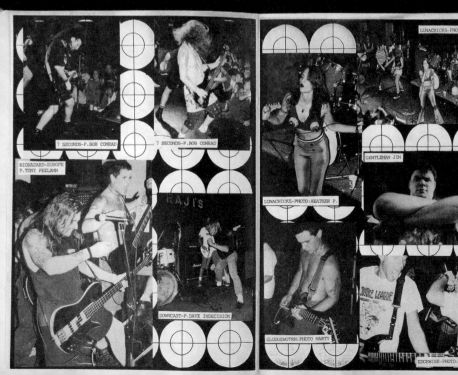

7 SECONDS-P.BOB CONRAD

7 SECONDS-P.BOB CONRAD

BIOHAZARD-EUROPE P.TONY PEELAMN

RAJI'S

DOWNCAST-P.DAVE INDECISION

LUNACHICKS-PHOTO:HEATHER P.

GENTLEMAN JIM

LUNACHICKS-PHOTO:HEATHER P.

SLUDGEWORTH: PHOTO MARTY

EDGEWISE-PHOTO:DAVE INDECISION

CHIA PET:P.JOHN HANDWERK

KILLING TIME-PHOTO DAN WERLE

EYE FOR AN EYE-PHOTO:JUSTINE De METRICK

TURNING POINT-FINAL SHOW PHOTO:GREG BROWN 6/91

EYE FOR AN EYE-PHOTO:JUSTINE De METRICK

TURNING POINT-FINAL SHOW PHOTO:GREG BROWN 6/91

BURN-5/4/91 D.C.

INTO ANOTHER P.JIM TESTA

L7

AGNOSTIC FRONT-EUROPE PHOTO:TONY PEELMAN

BURN 7/91 PHOTO GREG BROWN

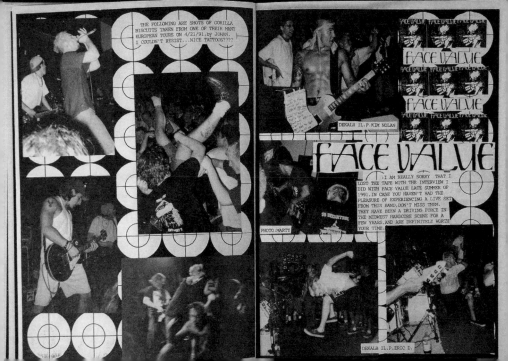

THE FOLLOWING ARE SHOTS OF GORILLA BISCUITS TAKEN FROM ONE OF THEIR MANY EUROPEAN TOURS ON 4/21/91,by JOHAN. I COULDN'T RESIST...NICE TATTOOS????

DEKALB IL.P.KIM NOLAN

FACE VALUE

:I AM REALLY SORRY THAT I LOST THE TAPE WITH THE INTERVIEW I DID WITH FACE VALUE LATE SUMMER OF 1991.IN CASE YOU HAVEN'T HAD THE PLEASURE OF EXPERIENCING A LIVE SET FROM THIS BAND,DON'T MISS THEM. THEY HAVE BEEN A DRIVING FORCE IN THE MIDWEST HARDCORE SCENE FOR A FEW YEARS,AND ARE DEFINITELY WORTH YOUR TIME.

PHOTO:MARTY

DEKALB IL.P.ERIC D.

THE FOLLOWING ARE QUOTES OR THINGS I HAVE READ AND SEEN
THAT I THINK DESERVE REPEATING. EVERY ONCE IN A WHILE, SOMEONE
SAYS SOMETHING THAT CATCHES MY ATTENTION AND MAKES ME THINK,
OR JUST STARTLES ME. SO, I WRITE THEM DOWN. HERE ARE A FEW.

"THOSE WHO DON'T KNOW THEIR OPPONENTS ARGUMENTS,
DON'T COMPLETELY UNDERSTAND THEIR OWN."

"IS BEING OPEN MINDED A CLOSED MINDED THING?"

"THERE IS NOTHING GOING ON OUTSIDE, IT'S ALL
GOING ON IN MY HEAD."

"A SMART PERSON HAS MORE QUESTIONS THAN ANSWERS."

"A ZINE IS A NON-MUSICIANS BAND."

"I THINK I'D BE A BETTER PERSON IF I DIDN'T HAVE A PENIS."

...God, I am so full of shit...

...Am I the lamest person you ever interviewed?

...God I am such a loser...

AN INTERVIEW WITH... ALYSSA CHUNX

Sorry for the extra small type. I didn't want to cut any of this.

LAST TO GO

SAY
NO MORE records...

$3.50 ppd. us
$5 world

"FIFTH SEASON"
7" EP
OUT IN SPRING

CHUMP RECORDS
3105 EMMAUS AVE. APT B
ZION IL 60099

BLOW'N CHUNX!

BLOWIN' CHUNX 4

Some people think little girls should be seen and not heard, but I think:
OH BONDAGE UP YOURS!

DORENE, KIM, AND ALYSSA

DUMPSTER PHOTO BY: YASMINE

BLOWIN CHUNX
N U M B E R   T W O
O N E   B U C K

A favorite past-time...Inhaling drinks

Wrecking Crew
Quicksand

Sheer Terror
Kingpin

SAY IT
411
THOUGHTS THAT FEED THE FIRE

411
411
411

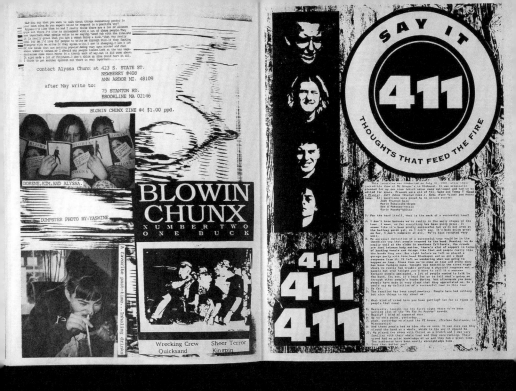

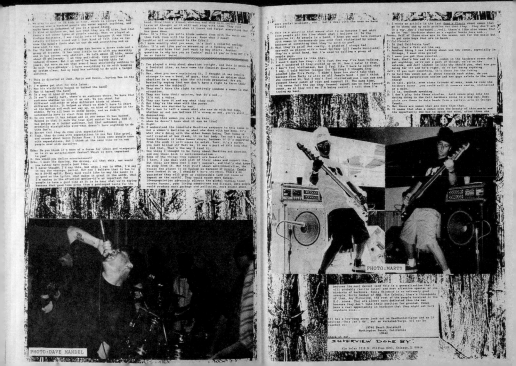

PHOTO: MARTY

PHOTO: DAVE MANDEL

INTERVIEW DONE BY:

I remember a long phone conversation I had a while ago with a female friend where she said that she thought that the worst thing that could be said about a guy,was that he is a "pussy".(I hate that word,but she did say it.)That is to say,there is no better way to get to a guy's ego,than to imply that he is a wimp,sissy,girlish,etc...At first, I agreed with that 100 percent,without a doubt.After a little more thought,I would have to say that doesn't apply in every case,to every guy.Let me try to explain.

I have been doing my weekly grociery shopping at the same place for the past 4-5 years, and since the place isn't that big,I figure they all recognize my face by now.On one particular day,I unloaded my food on the belt to be rung up by a woman,about in her 40's. She said something to me that to this day,I'll never forget.She said,"Do you want paper or plastic bags,MA'AM?"I looked up at her,knowing fully what she said,and burst into laughter.She did the same,and apologised.For weeks after,I'd see her working and say Hi, and talk for a bit.

A few months later,again I was doing my weekly shopping.This time I went to a young man's line.He rung up my stuff,and wouldn't you know it...He said the same thing,"Would you like paper or plastic,MA'AM?"I looked at him with a straight face and told him paper, as he tried to play like he didn't say it.He hurried up,and got me out of there.I did hear him,I just didn't want to make the situation more uncomfortable than it was for him.

Well,a few days ago,a similar thing happened to me.This time was a little different. I was at a gas station,going to pay for my gas that I had already pumped.I walk in the place,and I see the young cashier boy,(about 17),looking at me funny.He looked as if he wanted to comment on my appearance in some way that was unpleasant to me.So as I turned to look at the candy bars,he said to me as to ask if I needed help,"MA'AM?" I knew he knew I was a guy,but just trying to crack on me.I turned to him,and he tried to apologise,but didn't seem convincing about it.I paid and left.

I have to say,that in all three instances,I did not feel the slightest offended by being mistaken for a woman.Actually,in a funny way,I kind of enjoyed it.Sometimes in pictures,I do look like a girl,and not just because I have long hair.I know that a lot of my friends have told me I look like a girl.Maybe I do,or maybe people just don't look close enough when they speak to me.

I told this to another female friend of mine the other day.she told me of a similar instance that occurred to her when she was younger.She played on a softball team,and one day on the way home from practice,a car drove next to her.In the car were 2 young guys.They said,"Hey,are you a boy or a girl?"She immediately responded by pulling up her shirt and said,"What do you think?"I am sure this happens a lot to some people,and maybe once or twice to almost everyone.Everyone's reaction is different,and that is very natural.

In a book called "The Second Sex",by Simone de Beauvoir,it explains a lot of things about women and men,and life in general.One thing that I got out of it,was that all people should get in touch with all of their feelings,whether they be masculine or feminine.Both sexes have both feelings,,believe it or not.Maybe I give off an signals or actions of a female as I walk down the street,at work,or anywhere?I can't change that.I can lift weights,cut my hair,or wear "manly"clothes to change the way I look, but that wouldn't be me.I would be a person that society wants me to be.People are so hung up on labels and classifying others,that if someone doesn't fit in with a group, they are weird.I hate labels,but if you want to label me,I got one for you...Human. When I think of this,I always go back to something that Phil Rind of Sacred Riech wrote. He wrote,"Too many people are hung up on how people are different from each other.Be it race,religion,color,sexual preference,gender,or age.The fact is that we are more similar than different.We all want to love and to be love.we're all made of flesh and blood,we all laugh,and we all cry.If we could all just focus on our similarities than our differences,the world would be a better place.It seems so simple..."

I know there are things different about everyone in this world,and that is natural. But a lot of times these differences are used as an excuse for racism,sexism,and every form of prejudice there is.There is no excuse.I do not claim to be perfect,and I have had prejudice thoughts drilled in my head since I was born.Now,I think it's time for me to re-think and re-learn what I was taught to believe by my family,friends,and peers. It is a hard stuggle,but I have come this far,and hopefully someday I will be free of all my misinformation.Thank you to anyone that has helped me along the way.I learn from all my past,present and future mistakes.

Doc Hopper

DOCHOPPER IS:
MALCOLM-DRUMS
JON-BASS
CHRIS-GUITAR+VOX
GEORGE GUITAR

Dochopper probably isn't a household name amongst most of you,but that is understandable.They are a four piece out of the far northeast corner of the U.S.I met the guitarist/singer about 2 years ago,and thought he was a freak ever since.But,on top of being a freak,he is also cool,which is weird among freaks.I got a chance to see Dochopper play a set at the Rat in Boston,and was very impressed with them.Keep an eye out for these guys in the future,they definitely deserve a looksy from all.

I interviewed Jon and Chris a day before the show.It was the most humorous experience.Present for the interview,was Tom,Meg, Sean,and me.Thanks to all that participated.

G&P:What does Dochopper mean?

Chris:One night,Jon and I were sitting around playing with an oiji (sp?) board,and we summoned this spirit.He said his name was Dr. Hopper,so we shortened it,and he is referred to Doc Hopper.Every night we were summonsing him,and we found out a lot of stuff about him,like he was born in 1840,and he used to do these weird experiments on women,It was really weird. He would surgically remove their nipples.

Jon:We had to infer a lot of this.Most of it was garbled words,but that's what we got.

Chris:After a while,we just got so freaked,so we stopped.

G&P:So how long has Dochopper been playing?

Chris:About a year and a half.

G&P:Where do you claim to be from?You have members from different states.

Chris:We are all from Maine,but we're just Boston transplants.We live here cause it's more fun.We are from Maine deep in our hearts,but on the exterior,were from Boston.

G&P:You just recorded a demo,how did that come out?

Chris:It's ak.Good enough for a four track.It didn't cost us anything.It took us about six hours to do thirteen songs,just breezin' along.It's kinda silly when bands spend lots of money to put out demos,that noone ends up hearing.

Jon:That eventually becomes a collectors item.

Chris:Yeah,like our now legendary sold out demo,that led to our Revelation 7".

Sean:You guys and Sick Of It All.

Chris:We are down with the crew.

Sean:Yeah,but more importantly,are you down with OPP?

Chris:I'm down with HIV. (Jokingly)

G&P:What are some of your lyrics about, give me some insight.

1-92;the RAT P.GABE

Jon:Chris likes to sing about Megan,or food or coffee.

Tom:This is directed to Chris-What about side bands?I heard you have this band called Still Screaming.

Chris:Yeah,I sing for this band called Still Screaming.We're trying to bring back the original HC energy of the straight edge scene of about 3 years ago,when all the bands were good.We just played a show tonight actually,and the cops came and shut us down,man. Just like CB's,right before the mosh part,when we covered New Direction. Bringin' it back '92 style,the SE posse,boyee...Bidup bop.

Meg:Why do you guys cover GG Allin songs?

Chris:Cause GG is god.

Jon:They are awfully good songs.

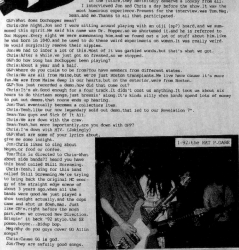

1-92:THE RAT P.GABE

Chris:GG is a fuck-nut,but he's a nice guy.When I talked to him he was nice.

Meg:Cause you are a man.

Chris:I think GG has a lot of good points.He's got a good go-tee.His facial hair is definitely a+.

G&P:Hitler had a mustache also.

Chris:He did.GG has the negative of Hitler's mustache.

Tom:What about him being a nazi?

Chris:GG is not a nazi.He hates everyone.He is indiscriminately hateful.He hates blacks,whites,he doesn't care if anyone knows that he fucked his brother or his brother's dog.He hates men and women,he just hates.No matter what anyone says,his first couple of records were awfully catchy songs.You find yourself going,"Du,du,dum,du."

Meg:What do you guys do when you aren't playing in the band?

Jon:I like to sleep.

Chris:Sleeping and eating are good.Masturbation is definitely A+.

Jon:Chris farts a lot.He spends a lot of time in the bathroom.

Tom:What are you guys trying to accomplish with this band?

Jon:We have a plan.

Chris:Jon,George,and Malcolm all want to pick up girls,and I want to keep mine.Actually,when the songs were written,I wanted to pick up girls too,it's just I wanted to pick up her,(Megan). Now with that done,I can move on to newer territory...It's a joke!

Sean:So you are moving onto deeper territory lyrically,that's what you meant?(laughter)

Tom:What are your influences?I hear a little Slayer in there sometimes.

Chris:Believe it or not,there's some Cro-mags,Old Agnostic Front,Sick Of It All,Raw Deal.

Meg:Really.So people can order your tape,so they know what you sound like.

Tom:Well they will order it if they sound like that! (laughter)

Chris:Somewhere in between the Monkees and Slayer.Although Nick says we sound like a cross between Black Flag and Green Day.

Meg:I think so,too.

Chris:I think if you were going to say a cross between anything,it would be Blast/Doughboys.

Jon:We pretty much rip everybody off.

Chris:I rip everyone off to write my songs.Especially Dag Nasty in one song.So if you like Dag Nasty,order our tape.You'll get mad and say,"These guys ripped off Dag Nasty!"

Meg:What's the meaning behind the little frogs you all wear around your neck?

Jon:It's kind of a unity thing.

Chris:The other night when we were at the Krishna ISKON temple, shopping for shoes,Lord Maharishinashnankuni told us that we would be invaded by a small reptilian creature.I interpreted that as a frog,even though they are amphobions.I forgot my biology.

Sean:So it's sort of a religious thing.Your spiritual master told you to.

Chris:Yes,he did. We are a very religious band.

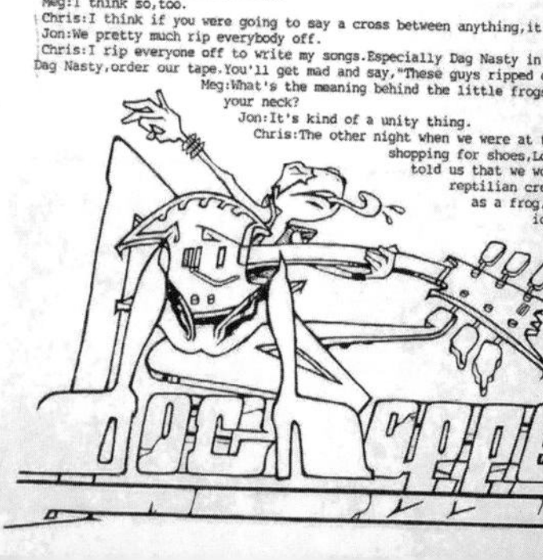

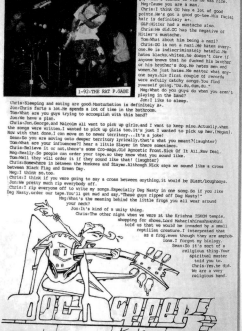

Meg:And what about your sideburns,are they religious also?

Chris:We got our sideburns when Ray Cappo shaved his head.We took his hair and superglued it to the sides of our face.

-the interview drags-

Chris:I'd like to read a bit from one of our best songs."Hey,listen up.I've got one thing to say.I want to talk about something that means,a fucking lot to me.It's a matter of pride.It's the way I feel...When there's betrayel.Where the fuck is your head man?And just how much does this mean to you?"...This is going to be the most idiotic interview G&P has ever seen.Except for maybe the Integrity interview,although they were trying to be serious.

Meg:So you are inspired by Wynona Ryder I hear?

Chris:Yeah,we drove all the way to Wynona Minnesota to where she was born.We drove 2100 miles to see it.

G&P:If your drummer Malcolm was here,what would he say about now?

Jon:He'd talk about clowns.He draws clowns on everything.

Chris:He had this prem-o Monkees poster,and he put a clown-face on Peter Tork.The first time I went to his place,I went to the bathroom,and I sat down to take a poo,and I saw on the wall, there was this big Kraft Clown,and on the wall in Duc Tape it said,"Hee,Hee,Hee, I C U P. It was the most unnerving thing.I couldn't go.I had to hold it until I went home.I was scared. I'd like to read another excerp from one of our songs."You've got nothing good to say about those that surround you.Think twice about the words that kill,this goes out to you and your crew.You ate your words.You drank your words.You smoked your words.Now I know the truth.

G&P:Tell me about all of the Bee-Gee's posters all over the Dochopper pad.What is the deal with all of that?

Jon:Oh,this summer,Malcolm and I were driving around,and we went to this lawn sale.They had all these old Teen Beat magazines from about 1979, and we bought a bunch.Stuff like old pictures of Ricky Schroeder,Erik Estada,The Dukes of Hazard.

G&P:How would you like to close this interview?

Chris:Don't use bean-o.

G&P:What is bean-o?

Chris:It's this stuff that gets rid of gas.So don't use it.Say no to bean-o.I also want to give a strong congrats to anyone with dreadlocks who isn't rastafarian,a deadhead,a hippie,or a crusty. I hate crusties,cause they smell.They smell worse than me.They smell worse than NOFX,which is pretty bad.So,if you aren't one of the people I named,if you have dreadlocks,sideburns,go-tees,and big geeky glasses,you are cool.

Sean:So basically,you have narrowed it down to Dochopper and the Doughboys.

Chris:Yeah,if you're in Dochopper or the Doughboys, you are cool.If not,you can only strive.

Girl Crazy
Wimp-Core
We May Be Wimps, But We Can Still Get Hard.

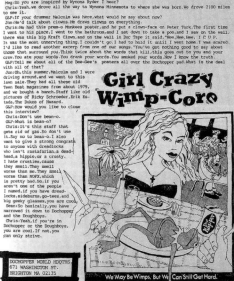

DOCHOPPER WORLD HDQTRS.
671 WASHINGTON ST.
BRIGHTON MA 02135

KINGPIN
I KNOW THIS LOOKS WEIRD, BUT IN A COOL KINDA WAY...PHOTO:ALYSSA CHUNX

In the search for good,young bands in recent times,I have often come up short. Recently,a friend of mine made me a tape with a load of bands,one of which was a band called Kingpin.I'd have to say,that before long,they did become a stand-out on that tape.If I had to describe them,first of all it wouldn't be easy.But since I hate it when I see interviews with bands,and I want to know what they sound like, but nowhere does it say,so I get pissed,I'll try.If you were to take the 7" from Quicksand,and blend in Can I Say by Dag Nasty,that would be my best description. I hope that is a good description.I recently had a chance to catch up with Kingpin, while in Boston myself.I highly recommend everyone to keep an eye out for this young four piece from Boston.Present for the interview,and helping out with the questions, were Sean Coleman,and Alyssa Chunx,and myself.Read on...

KINGPIN IS:
ALEX-DRUMS
MATT-GUITAR
KEITH-BASS
MARK-VOCALS

date of interview: 1/3/92

G&P:How long has Kingpin been together?
Matt:About a year and a half.
G&P:Why did you guys decide to form a band?
Alex:We were all friends and stuff.When we were younger,we'd get together and play Black Sabbath covers.Then we got better and started doing our own music.
G&P:Right now,if you had to describe your sound,what would you say?
Matt:I suppose,if someone asked me what music Kingpin plays,which happens often,I'd have to say hardcore, because I guess there's no other word to describe it...I don't know.Keith,do you want to put your ¢2 in?
Keith:It's metal/funk/oi. (laughter)
G&P:Do you think you guys fit in,as far as the Boston hardcore scene is concerned?
Matt:When we first started ,we sounded totally different.Our sound was real heavy like mosh-core.Mark used to scream/We weren't accessible with the Boston hardcore scene.Now,everyone shows a lot of support at shows and stuff,so it's pretty cool.
Mark:I think it's pretty cool.
Matt:lets say some more interesting things than "it's pretty cool".(to Mark)
Keith:About what?About how we fit in,who cares.
Sean :Is there any sense of unity between the bands,and if there is,is there any sense of direction that these bands are taking?
Alex:We are friends and stuff.
Matt:I think each individual band is doing there own thing.But at the same time,the bands seem to work well when they play together.Bands like Said and Done,Eye For An Eye,Third Degree...if we had a show and we'd all play together,even though each band sounds different,they attract sort of the same scene.
Mark:Each band tries to help the other bands.
Keith:Did you mean unity towards music,or as to try and build something.
Sean :I meant more like the sense of a scene,and building it.
Mark:We're all trying to help each other out.It's like,if we were trying to get an out-of-state show,we'd try to get someone else on the bill from Boston.We're not worried about who is going to become more popular. It's not like a race,It's more like a team.
G&P:You guys have a seven inch out now,on Suburban Voice Records.Are you happy with the way it came out?
Mark:I like it.
Keith:It's round,and it's black and it has a small hole.So in that aspect it came out good.
Matt:We're not too happy with the way he handled promotion,and things like wethat.We're grateful that he put out our record,but at the same time,I don't feel that he did an adequate job promoting it.I think we could have sold a lot more copies if more people knew about it.
Keith:We sold them all.
Matt:I know.We sold the first pressing,but most of them were sold in Boston.
Alex:I think he did a good job in that,he put up the money for us,and the distribution that it did get was all from him.
Mark:He did take a big chance on us.

7-13-91:THE EDGE P.CHRIS KING

Alex:Personally,I don't know if anyone else in the band agrees with me,but I think hardcore bands should more try to do things for themselves,rather than allowing ourselves to worry about how anyone is going to handle how well our record goes out.I think from now on,we should do everything ourselves. From tonight on.
Matt:that's exactly what's gonna happen.That's exactly the direction that we are taking right now. This guy Pete and I are starting our own label.We are gonna do a Kingpin record,and probably an Arise 7",and hopefully a compilation.
:Keith:There's going to be a comp. with prohibition on it.
G&P:I am n ot sure if this is true,but there has been word of a Kingpin song that may pop up ao an Equal Vision compilation in the future.
Matt:There was.I don't know.-It's not like a Krishna conscienceness song or anything like that.It is basically,Ray asked us if we wanted to be on a comp.
G&P:Is that going to happen?
Matt:I think it's been put on hold for now.
Sean:If you were to do a song for Equal Vision, don't you feel that recording for that company is like supporting a dogmatic religious organization?
Matt:I suppose it would actually,when it comes right down to it.We agreed to do it a while ago,and I don't think,that if the comp were to start rolling now,that we would be on it.
Keith:the Krishnas don't like Matt anymore.
Sean:oh yeah,is that something you would like to share?They don't like me either,I'm just curious.
Matt:Actually,Ray is pretty mad at me,because I was supposed to go down and play 3 shows with Shelter this past weekend,and I bailed out on them.
Mark:As far as it being dogmatic,I mean,I like dogs.The are cool.(laughter)
Matt:No one in the band is Krishna conscienceness at all.
Keith:I think if everybody forgot about it and ignored them...Let them do what they want.I don't agree with what they say,but i don't see them forcing it upon anyone.I'm not going to denounce them.
Sean:People can argue and say not to denounce them,but the reason I denounce them isn't because they are a religion,it's because they are sexist,and they are homophobic.They promote hat towards women,and they promote hate towards homosexuals.That's my main gripe.
Keith:Well,in that respect,I'd agree.
Matt:One thing just to say for the record,that we have been labeled,I wouldn't sa unjustly,because we have done an interview with Enquirer Zine,but we've been labeled as a Krishna band.I want to set the record straight that we are not,and noone in the band participates in it.
Keith:I like onions too much.
Mark:These are Krishna beads,(on his neck)but they aren't to be worn around your neck.It's kinda like, I'm rebelling.
Alyssa:Lately the Boston scene has been dominated by big business promoters,like Cringe and stuff like that; That has pushed a lot of bands out perhaps,and some touring bands won't be able to play here.-
Matt:It's done more than push touring bands aside.We've played Boston only 3 times in the past year,which is ridiculous...I think it sucks right now.When Shawn Cringe first started doing shows in Boston,and Jon Regan,I guess it got too much for him to handle for him.When they first did shows,they had bands like Starkweather play,from Philly,and smaller bands. But they weren't making any money,so they started doing bigger ones.Now, the only bands that play around pretty much are the bands that he manages, like Slapshot,and Sam Black Church.
Alyssa:Are there any shows coming up for you in Boston?
Keith:Not at all.
Matt:Between the 2 times we played Boston,we played 3 time in New York.
Mark:that was about a 6 month gap between our 2 Boston shows.

11-24-91:THE CHANNEL P.MIKE DAHILL

PHOTO:TINA A.

G&P:I saw on the blacklist mailorder catalogue,next to the Kingpin 7" for the description it said,"Straight Edge Mosh Core."(laughter)Is Kingpin a straight edge band?
Keith:We're all straight edge,but we don't have any SE songs.If someone would call us a SE band,I wouldn't be offended.
Matt:Individually,the members are SE. Collectively,we probably wouldn't want to be labeled as a SE band,just because of the negative connotation that goes along with it.Straight edge has this parallel that a lot of people find with being generic.I don't think our music is generic,and I'd be offended in that respect.I don't mind being called a SE band,if people know what we sound like.
Keith:But we are Mosh-core,that pert was pretty accurate.(laughter)
Sean:This is a political question,trying to get people to think.What is your opinion on the situation in the Persian Gulf,and the U.S. foreign policy,and do you think the people of the US were completely manipulated by the media.
Matt:They were led like sheep.
Keith:Yeah,noone really knew what was going on...This isn't information that I found out myself,I read this in Dear Jesus.This isn't to make me look smart.We were led to believe that the people of Iraq are mean,bad people,where there is no justice,and have public executions and stuff.But they have the same stuff happening in Kuwait,which is who we were defending.We went in,killed 100,000 people,and nothing has really changed. Except,you don't have to pay as much for gas.
Mark:This is the most overdone statement,but it's really true.All it was,was blood for oil.That's what I think.it was stupid.
Matt:We were led into this macho image of being the defender of this poor little country of Kuwait.
Sean:So,do I forsee any songs about Iraq or Kuwait on a future Kingpin 7"?
Mark:Probably not...It's pretty sad,I saw an infant somewhere wearing a desert storm shirt.He doesn't know what the hell is going on.It's just pathetic.
Sean:Would you like to comment on the situation with the William Kennedy Smith trials.What kind of impact do you think it is going to have on society as far as the feminist movement goes?
Keith:Is that to say that you think he was guilty?
Sean:I don't want to assume that anyone was guilty.More to say,that if he was guilty,the evidence was kinda backlashed in the fact that she had a poor lawyer.
Keith:As far as I know,regarding evidence,her clothes weren't torn,and noone heard any screaming.
Sean:Don't you think that is a ridiculous way to prove rape?
Keith:The point is,you have to prove that she was raped.As far as the legal system goes,the burden of proof is on the prosecution.If you can't come up with the proof,I don't think he should go to jail.I don't know whether he was guilty or not.But you can't just say,that if someone says they were raped,that they were,and that guy did it,and he has to go to jail.There has to be order for things.
Sean:At the same time,now it's going to be even harder for women to come out,and admit that they were raped.
Keith:The most difficulty in coming out,accusing somebody of rape,is that you pretty much go on trial yourself,cause you get questioned so much.
Matt:My feeling about the whole case is,because the case was so publicized,and it was on prime-time t.v.,-you could sit at home and watch the whole questioning process,because of all that,and the verdict was not guilty,I think it's going to have a tremendous effect on people that were raped.They are going to be afraid that because they were raped,they might have to prove it,and things could be worse afterwards.
Keith:The legal system may be messed up,but what's not messed up is that you have to prove someone is guilty. I think if anything is messed up,it's the fact that the media can go in and televise events such as that.
G&P:There seems to be more awareness about womens issues in hardcore,and such.What is Kingpin doing to either help or hinder this issue?
Matt:Kingpin is doing nothing to hinder or help.
Keith:Basically,we play music to get chicks.(sarcastically)
Matt:One thing,we were playing a show a few weeks back,and Mark made a statement about dancing,in the pit, about it being a human thing-not male or female.Because there were some girls dancing,and he pointed that out.
Mark:This probably doesn't do much, but if anyone is influenced by what

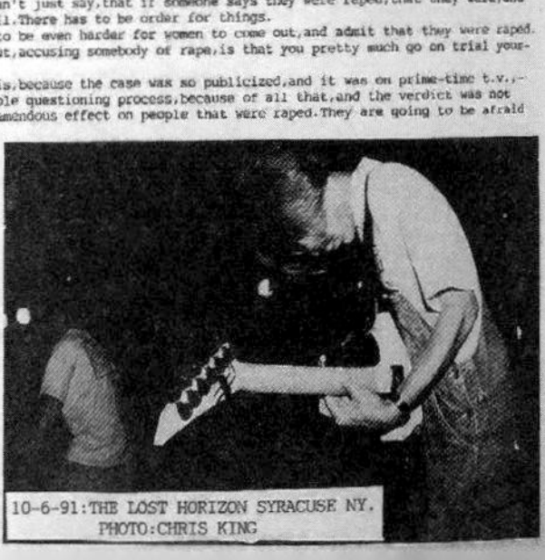
10-6-91:THE LOST HORIZON SYRACUSE NY. PHOTO:CHRIS KING

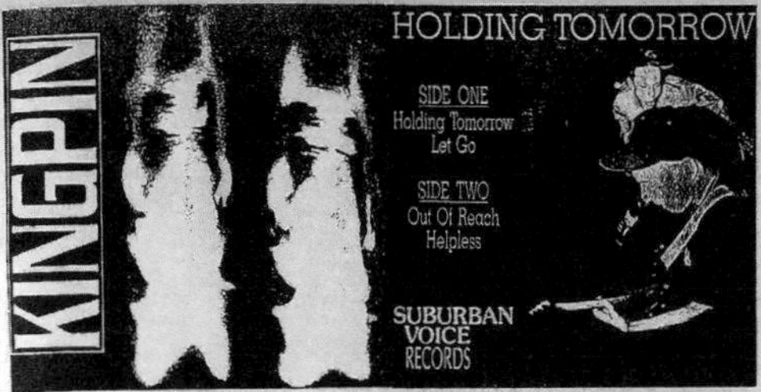
KINGPIN
HOLDING TOMORROW
SIDE ONE
Holding Tomorrow
Let Go
SIDE TWO
Out Of Reach
Helpless
SUBURBAN
VOICE
RECORDS

Alex:I am.
Mark:All right.At one of our shows,I said,"Fuck sexism,fuck racism,fuck homophobia."and stuff like that.If someone listens to something I say,and maybe they agree,maybe they'll do something about it.
G&P:Maybe in the same breath that you said that,later you jumped on 5 people in the front row while stagediving,and brought them down to the floor.
Mark:What does that have to do with sexism?
G&P:It's not directly about sexism,but more about peoples rights.
Keith:That's what happens up at the front.It is what is expected.
Alyssa:If I'm up front,because maybe some of my friends are in the band,or something,-to be up front and to have to worry...I'm not down on stagediving,because I have done it.
Matt:I have to agree with Alyssa on this point.I'm not down on stagediving,but there are certain times when I want to stand up front,so I can see the band better,and not have to worry about some clod kicking me in the face.
Alyssa:Unfortunately,there is this thing about space,-or maybe it's not so unfortunate.It's like,there is space,and space does get violated,over your head or whatever.
Matt:That's why I don't stagedive.
Sean:I'm not saying everybody,but at least for a lot of people it turns into sort of a macho proving ground,almost parallel to a football game,where they have their girlfriend stand on the sideline,holding their jacket,or camera while they go in and "mosh it up".
Keith:Personally,I don't know anybody in that situation.It may be that way.But as far as stagediving goes,it is totally fun,and I don't think there is anything wrong with it at all.If you're at a hardcore show,it's not that difficult to avoid someone jumping on your head,if you don't want them to.I think it's all a part of hardcore.
Tom:(interjecting his two cents)And Gabe,you are the first person to dive at times.
G&P:I didn't say I have never done it before.I am just throwing out some thoughts.(as far as my personal beliefs, I think stagediving is more of a hinderance than anything else at shows,and I don't paticipate anymore.)
(the conversation goes on about stagediving)
Matt:This is exactly the opposite of what a Kingpin show is.If anyone has ever been to a Kingpin show,like when we played with Sick Of It All,we played before them,and for them the pit was totally violent.But during our set,it's always fun first.Our lyrics are all serious,we don't have any funny songs,but when we are on stage,what it all boils down to is just the personalities...Everything turns out to be fun.The whole point of why we play,and playing HC has to do with fun.At Kingpin show,there is stagediving and dancing,but it's never violent,and if it is,we point it out and eliminate it to the best of our ability.
G&P:(on to a lighter subject)What do you guys eat for breakfast?
Keith:I eat only Cap'n Crunch.
Matt:I eat granola,and Cream of Wheat.
Alex:Kelloggs Corn Flakes with bananas,
Mark:Cookie Crisp or Cocoa Crispies.
What is in the future for Kingpin in '92.
Matt:Hopefully,since Pete and I are starting a label,we have a few songs recorded for comps,but if they don't come out,maybe we'll do it as a record.Hopefully,a lot of vinyl will come out this year.
Alex :How come,when bands get interviewed,they talk about issues and stuff.Noone talks about music.
Keith:What about music.
Matt:To me,being a musician takes a backseat to playing hardcore.
G&P:Don't you think hardcore is more than music?
Matt:Hardcore is definitely more than music.I like being in a band,and I like playing guitar,because it gives me a good feeling.Being in a hardcore band,is a completely different feeling,because it's not just playing music,like metal.I don't look at myself as a musician.I'm just a kid that plays guitar in a hardcore band.It's cooler to me than some dude who goes to Berkeley...I'm talking about musicians that spend their whole lives schooling themselves and can only read sheet music.I'm not trying to rank on Al for going to music school,but I'm just trying to say,for me,this is a lot better than schooling music,and only being able to read sheet music,and having it all come from your head,and not your heart.All the music and lyrics I have written are expressions.This is the way I like expressing myself,through playing hardcore.
Sean:Do you guys wear boxers or briefs?
Kingpin:Boxers.
Sean:All right,that determines the coolness of a band.
G&P:Closing comments?
Matt:I always say this at the end of every interview,and no one ever pays attention.But,we're always looking for out of state shows.Anyone putting on shows,and would like us to play,please contact us.

Keith:I want to say something that I didn't have a chance to say before.Lately,I have been thinking about alternative rock-and the whole idea is totally fake.You see all these bands on MTV,and they call themselves "alternative rock",and all the kids who listen to them think they are alternative rockers,different from everyone else.What I don't understand,is it's pretty much the same music,coming out of the same major labels,and you are paying the same high prices for the record and everything,so...What's the alternative?So,if you're gonna buy that alternative rock tape,just think to yourself,What's the alternative? Just because they look different,doesn't mean they are different.They are still screwin' you over for a whole bunch of money.

KINGPIN
49 GROVE ST.
HOLLISTON MA.01746

PHOTO:JUSTINE De METRICK

DAG NASTY

FOUR ON THE FLOOR

10 GREAT SONGS FROM ALL ORIGINAL MEMBERS!
Compact Disc, Album, and Cassette on Epitaph Records 6201 Sunset Blvd #111 Hollywood CA 90028

MILWAUKEE WI. P.GABE

MILWAUKEE WI. P.GABE

Say No More
Billingsgate
BLOODLINE
Monday, July 1 at 7:00 pm
ALLADES $4.00
Speedway Gallery

GILMAN ST. PHOTO:BOB CONRAD

PHOTO GREG BROWN

UNDERMIND
BILLINGSGATE
SAY NO MORE
TUESDAY
AUG.
SIXTH

SNAGILWET
DOORS OPEN 4:00

PHOTO:DAVE INDECISION

GILMAN ST. P.BOB CONRAD

FINAL CONFLICT
GENERATOR
SAY NO MORE
Billings Gate Smog
SAT JUL 13
3:00 $5

924 Gilman

SOMEWHERE IN CA. PHOTO:DAVE INDECISION

THE END

Exploring Boston

I recently spent the new year in Boston and had a fabulous time. Me and my friend Tom drove 1000 miles to get away from the norm. That we did... we used a lot of film on the trip and I thought I'd share a few shots. I couldn't resist this one → Alyssa, Tom, + Shawn on the run.

JAN. '92 P.GABE

JAN. '92 P.GABE

At 4:00 A.M. on a weeknight, chris, tom and shawn decide to relive the past. It was breaking up the police. try explaining that one to the cops.

Here we were introduced to a teams fastlane amongst the locals. Only asking so we have never tried it, so try this at home. So don't stage dive. Pictured: Gabe, Jon Reed Tom?, Nysim, + Leah on top.

these two days were definitely unforgettable, to say the least. thanks to all who helped to fuck shit up!!!

P. Justine De METRICK

WHaTs HOT?

PAUL RODRIGUEZ
ALL IN THE FAMILY
"HERE"
BOWLING
13-(the tv show)
GRUNGE ROCK
LOVE ROCK
VINYL
HEDGEDIVING
TACO BELL

GABE'S TOSTADAS
GREASY HAIR
70'S BAD COMPANY
ALL AGES SHOWS
FLANNEL
RIVER DEEM
LOOKOUT RECORDS
ZINE REVIVALS
CHICAGO
BEAN-O
CHUMP CHANGE PRODUCTIONS
RED/PINK/PURPLE HAIR
MIKE JUDGE SOLD UP.
VELCRO WALLETS

WHaTs NOt?

ANDREW DICE CLAY
HARDLINE
FALLAFEL
SHAMPOO
RAY + PORCELL
AGE LIMIT SIGNS
PERKS
CHICAGO
GOOD & PLENTY PRODUCTIONS
SISTER SOULJAH
DANCEPIT VIOLENCE
MURPHY'S LAW
CHICAGO BEARS
ZINE DEATHS
CHAIN WALLETS
ROSEANNE
METALLICA
SCARLET PIMP

BASEBALL
BELINDA CARLISLE
NICKELODEON
THE GUESS WHO

MTV'S BAD COMPANY
STRAIGHT EDGE
HATE CORE
REVELATION RECORDS
COMPACT DISCS

BASKETBALL
PAULA ABDUL
BLONDE HAIR
COMBS
STAGEDIVING
WHINING
LYNYRD SKYNYRD

If anyone would like me to explain these, just write. There is a story behind most of them.

In the last issue of G&P, I did a section called "What's Hot, What's Not," and I think it went over well. Here is a list again that me and a few friends could agree upon. This time around. There's a reciprocal for most of these. It's your job to find them. These are subject to a bit of humor again.

"COME SEE WHAT THE BUZZ IS ABOUT...
THE G&P BUZZ CLIP. LOCAL H. SEND SASE
FOR NEWSLETTER, STICKERS AND INFO TO...
LOCAL H
C/O INNER THOUGHT
PO BOX 9161
WAUKEGAN IL 60079-9161

Interview with Gabe Rodriguez
Walter Schreifels

Walter Schreifels: I know you had a lot of people helping you with the *Good and Plenty* but is it fair to say it was your zine? Perhaps it varied from issue to issue.

Gabe Rodriguez: *G&P* was definitely my baby, with a little help from my friends. In the beginning, my buddy Mike Good and I started the zine *Good and Plenty*. The original name came when we were talking on the phone. I was looking through my kitchen pantry. I suggested "Open Pit," and eventually we got around to *Good and Plenty*. His name being Mike Good, I became Gabe Plenty.

There were a couple of other collaborators through the era, including Matt Garcia, the original bassist for Local H. The bulk of the design, interviews, reviews, and content was me with a lot of Mountain Dew.

How did you make the zines? Kinkos didn't exist. Did you have staple parties with friends? What was the process?

I studied graphic communications in high school and was heavily into printing. My father was a pressman at a family-owned print shop, which came in handy for future issues when the volumes were in the thousands. In the beginning, there was a quick print franchise [Sir Speedy Printing] we used for the half-page zines, where they would collate, staple, fold, and staple. They used a Xerox printer. By the time I got to a full-size fanzine, we had gone to offset printing, and good ole fashioned collate and saddle-stitch. I was working in the family-owned print shop after high school, so had access to the equipment. There were collating parties where I would bribe my friends to help. We always had the boombox blasting the classics, (Misfits, 7 Seconds, and the occasional Iron Maiden to round it out.)

Did you have help with mail order?

I did all the mail order. We advertised in *MRR*, and other fellow zines such *No Answer* and *Stop and Think* among others. Mail order was cool because it involved a personal touch. Before email, people used to communicate through the mail, and I honestly made some really cool penpals over the years. Some of those people are still in the scene today, and some influenced me tremendously. I took road trips to the East Coast to experience some killer shows at the Anthrax, The Ritz, and The Rat. It all came together because of my connections through mailorder.

Making the zine was hard work. This was before computers made it easy to do desktop publishing; it was guerilla zine-making at it's finest. A good old Sears typewriter was my tool of choice while laying out the pages with a blue pencil and typing around the shapes where the pics would go. It was DIY with glue-sticks and scissors. My favorite part of the layout was the pictures. I made sure I had content that included action-packed pics from shows. Of course, this was before iPhones, so we had to develop the film from our cheesy 35mm camera at Walgreens.

If you had a camera at shows back in those days, you were almost always doing a zine. I got the nerve to ask bands for interviews and get involved with the scene the best I could. When it came time to put it all together, I would gather all of my friends to the print shop, and we would be jamming 7 Seconds in the background while we collated pages and saddle-stitched the zine.

Of course, we would take road trips to shows in the Midwest, and even out east; we hocked zines at shows, record stores, and wherever we could. The people and memories are the best part.

Eventually, we grew up and ran out of time and passion to keep doing *G&P*, but the kids kept the scene alive. The music and the message are still in my heart. The straight edge scene evolved, and I did not keep up with it past the 1990s.

But hardcore will never die. The kids keep it going, the old folks reminisce about the early days, and reunions bring them all together. I get a smile every time I think about the *Good and Plenty* days. The music will never get old.

It is sad to hear about the people that have passed on, as it is a sign that we are all getting older, and we miss our hardcore family. Although I do not know them all personally, they all have had an impact on a lot of us in some way. We ordered merch and records from them, saw them at shows either on stage or in the crowd, hung out late at night on weekends. It was an extended family. I am glad to have been a small part of the hardcore scene in the Midwest and brought some of the experiences from the East Coast back with me—it is some of my favorite music in the genre. I was a fan who could not play guitar, but I could make havoc with paper, scissors, and glue!

Hardcore Fanzine:
Good and Plenty, 1989-1992

Published by
Draw Down Books
42 Water Street, Box 609
Guilford, CT 06437
hello.drawdown@gmail.com
www.draw-down.com

First edition

Designed by Partition
Typeset in Atlas Grotesk and Atlas Typewriter

Printed in the United States

ISBN: 978-0-9857337-9-7

Photo Credits

Front cover: (middle left)
Cover of *Good and Plenty*,
issue 3, 1989. (lower left)
Photograph of Gorilla Biscuits
in Chicago from *Good and
Plenty*, issue 4, p. 14, 1990.

Back cover: (upper right)
Photograph of Insted singer
Kevin Hernandez and
guitarist Burt "Bear" Barret
at The Anthrax, Stamford,
Connecticut. Credited to
Brian Boog, from *Good and
Plenty*, issue 4, p. 25, 1990;
(center) Masthead, *Good and
Plenty*, issue 4, 1990; (lower
right) Cover of *Good and
Plenty*, issue 7, 1991-1992.

Frontispiece: © Gabe
Rodriguez. Paste-up of *Good
and Plenty*, issue 7, p. 36, 1991
(detail), with photos of Gorilla
Biscuits in Europe, 1991 April
21, credited to "Johan."

p. 7: © Gabe Rodriguez.
Paste-up of *Good and Plenty*,
Issue 4, p. 21, 1990 (detail),
with photographs of Gorilla
Biscuits in Chicago.

p. 36: © Gabe Rodriguez.
Paste-up of *Good and Plenty*,
Issue 7, p. 23 (detail), with
photos of Chaka Malik of
Burn and L7. Burn photo, July
1991, credited to Greg Brown.

p. 37: © Gabe Rodriguez.
Paste-up of *Good and Plenty*,
Issue 7, p. 17 (detail), with
photos of Jawbox and Inside
Out. Jawbox photo, April 1991,
credited to "Marty." Inside
Out photo credited to "Dave
Indecision" (Dave Mandel).